EMINENT ORIENTALISTS

INDIAN, EUROPEAN, AMERICAN.

EMINENT ORIENTALISTS
INDIAN, EUROPEAN, AMERICAN.

Published by

GYAN

Gyan Publishing House
5, Ansari Road
Daryaganj, New Delhi-110002
Phone: 011-47034999, 9811692060
E-mail: books@gyanbooks.com

Distribution Network
gyanbooks.com
India, USA, Canada, UK, Australia, France

ISBN : 978-81-212-3347-7 (PB)
First Published, Madras, 1922

2nd Impression 2020

Printed at: Gyan Press, Delhi.

Eminent Orientalists
Indian, European, American.

PREFACE.

THIS is the first attempt to present under one cover a succinct account of the lives and achievements of well known Orientalists, like Sir William Jones, Buhler, Fleet, Fergusson, Rajendra Lal Mitra, Max Muller, Whitney, Vincent Smith, Macdonell, Tilak, Dr. Bhandarkar, and Sylvain Levi who have done pioneer work in the field of Indology. The activities of this group of Savants—English, Scotch, French, German, American and Indian, have been many-sided They have explored the regions of archæology, epigraphy and palæography, not to speak of their valuable researches in regard to the religion of the Vedic Aryans and have thus opened out vistas of knowledge in directions never before thought of. Inspired by a noble desire to understand and interpret the genius of India and her civilization, they have left us a legacy of inestimable value. It is hoped that this modest collection of critical sketches will serve to remind us of their achievements and inspire us to continue their work with becoming devotion.

THE PUBLISHERS.

INTRODUCTION.

THE world has travelled far indeed since Macaulay with characteristic cocksureness, talked lightly of the wisdom of the East. His profound ignorance of Eastern literature betrayed him into an attitude of unreasoning contempt for anything that did not savour of European civilization. Time has had its revenge and the verdict of Macaulay no longer holds the field. The East has come into its own. Its deep wisdom and its hoary traditions have come to be recognised as an important contribution to the sum of human knowledge. Nay more. As the mystery of the Orient is unveiled, a deep sense of gratitude as of veneration has come over the rest of the modern world which has learnt to look upon the East as the lamp of ancient wisdom.

In this task of unveiling the wisdom of the East, a handful of European and Indian scholars have co-operated with admirable results. It was during the days of Warren Hastings that the first impetus was given to Oriental research and a devoted band of scholars under the lead of Sir William Jones founded the Asiatic Society of Bengal in 1784. Colebrooke and Wilson followed his tradition and enriched the proceedings of the Society with their contributions, with a view to popularise the abstruse scriptures of the Sanskrit classics. The bright example set by these illustrious Sanskritists inspired a host of savants intent on Indo-Aryan research. Every department of Oriental life and thought came to be scrutinised from a new angle of vision, a vision disciplined by the critical methods of science and inspired by the wealth and splendour of the half-hidden world of culture. The votaries of ancient Indian history examined her records with a keen and sympathetic understanding. Dr. Vincent Smith took the whole field of ancient India under his ken, while the dynasties of the Kanarese districts and the history of Gujarat were explored by Dr. Fleet and Bhagavanlal Indraji. The pioneer in this fruitful field of historical research is Dr. Bhandarkar, whose Early History of the Deccan is still a model of what indefatigable research and erudition can achieve. Meanwhile the study and investigation of Indian archæology facilitated the difficult task of deciphering ancient inscriptions and the achievements of Prinsep and Cunningham in Europe have been nobly followed in India by Bhau Daji and Rajendralal Mitra. Indian Epigraphy and Palæography to which Buhler gave so much of his life time found in Dr. Fleet a worthy disciple, and students of Epigraphy are indebted to the labours of Prof Senart "whose epoch making work" on Asokan Incriptions has revealed a wonderful world of new knowledge. Fergusson's Architecture and Vincent Smith's interpretration of the fine arts are among the other treasures of Eastern art and craft. Above all, the study of religions as embodied in the writings of Max Muller, B. G. Tilak and Paul Deussen, are domain of perpetual wonder and deep content, while the efforts of Macdonell and others have unravelled the beauty of Sanskrit, the mother of languages. Nor could we forget the enchanting territories opened out in recent years by Prof. Sylvain Levi of the extra-territorial influence of Indian civilisation in distant lands. Above all, we are indebted to the muse of Arnold and Griffith and the eloquence of Sister Nivedita, who, by a strange affinity, were inspired by the life and thought of the East, and dedicated themselves to the interpretation of the best and loveliest in Oriental literature.

CONTENTS.

SIR WILLIAM JONES

INTRODUCTION.

IN one of his poems Sir William Jones said:—

Give me (thus my high pride I raise)
The ploughman's or the gardener's praise,
With patient and unceasing toil
To meliorate a stubborn soil
And say (no higher need I ask),
With zeal hast thou perform'd thy task."

We cannot introduce such a worker of such strenuous self-dedicatedness better than with such words of his own, because his zeal for work was remarkable, his search for virgin soil was rewarded, his tillage of it was scientific and thorough, his love for it was deep and true, and his harvest was golden and abundant and valuable to all men and for all time. It is through men of his type and temperament that the true spirit of fraternity between the West and the East will be born. It is through the co-operative work of scholars and scientists and artists and philosophers and humanitarians that the bridge of friendship can be thrown across the gulf of separation in spirit. Statesmen may proclaim the need of such kinship of feeling. Diplomats may proclaim that it exists already. But statesmen and diplomats and soldiers and civil officials can only keep up a patched-up outer peace often rent asunder by the frequent convulsions of inner estrangement. Sir William Jones was one of those with whom Indian scholars could and did feel that

> **We were nursed upon the self-same hill,**
> **Fed the same flock by fountain, shade and rill;**
> **Together both, ere the high lawns appeared**
> **Under the opening eyelids of the Morn**
> **We drove a-field.**

HIS LIFE.

Sir William Jones was born in 1746. He studied at Harrow School.. In his ninth year he fractured his thigh-bone and was confined to his bed for a year. It was during this time that he studied the best English poets. He had an extraordinary memory. On one occasion when he and his friends proposed to act *the Tempest* but had no copy at hand, he wrote it for them correctly from his memory. He composed a tragedy on the story of Meleager which was acted by his school-fellows. Learning was always uppermost in his mind. Dr. Bennett says that "great abilities, great peculiarity of thinking, fondness for writing verses and plays of various kinds, and a degree of integrity and manly courage, distinguished him even at this period." Dr. Thackeray, the master of the school, said that "he was a boy of so active a mind, that if he were left naked and friendless on Salisbury plain, he would nevertheless find the road to fame and riches."

He entered the University College, Oxford, in the spring, 1764. Mr. Chalmers says: "Oriental literature presented itself to his mind with unusual charms, as if the plan of his future life and the avenues to his future fame had been regularly laid down before him."

In 1765 he became private tutor to Lord Althorpe. In his twenty-first year he began his commentaries on Asiatic poetry, in imitation of Dr. Louth's Prelections at Oxford on the sacred poetry of the Hebrews. He translated the manuscript of the Life of Nadir Shah brought by the King of Denmark, then on a visit to England. He then resolved to study law and was admitted into the Temple on 19th September 1770. Mr. Chalmers says:

> Those who consider the study of the law as incompatible with a mind devoted to the acquisition of polite literature, and with a taste delighting in frequent excursions to the regions of fancy, will be ready to conclude that Mr. Jones would soon discover an invincible repugnance to his new pursuit. But the reverse was, in a great measure, the fact "...He was stimulated by what appears to have predominated through life, an honest ambition to rise to eminence in a profession which, although sometimes successfully followed by men of dull capacity, does not exclude the most brilliant acquirements."

In 1772 he published a volume of poems and two essays on Eastern poetry and on the arts commonly called imitative.

He was called to the Bar in 1774 and tried to make himself "not only the technical but the philosophical lawyer." Mr. Chalmers says: "For some time he had but little practice, but it gradually came in, and with it a very considerable share of reputation." In 1776 he was appointed a commissioner of bankrupts. He took to the study of Greek orators and translated the most useful orations of Isaeus. He was elected a Fellow of the Royal Society in 1772. He then published a Latin Ode to Liberty. In 1780 he published *An Enquiry into the Legal Mode of Suppressing Riots, with a Constitutional Plan of Future Defence*, a pamphlet suggested by the dreadful riots in London at that time. He tried to prove in it "that the common and statute laws of the realm then in force, give the civil state in every country a power, which, if it were properly understood and continually prepared, would effectually quell any riot or insurrection, without assistance from the military and even without the modern Riot Act." In 1780-81 he translated seven ancient poems of the highest reputation in Arabia. He published also an *Essay on the Law of Bailments*. "His object in all legal discussions" says Mr. Chalmers "was to advance law to the honours of a science." In 1782, he took a very active part in the societies formed to secure a more equal representation in the House of Commons. He wrote a *Dialogue between a Farmer and a Country Gentleman on the Principles of Government.*

In March 1783, he was appointed a Judge of the Supreme Court of Judicature at Fort William, on which occasion the honour of a knighthood was conferred on him. In April following he married Anna Maria Shipley. His friend, Lord Ashburton, congratulated him on securing "two of the first objects of human pursuit, those of ambition and love." He arrived in Calcutta in September. Mr. Chalmers says: "He had not been long in his new situation before he began, with his usual judgment, to divide his time into such regular portions, that no objects connected with duty or science should interfere." He formed in Calcutta a society for scientific work and he was appointed as its President. He soon began the study of Sanskrit. About the Sanskrit language he has said: "The Sanskrit language, whatever be its antiquity, is of a wonderful structure, more perfect than the Greek, more copious than the Latin, and more exquisitely refined than either." He compiled a Digest of Hindu and Mahomedan Laws to help him in his administration of justice. In 1789 he published his first volume of the Asiatic Researches, as also a translation of Kalidasa's immortal play, *Sakuntala*. In 1794 he published a translation of the ordinances of Manu "who is esteemed by the Hindus the first of created beings, and not only the oldest, but the holiest of legislators." He said about Manu:—

> A spirit of sublime devotion, of benevolence to mankind, and of amiable tenderness to all sentient creatures pervades the whole work; the style of it has a certain austere majesty, that sounds like the language of legislation and extorts a respectful awe; the sentiments of independence on all beings but God, and the harsh admonitions even to kings are truly noble: and the many panagyrics on the Gayatri, the mother, as it is called, of the Veda, prove the author to have adored not the visible material sun, but that divine and incomparably greater light, to use the words of the most venerable text in the Indian Scripture, which illumines all, delights all, from which all proceed, to which all must return, and which alone can irradiate not our visual organs merely but our souls and our intellects.

In 1794 he became ill of inflammation in the liver and succumbed to that disease on 27th April 1794.

Sir William Jones, the Author, the Judge and the Man.

Mr. Chalmers well says of him "Thus ended the life of a man who was the brightest example of rational ambition, and of extensive learning, virtue and excellence that modern times have produced, a man who must ever remain the subject of admiration, although it can happen to the lot of few to equal and perhaps of none to excel him." He was of encyclopædic learning but as Lord Teignmouth says: "No writer perhaps ever displayed so much learning with so little affectation of it." On the bench he was "laborious, patient, and discriminating." In him integrity and courtesy and learning were admirably combined. Lord Teignmouth well refers in his biography to "the exertion of his talents and abilities, of energies well directed and usefully applied to the benefit of his country and mankind."

His Letters.

Lord Teignmouth's Life of Sir William Jones is in two volumes and is as well-written as it is just in its estimate of the great scholar and judge. It contains many of Jones's excellent letters from which we give the following few extracts by way of illustration:—

The life of no man can be pronounced either happy or miserable, virtuous or abandoned, before the conclusion of it.

Fondness for polite literature, congenial pursuits, and conformity of sentiments are the great bonds of intimacy amongst mankind.

If it ever should be my lot to be concerned in the administration of affairs, I will renounce gain and popularity, and pursue one object, and one only, to preserve our beautiful constitution inviolate.

Let me ever retain a place in your affection, as you do in mine; continue to cultivate polite literature; woo the muses; reverence philosophy; and give your days and nights to composition, with a due regard, however, to the preservation of your health.

If I am disappointed, philosophy remains; the bar is open, and I shall not, I trust, want employment; for the harvest of litigation is always abundant..

To tell you my mind freely, I am not of a disposition to bear the arrogance of men of rank, to which poets and men of letters are so often obliged to submit,

Seven hours to law, to soothing slumber seven,
Ten to the world allot and *all* to heaven.
"Think how Sully shone,
Think how Demosthenes with heavenly fire
Shook Philip's throne and lightened over his towers.
What gave them strength? Not eloquence alone,
But minds elate above each low desire."

SIR WILLIAM JONES'S CHARGES TO THE GRAND JURY.

These are replete with wise and valuable thoughts. They cannot be dealt with in any great detail in this sketch. But the following passages may well be referred to here.

Legislative provisions have not the individual for their object but the species; and are not made for the convenience of the day, but for the regulation of ages.

Justice must be administered with effect, or society cannot long subsist.

The use of law as a science is to prevent mere discretionary power under the colour of equity; and it is the duty of a Judge to pronounce his decisions, not simply according to his opinion of justice and right, but according to prescribed rules.

I aspire to no popularity and seek no praise, but that which may be given to a strict and conscientious discharge of duty, without predilection or prejudice of any kind, and with a fixed resolution to pronounce on all occasions what I conceive to be the law, than which no individual must suppose himself wiser.

Be it our care, gentlemen, to avoid by all means the slightest imputation of injustice among those, whom it is the lot of Britain to rule; and by giving them personal security, with every reasonable indulgence to their harmless prejudices, to conciliate their affection, while we promote their industry, so as to render our dominion over them a national benefit and may our beloved country in all its dependencies enjoy the greatest of national blessings, good laws duly administered in settled peace! for neither can the best laws avail without a due administration of them, nor could they be dispensed with effect, if the fears and passions of men were engaged by the vicissitudes of war, or the agitation of civil discontents.

Sir William Jones on the Legal Mode of Suppressing Riots.

This pamphlet is of great value and excellence and presents, in a succinct form, the basis of personal security and public peace. He says well:

The power of the country, therefore, includes the whole civil state from the duke to the peasant; while the military state as such, forms no part of that power, being under a different command, and subject to a different law.

He concludes his essay with the following true and wise words:

As every soldier in England is at the same time a citizen, I wish to see every citizen able, at least for the preservation of the public peace, to act as a soldier; when that shall be the case the liberty of Britain will ever be unassailed; for this plain reason—it will be unassailable. The security, and consequently the happiness of a free people do not consist in their belief, however firm, that the executive power will not attempt to invade their just rights, but in their consciousness that any such attempt would be wholly ineffectual.

I may quote here, from his speech on the Reformation of Parliament, the following fine passage:

Be persuaded also that the people of England can only expect to be the happiest and most glorious while they are the freest, and can only become the freest, when they shall be the most virtuous and most enlightened of nations.

His Plan of a Treatise on Education.

This is very interesting, though he did not write out the treatise itself. It begins thus:

The perfect education of a great man consists in three points: in cultivating and improving his understanding: in assisting and reforming his countrymen; and in procuring to himself the chief good, or a fixed and unalterable habit of virtue.

He shows how education should improve our natural reason so that we may know and practise what is good. This can be best done only by assimilating the accumulated experience and wisdom of all ages and all nations. Hence we must study the languages and literatures of the great races of the world; and we must convey to other races our great ideas. "It follows, therefore, that the more immediate object of education is to learn the languages of celebrated nations both ancient and modern." Science and art must be equally attended to, as also manly sports. Ideas like these deserve to be emphasised again and again in modern India where education is being steadily forced away from healthy and proper channels and is getting more and more divorced from the great summations of Indian thought, the traditional methods and ideals of our outer and inner life, the supreme lessons and proclamations of Indian art and religion, and is not rooted in the past or alive to the present or clear-sighted about the future that is to be.

DISCOURSES AT CALCUTTA.

These display his deep insight into the Indian culture and his comprehensive knowledge of Indian literature and philosophy. He says:

> The six philosophical schools, whose principles are explained in the Darsana Sastra, comprise all the metaphysics of the old Academy, the Stoa, the Lyceum; nor is it possible to read the Vedanta, or the many fine compositions in illustration of it, without believing that Pythagoras and Plato derived their sublime theories from the same fountain with the Sages of India.

He says further:

> We are told by the Grecian writers that the Indians were the wisest of nations, and in moral wisdom, they were certainly eminent.

The addresses treat also of the Arabs, the Tartars, the Persians, the Chinese and other races of Asia. About Sri Sankaracharya's *Bhashya* on the Vedanta Sutras he says :—It is not possible, indeed, to speak with too much applause of so excellent a work." He says further :

> The fundamental tenet of the Vedanta school, to which, in a more modern age, the incomparable Sankara was a firm and illustrious adherent, consisted, not in denying the existence of matter, that is, of solidity, impenetrability, and extended figure (to deny which will be lunacy) but, in correcting the popular notion of it, and in contending, that it has no essence independent of mental perception, that existence and perceptibility are convertible terms, that external appearances and sensations are illusory, and would vanish into nothing, if the divine energy, which alone sustains them, were suspended but for a moment.

THE ASIATIC MISCELLANY.

It consists of various translations, imitations, fugitive pieces, and original productions. The first poem in it is a *Hymn to Camdeo* and describes Cupid (Kama). The opening stanza runs thus :

> Hail, pow'r unknown ! for at thy beck
> Vales and groves their bosoms deck,
> And ev'ry laughing blossom dresses
> With gems of dew his musky tresses
> I feel, I feel thy genial flame divine,
> And hallow thee and kiss thy shrine.

The poem recalls the heavenly beauty of the description of the triumphant advent of Cupid in the third Canto of Kalidasa's *Kumarasambhava*. Jones addresses Kama and Rati thus :

God of each lovely sight, each lovely sound,
  Soul-kindling, world-inflaming, starry-crown'd,
  Eternal Kama!
  Thy consort mild, *affection* ever true,
  Graces thy side, her vest of glowing hue,
  And in her train twelve blooming girls advance,
  Touch golden strings and knit the mirthful dance.

Equally interesting is Jones's poem *A Hymn to Narayana.* He well describes the Hindu theory of creation when he says:

The whole creation was rather an *energy* than a *work*, by which the Infinite Being, who is present at all times and in all places, exhibits to the minds of his creatures a set of perceptions, like a wonderful picture or a piece of music, always varied, yet always uniform; so that all bodies and their qualities exist, indeed to every wise and useful purpose, but exist only so far as they are perceived; a theory no less pious than sublime, and as different from any principle of atheism, as the brightest sunshine differs from the blackest midnight. This illusive operation of the deity the Hindu philosophers call Maya.

The poem begins thus:

Spirit of spirits, who, through ev'ry part
Of space expanded and of endless time,
Beyond the stretch of lab'ring thought sublime,
Badst uproar into beauteous order start,
  Before Heaven was, Thou art.
Ere spheres beneath us roll'd or spheres above,
Ere earth in firmamental ether hung,
Thou sat'st alone; till, through thy mystic love,
Things unexisting to existence sprung,
  And grateful descant sung.
What first impelled thee to exert thy might?
Goodness unlimited. What glorious light
Thou power directed? Wisdom without bound.

This work contains also fine translations of extracts from Jami's *Yusuf Zuleika* by Thomas Law, Najnoon, etc. These are by other writers and not by Sir William Jones.

POEMS.

A collected edition of his poems was published in 1772. They are not of a high order of achievement but are certainly full of occasional beauty and general refinement. The following stanza is from an imitation of Horace written by him when he was fourteen years of age.

> How quickly fades the vital power!
> Alas my friend! each silent hour
> Steals unperceived away.
> The early joys of blooming youth,
> Sweet innocence and dove-eyed truth,
> Are destin'd to decay.

Arcadia is a pastoral poem written by him in 1762. In it occur the following fine lines:

> A graceful ease in every step was seen,
> She moved a shepherdess, yet looked a queen.
> Now deeper blushes ting'd the glowing sky,
> And evening raised her silver lamp on high.

Caissa or the Game of Chess was a poem written in 1763. It is very ingenious and elegent and concludes thus:

> Low in their chest the mimic troops were laid.
> And peaceful slept the sable hero's shade.

The *Seven Fountains* is an eastern allegory written in 1767. *Solima* or an Arabian eclogue was written in 1768. It contains the following fine lines:

> Love-tinctured cheeks, whence roses seek their bloom,
> And lips, from which the Zephyr steals perfume.
> Till morn with pearls has deck'd the glowing east.

Laura, an elegy from Petrarch, is in the style of the eighteenth century poetry but Jones's study of Indian poetry enabled him to get a release from the shackles that chained the poetic imagination and emotion of the age. Another poem contains the following fine refrain:

> Come, smile, damsels of Cardigan,
> Love can alone make it blissful to live.

The following two brief poems are of real beauty:

> As meadows parch'd, brown groves, and withering flowers,
> Imbibe the sparkling dew and genial showers,
> As chill dark air inhales the morning beam,
> As thirsty harts enjoy the gelid stream,
> Thus to man's grateful from heaven descend,
> The mercies of His father, Lord, and Friend.
> Before thy mystic altar, Heavenly Truth,
> I kneel in manhood, as I knelt in youth
> Thus let me kneel, till this dull form decay,
> And life's last shade be brightened by thy ray,
> Then shall my soul, now lost in clouds below,
> Soar without bound, without consuming glow.

Equally fine is his Ode in Imitation of *Alcaeus* in which he says:

What constitutes a state!

. . . .

Men, high-minded men,

. . . .

Men, who their duties know,
dare maintain,
Prevent the long-aimed blow,
And crush the tyrant while they rend the chain,
These constitute a state
And sovereign Law, that state's collected will,
O'er thrones and globes elate,
Sits empress, crowning good, repressing ill.

Another *Ode* sums up England's ideal thus:

Rise Britannia! Dauntless rise!
Monarch good, and nobles wise,
People valiant, firm, and free.

A Chinese Ode contains the following ideal of true manhood:

What soft, yet awful dignity!
What meek, yet manly, grace!
What sweetness dances in his eye
And blossoms in his face!

A Turkish Ode contains the following fine lines:

See! yon anemones their leaves unfold,
With rubies flaming and with living gold.
The plants no more are dried, the meadows dead,
No more the rosebud hangs her pensive head:
The shrubs revive in valley, meads and bowers,
And every stalk is diadem'd with flowers;
In silken robes each hillock stands arrayed.
Be gay; too soon the flowers of spring will fade.

A special place in our thoughts and hearts must be given to his two excellent poems called *Two Hymns to Prakriti.* In one of them the wonderful episode in Canto V of

Kalidasa's Kumarasambhava where Uma moves away in anger from the self-ridiculing and self-concealed Siva is thus described:

She spoke and o'er the rifted rocks
Her lovely form with pious frenzy threw;
But beneath her floating locks
And waving robes a thousand breezes flew,
Knitting close their silky plumes,
And in mid-air a downy pillow spreading;
Till, in clouds of rich perfumes
Embalmed, they bore her to a mystic wood;
Where streams of glory shedding,
The well-feign'd Brahman, Siva, stood.

In the other occurs the following stanza full of exalted feeling:

Mother of Gods, rich nature's queen,
Thy genial fire emblaz'd the bursting scene;
For, on th' expanded blossom sitting,
With sunbeams knitting
That mystic veil for ever unremoved,
Thou bads't the softly—kindling flame
Pervade this peopled frame,
And smiles, with blushes tinged, the work approved.

In his *Hymn to Indra*, Mount Meru is thus described:

Hail, mountain of delight,
Palace of glory, bless'd by glory's king!

The sun is thus addressed in his *Hymn to Surya*:

Fountain of living light,
That o'er all nature streams,
Of this vast microcosm both nerve and soul;
Whose swift and subtle beams,
Eluding mortal sight,

Pervade, attract, sustain the effulgent whole;

. . . .

Lord of the lotus, father, friend, and king,
O Sun! thy powers I sing.

. . . .

Since thou, great orb! with all-enlightening ray
Rulest the golden day,
How far more glorious He, who said, serene,
Be, and thou wast—Himself unformed, unchanged, unseen

The *Hymn to Lakshmi* is equally fine. It says:

Daughter of ocean and primeval night,
Who, fed with moon beams dropping silver dew,
And cradled in a wild wave dancing light,
Saw'st with a smile new shores and creatures new,
The goddess! I salute; thy gifts I sing.

. . . .

Shall man unthankful riot on thy stores?
Ah, no! he bends, he blesses, he adores.

. . . .

Oh! bid the patient Hindu rise and live.

The companion *Hymn to Saraswathi* says:

These are thy wondrous arts,
Queen of the flowering speech,
Thence Saraswathi named and Vani bright!
Oh, joy of mortal hearts,
Thy mystic wisdom teach.

The *Hymn to Ganga* is equally fine:

How sweetly Ganga smiles, and glides,
Luxuriant o'er her broad autumnal bed!
Her waves perpetual verdure spread;
Whilst health and plenty deck her golden sides.

Jones's poems contain also two Indian tales in verse—*The Palace of Fortune* and *The Enchanted Fruit* and various Latin poems.

Special mention may here be made of a few fine lyrics by him. Out of these we cull the following lines :

> Beauty like thine, all nature thrills ;
> And when the moon her circle fills,
> Pale she beholds those rounder hills,
> Which on the breast thou wearest.

HIS THEORY OF POETRY.

Sir William Jones's *Essay on the Arts, commonly called Imitative*, is of great value. In it he discusses the theory that all poetry consists in imitation. He shows how poetry originated in a strong and animated expression of the human passions; how cadence and measure accompany strong feeling ; and how love and war were the chief inspirers of song. Elegy and Satire also came into being as poetic forms. Music with its harmonies of accessory sounds is also as old as man. He says :

> What has been said of poetry may, with equal force, be applied to music, which is poetry dressed to advantage ; and even to painting, many sorts of which are poems to the eye, as all poems, merely descriptive, are pictures to the ear.

He shows how the real power of art is in creative power, not in mere imitative accuracy. He says :

> Thus will each artist gain his end, not by imitating the works of nature, but by assuming her power, and causing the same effect upon the imagination, which her charms produce upon the senses : this must be the chief object of a poet, a musician, and a painter,

who know that great effects are not produced by minute details, but by the general spirit of the whole piece and that a gaudy composition may strike the mind for a short time, but that the beauties of simplicity are both more delightful and more permanent.

HIS INTERPRETATION OF HINDU CULTURE.

Sir William Jones was one of the earliest and best interpreters of Hindu culture to the world. His was a calm and balanced soul with an inborn and indomitable Indian outlook on life; and this was the reason of his sympathetic insight into Indian culture. Though great and varied is his work in other directions, it is this spirit of sympathetic insight that is of even greater importance than his actual achievement.

He knew what few others have cared to know and what may ignorantly deny that the Hindus are as much lovers of poetry as of philosophy. He says:

> In all our conversations with learned Hindus, we find them enthusiastic admirers of poetry, which they consider as a divine art, that had been practised for numberless ages in Heaven, before it was revealed on earth by Valmiki, whose great heroic poem is fortunately preserved.

Here we have an indication as to what the Indians must do now and hereafter to preserve and perfect their self-consciousness, to redeem their fair name so proud and revered in the past from the charge of senility or sterility in the present, and to make their future brighter than their wonderful past. We must understand and realise the *differentia* of Indian culture. Till then mere additions of thought from the West will hang loosely about us and will never become an integral portion of our inner life and enrich the treasury of our national consciousness.

SIR WILLIAM JONES ON INDIAN LITERATURE AND ART.

He says about the *Vedas* as the fountain of Indian literature:

> From the Vedas are immediately deduced the practical arts of Surgery and Medicine, Music and Dancing, Archery, which comprises the whole art of war, and Architecture, under which the system of mechanical arts is included.

About Indian medicine he says with a prophetic warning and by way of wholesome advice:

> Infinite advantage may be derived by Europeans from the various medical books in Sanskrit, which contain the names and descriptions of Indian plants and minerals, with their uses, *discovered by experience*, in curing disorders.

The West is yet to learn this great truth and act on this wholesome advice. Sir William Jones was always impressed by the vastness of Indian literature. He says:

> Wherever we direct our attention to Hindu literature, the notion of infinity presents itself.

A great fact to which he drew repeated attention was the wonderful metrical system of Sanskrit poetry. He says:

The Hindu poets never fail to change the *metre* which is their *mode*, according to the change of subject or sentiment in the same piece; and I could produce instances of poetical modulation (if such a phrase may be used) at least equal to the most affecting modulations of our greatest composers.

Sir William Jones has translated the *Gita, Garuda, Ritu Samhara, Sakuntala,* and *Hitopadesa,* as also Manu. He calls Kalidasa the Shakespeare of India and says:

Dramatic poetry must have been immemoriably ancient in the Indian Empire.

He says of *Ritu Samhara* by Kalidasa:

Every line composed by Kalidas is exquisitely polished; and every couplet in the poem exhibits an Indian landscape, always beautiful, sometimes highly coloured, but never beyond nature.

Jones's discourse on the *Musical Modes of the Hindus* is of great value. He says about music:

Considered as an *art*, it combines the sounds, which philosophy distinguishes, in such a manner as to gratify our ears, or affect our imaginations, or by uniting both objects, to captivate the fancy while it pleases the sense, and, speaking, as it were, the language of beautiful nature, to raise correspondent ideas and emotions in the mind of the hearer; it then and then only becomes what we call a *fine art*.

He says further about the Indian conception of art:

In the literature of the Hindus all nature is animated and personified; every fine art is declared to have been revealed from heaven; and all knowledge, divine and human, is traced to its source in the Vedas, among which the Sama Veda was intended to be sung.

He quotes the following beautiful stanza as descriptive of the Hindu idea of Ragas. It describes the Sri Raga.

लीलाहिहारेण वनान्तराले

चिन्वन्प्रसूना निवधसहाय: ।

विलासिवेषोदित दिव्यमूर्तिः

श्रीरागएषः प्रथितः पृथिव्यां ॥

(The demigod Sri Raga, famed over all this earth, sweetly sports with his nymphs, gathering fresh blossoms in the bosom of yonder grove; and his divine lineaments are distinguished through his graceful vesture).

He then points out that Hindu musicians give "their modes a distinct character and a very agreeable diversity of expression." He knew further that the great Hindu Musicians were masters of "modulation, or change of mode, to which passionate music owes nearly all its enchantment."

SIR WILLIAM JONES ON ARAB POETRY.

Not only was he alive to the beauties of Indian culture. His mind took in all oriental culture. He gives in his *Essay on the Poetry of the Eastern Nations* many just and noble ideas about Arab poetry He points out how the Arab life has lent its glow to Arab poetry. He says:

"It is very usual in all countries to make frequent allusions to the brightness of the celestial luminaries, which give their light to all, but the metaphors taken from them have an additional beauty if we consider them as made by a nation, who pass most of their nights in the open air, or in tents, and consequently see the moon and stars in their greatest splendour."

He shows also how "they have never been wholly subdued by any other nation" and how this also has given a grace and power to their poesy. He further says that, in a hot country like Arabia where the intense heat of the sun is tempered by the shade of trees, the notions of felicity are naturally taken from freshness and verdure. "It is a maxim among them that the three most charming objects in nature are a green meadow, a clear rivulet and a beautiful woman." Love poetry is predominant in Arabian literature. It compares the maiden to a wanton fawn playing among the aromatic shrubs. He says:

Their language is expressive, strong, sonorous and the most copious, perhaps, in the world.

Arabian poetry inspired Persian poetry which, in its turn, inspired Turkish poetry. He concludes thus:

I must once more request that, in bestowing these praises on the writings of Asia, I may not be thought to derogate from the merit of Greek and Latin poems, which have justly been admired in every age; yet I cannot but think that our European poetry has subsided too long on the perpetual repetition of the same images and incessant allusions to the same fables.

Sir William Jones on Sufism.

He points out in his discourse on the *Mystical Poetry of the Persians and Hindus* the points of identity between Vedantism and Sufism. The Sufi doctrine is thus summed up by him:

That the souls of men differ infinitely in degree, but not at all in kind, from the divine spirit, of which they are particles and in which they will ultimately be absorbed; that the spirit of God pervades the universe, always immediately present to his work, and consequently always in substance; that He alone is perfect benevolency, perfect truth, perfect beauty; that the love of Him alone is real and genuine love, while that of all objects is absurd and illusory; that the beauties of nature are faint resemblances, like images in a mirror, of the divine charms; that from eternity without beginning to eternity without end, the supreme Benevolence is occupied in bestowing happiness or the means of attaining it; that men can only attain it by performing their part of the primal covenant between them and the Creator; that nothing has a pure absolute existance but mind or spirit; that material substances, as the ignorant call them, are no more than gay pictures presented continually to our minds by the sempiternal Artist; that we must beware of attachment to such phantoms and attach ourselves exclusively to God, who truly exists in us, as we exist solely in Him; that we retain even in this forlorn state of separation from our beloved, the idea of heavenly beauty and the remembrance of our primeval vows; that sweet music, gentle breezes, fragrant flowers, perpetually renew the primary idea, refresh our fading memory, and melt us with tender affections; that we must cherish those affections, and by abstructing our souls from vanity, that is, from all but God, approximate to His essence in our final union with which will consist our supreme beatitude,"

His Miscellaneous Works.

The range of his miscellaneous works is immense. It includes such varied subjects as *The Chronology of the Hindus, The Indian Zodiac, The Lunar Year of the Hindus, The Cure of the Elephentiasis, The Indian Game of Chess, Tales and Tables by Nizami, The Spikenard of the Ancients, Botanical Observations in select Indian plants, A Grammar of the Persian Language, The History of the Persian language, The Mahomedan Law of Inheritance, The Speeches of Isaeus, A Catalogue of Oriental Manuscripts, A Short History of Persia, A Description of Asia, etc.*

Conclusion.

Such was the great man and such was his great work. We cannot take leave of him better than by feeling and saying that he has amply won the praise coveted by him in his trees :

Give me (this my high pride I raise,)
The ploughman's on the gardener's praise,
With patient and unceasing toil,
To meliorate a stubborn soil,
And say (no higher need I ask),
With zeal has thou performed thy task.

Sir Charles Wilkins

CHARLES Wilkins was not a Londoner like his famous contemporary, Sir William Jones; he hailed from Somersetshire, where at Frome he was born about the year 1750. He was the son of Walter Wilkins of that town and his wife Martha Wray, niece of Robert Bateman Wray, the well-known engraver. Very little is known of his early life. His parents were probably all but poor, and their boy grew up amidst humble environments. Young Wilkins was not much taken care of; he was almost left to shift for himself. If he received any education at all, it was very scant and certainly did not hold out any promise of the big eminence to which he afterwards attained. Finding that his prospects at home was all but gloomy, he cast his longing eyes towards the Far East, and having somehow secured a 'writership' in the service of the East India Company, came out to India when he had just passed out of its teens. After his arrival he stayed for a few months at Calcutta, whence he was sent to Malda as an Assistant to the Superintendent of the Company's Factory there. But factory business did not engross his attention: in his leisure hours he commenced to learn Persian and Bengali, the two dialects there in common use, and without a knowledge of which no foreigner could hope "to get on" well. It would seem that Wilkins possessed a remarkable aptitude for learning languages, and it was not long before he acquired a fair mastery over those two popular languages. This proficiency gave an impetus to his capable mind, and he took to learning Sanskrit, the most ancient as well as the most difficult of languages that are in vogue in the world. It so happened that at this time his friend, Nathaniel Brassey Halhed, was also learning the language, and it is only natural that he should follow his friend's example in this respect. As he himself writes: "About 1778, curiosity was cxcited by the example of my friend, Mr. Halhed, to commence the study of the Sanskrit." He, too, began to study it, and has brought his usual zeal and assiduity into requisition, acquired a fair knowledge of it in a comparatively short time.

Having thus gained something like a mastery over the languages in use, Wilkins directed his attention towards the dissemination of knowledge. The same, he thought, he could not do better than by introducing the art of printing in India. This all-important undertaking which has made his name almost a household word in this foreign land, he took up in right earnest. He invented and cast types in Persian and Bengali characters, the first few of which he prepared with his own hands. Here he was not only an organiser but also (in the words of Halhed) 'metallurgist, engraver, founder and printer' of types of alphabets so elaborate and distinct from one another as Bengali and Persian. In passing, it is worthy of notice that the Governor-General, Warren-Hastings, had at first asked Mr. Bolts, the author of the *Consultations*, to do the thing, but though an expert, the latter could not execute even the primary alphabets; whereupon Wilkins was called in, and as he gave his heart and soul to the work, it was done so well and admirably as to have left very little to be desired. In fact, his method had since been followed without any attempt at innovation or improvement. This shows that Wilkins was a thorough master of the art which he introduced in this country, and the cognomen of "the Caxton of Bengal" would not be inappropriate in his case.

As Hooghly on the Bhagirathi was then a place of great importance and drove a brisk trade, Wilkins established his printing press in that historic town. As this was the only press in the land, for the three well-known Baptist Missionaries, Carry, Marshman and

Ward, who set up a press at Serampore had not then come out to Bengal—it did all but a roaring business and issued out in rapid succession many useful and interesting publications. Like Wilkins, his friend Halhed had also learned, among a few other languages, Bengali. Indeed, his knowledge of this tongue was far above the average, so much so that he was in a position to write a grammar on it. This was no ordinary feat, more especially for a foreigner, as his was the first attempt in that direction. It was only natural that this altogether new work should be printed in the press established by Wilkins at Hooghly. In fact, the author had but Hobson's choice in the matter, he having had no other alternative. With the Bengali types cut and cast by Wilkins, Halhed's *Bengali Grammar** was printed; and with his Persian types, Balfour's *Forms for Herkern* was printed. This latter work was nothing but a collection of letters in Persian intended to serve as models for correspondence. Similarly, all the Laws and Regulations of the East India Company which

* In the title-page, the author states that the book was written for the purpose of teaching Grammar to the Feringhees, meaning thereby Europeans in general. And the necessity for this knowledge he founds upon the well-known political view that, to smooth the feelings and to gain popularity the conquerors should understand the language of the conquered, as the ancient Romans had done in the case of the *Greeks*.

were translated by Edmonstone and others continued to be printed with his Persian types.

In September 1783, Sir William Jones, an honored name in the republic of letters, arrived in Bengal and joined the Supreme Court at Calcutta as one of its Puisne Judges. His reputation had preceded him, and his coming to this country was hailed with general satisfaction. His first act in the direction of the cultivation and propagation of Oriental learning in Bengal—an act which has secured for him a glorious immortality—was the establishment of the Asiatic Society of Bengal, an institution of researches planned and formed on the lines of the Royal Society of London. The new Association met for the first time in 1784 under the presidency of its noble founder. In this laudable enterprise, Sir William was aided and supported among a few others by Charles Wilkins. In fact, the latter who had the good of this country at heart was always to the fore to do all for it that lay in his power.

The next work which engaged the attention and employed the labour of Wilkins was an English translation of that masterpiece of Hindu philosophy, in which are harmoniously combined the sweetness and elegance of poesy with the stiffness and severity of philo sophy. Need I say that I refer to that Canti cle of Canticles, the *Bhagvat Gita*, a didactic poem of a very high order. It contains, as F. Schlegel* says, the modern system of Indian thought connected by a common origin with the doctrines of the religious sect formed in India by the Greeks and called by them Samaneans in contradistinction to the Brahmans. It is an episode of the grand Sanskrit poem the *Mahabharata*; but though part of an Epic, it is philosophical throughout. It is done up in the form of Dialogues between Sree Krishna and Arjuna, and contains a fair and faithful exposition of some of the most difficult problems of Hindu Philosophy and Theology. It may almost be styled, says the eminent German scholar whom we have quoted above, a manual of Indian Mysticism; it is in great repute and the best exponent of the actual Indian mind. There is a remarkable peculiarity about this Book of Books, as regards the unmeasured praise bestowed on leading Deities, either not found at all in Manu's Institutes, or almost passed over without comment, while the old doctrines, the Vedas, and Polytheism generally are roughly handled. The essential creed expounded is that of an absolute divine unity absorbing all distinctions and engulfing all things. Yet in so far as it is connected with

* See his *History of Literature*, translation, pp. 122,123 (Bohn's Library), 1877.

mythology, it may be termed poetic pantheism, not unlike the Neo-Platonic philosophy, which, it will be remembered, combined under somewhat similar circumstances with the then popular belief, in its last throes, expecting by these means to revive its drooping energies. This pantheism, according to the Vedanta doctrine, pervading the whole of Indian literature since the time of Vyasa, is satisfactorily epitomised in the *Bhagavat Gita*, and is abundantly known to us, inasmuch as all classical Hindu Works in every branch of literature are more or less composed, or at any rate remodelled in the spirit of this doctrine. The worship of Vishnu and Krishna, now universally prevalent in Hindusthan, differs only in one particular—that of retaining the division into castes—from the religion of Buddha and which was transplanted from India to Tibet and China in the first century of Christianity, and disseminated throughout Central and Northern Asia.

Such being the character and importance of the *Bhagavat Gita*, it is not at all surprising that its English rendering, executed as it was so very admirably by Wilkins, attracted the attention of that liberal patron of oriental learning, the great Indian Satrap, Warren Hastings of laudable memory. In fact, His Excellency was so highly pleased with it that he sent up the work with his strong recommendation to the Honourable Directors of the East India Company to be published in England. The Directors, too, in accordance with his recommendation published in London the translation in 1785. But not only did it receive favour in England, it also moved the minds of the great in some other countries of Europe, and the result was that it was re-translated in rapid succession into French, Russian and German. Thus, this jewel of Hindu literature and learning became known and appreciated all over the far West. Not only did Wilkins distinguish himself by his translation of the *Bhagavat Gita*, he also deciphered some ancient inscriptions on copper plates and stone pillars which had hitherto baffled the attempts of sages and savants at explaining and translating them. This he did in connection with his labours in the field of Oriental researches. The first inscription brought to the notice of the Asiatic Society of Bengal was a copper-plate grant of Vigrahpala, the fifth king of the Pala dynasty. It had been discovered amidst some ruins at Monghyr, the Mudgagiri of the Sanskrit writers, and was translated by Mr. Charles Wilkins in 1781, three years before the foundation of the Society. The translation was published in the first volume of the Asiatic Researches, the organ of the Society, but without any facsimile or transcript of the original. The original is lost, and so many doubtful points in it cannot now be solved. It opens with the name of Gopala, the first of the Pala dynasty. He was a pious king who acted according to what is written in the Shastras and obliged the different sects to conform to their proper tenets. His religion is not distinctly mentioned, but he was evidently a Buddhist, as almost all the other Pala kings were, for the documents begin with a comparison between him and Sugata Buddha. But though a Buddhist by faith, he was the very reverse of a bigot, and was perfectly tolerant in respect of the religions of his subject-people. The grant also makes some mention of the successors of Gopala. From the conclusion it would appear that the document was executed in the seventeenth year of the reigning sovereign, on the 9th day of Baisakh, when the royal grantor lay encamped near Mudgagiri, modern Monghyr, and that by it the village of Mukatika was presented for the support of Siva-Bhattaraka and his followers. The record was composed by Bhatta-guraka, the minister, who erected the Budal pillar, which we shall presently notice.

Soon after the discovery of the Monghyr copper-plate, another monument of the Pala dynasty was found at Budal in Dinajpur.

This inscription, too, was translated by

Wilkins. It was a record inscribed on a stone pillar set up by the minister referred to above. As in the case of the Monghyr inscription, so in this the translation was published in the "Asiatic Researches" without any text. The inscription records the merits of the founder's ancestors who seem to have been all officers of the Pala family. Trusting to the wisdom of one of them, the chronicler states: "The king of Gaur for a long time enjoyed the country of the eradicated race of Utkala, of the Hunas of humbled pride, of the kings of Dravida and Gurjara whose glory was reduced, and the universal sea-girt throne."

After having thus laboured hard and incessantly in the field of Oriental learning, Wilkins found to his deep regret that his health, which was unusually strong, had been considerably shaken, and he, therefore, longed for the bracing air of his native Albion. He accordingly bade a long adieu to the land of his adoption in 1786, and sailed for the land which had given him birth. On his arrival in "Merry England," he took up his quarters at Bath, so well known for its pure wholesome air and waters. Here, however, he did not live an idle invalid life, but occupied himself with translations from the Sanskrit, the language which, of all others, he loved so much and in which he had acquired a wonderful proficiency for a foreigner. At Hawkhurst he began the formation of a fount of Nagari types for printing Sanskrit. In 1787, at Bath, he translated, with explanatory notes from an ancient Sanskrit manuscript, the *Hitopadesa* of Vishnu Sarma, who is facetiously called Pilpay.*

This excellent book of 'proverbial philosophy' contains some admirable fables in easy prose, but the prose is interspersed with difficult metrical precepts, and it is these illustrative quotations which often prove to be the rocks on which dull students suffer shipwreck, so very hard are they of comprehension to ordinary minds. This fable-book may well be styled the *Nitishastra* of the Hindus, and is the source of so many other collections of fables. The author occupied almost the same position in Hindu literature as Aesop does in Greek, and Lokman in Persian

* This is certainly a queer name, but its origin is not difficult to trace. In 1709 "Kutiladuma," a Persian work, was translated into French under the title of "Less-conceils-et-les-Maxims-de-pilpay-Philosophe-Indian sur-les divers itals-de-la vie." This translation was the direct source from which the English "Instructive and Entertaining Fables of Pilpay an ancient Indian Philosopher," was written and the latter book at once became so very popular that it passed through five editions in one single year, 1775. In this way the Indian Philosopher and Moralist, Vishnu Sarma, came to be called, almost in derision, Pilpay

Clearness of narrative is a distinguishing feature of the book : a selection of beautiful passages from old poems and maxims of wisdom are harmoniously combined. The narrative, indeed, mainly subserves to string the aphorisms and wise sentences together as a poetic garland intended to arouse reflection as well as to exercise the memory of youths The book is deservedly very popular and has been translated into many a language. In fact, with the exception of the holy Bible, there is hardly any book in the world which has been translated into so many languages as this fable-book of the Hindus. It is not known for certain when the *Hitopadesa* was first composed, but there is no doubt that it is an old work and has been in existence for many centuries together.

In this way Wilkins gained great celebrity as a Sanskrit scholar, and his learned labours in the field of Oriental learning attracted the notice of the powers that be, so that when a Library was founded in connection with the India House in the initial year of the nineteenth century, Wilkins was appointed its first Librarian on a salary or rather stipend of £ 1000 a year, an office then established mainly for the custody of Oriental manuscripts taken at Seringapatam and elsewhere. The Library proved very useful to the servants of the East India Company as it afforded them opportunities for learning almost all matters connected with India. Many of the Company's people helped this institution materially, amongst whom the name of Mr. Henry Thomas Colebrooke, so well known as a Sanskritist, deserves to be prominently mentioned, he having presented to it his very valuable collection of Sanskrit manuscripts numbering about two thousand.

As ancillary, to the office of Librarian, Wilkins was on the establishment of Haileybury College, in 1805, appointed Oriental Visitor at that College, whose duty was to co-operate with the Professors and to personally conduct the *viva voce* portion of the examinations. Like the Librarianship this office, too, he held till his death which took place in London more than three decades after.

Wilkins was succeeded in the visitorship by that distinguished Oriental scholar, Mr. Horace Hayman Wilson, then occupying the Boden Chair of Sanskrit at Oxford. In those days the Boden Professor was only required to reside three weeks in every term at Oxford, and was allowed to hold simultaneously the office of Librarian at the India House and of Oriental visitor at Haileybury. Professor Wilson held the office of Oriental Visitor till 1857, when old Haileybury was abolished.

One peculiar feature of the Haileybury College was that Sanskrit formed a part of its curriculam; Indeed, this venerable parent of world's languages was made compulsory so that no student could do without it. Thus, a good Sanskrit grammar was felt as a desideratum; but this want did not remain a want long. In 1808, Wilkins produced a *Grammar of the Sanskrit language*; but as it was the first attempt of its kind, it is not to be wondered at that it contained good many errors. But all the same it materially aided the learners in their first attempt at acquiring a knowledge of Sanskrit. The author, so far from bragging of his production, says at the very outset that it was not likely to be free from errors and he accordingly invites or rather exhorts sages and savants to point them out in order that he might correct them in a future edition.

In the introduction, Wilkins rightly observed that scholars in every branch of knowledge would find a fruitful field in the literature of the Hindu The Sanskrit lofe bristles with original treatizes on Astronomy, Mathematics, Philosophy, Metaphysics, Poetry, Music, Medicine, Ethics, Politics, Grammar and what not. He notices, in particular, the Puranas, poems of mythological treasures, as a collection of charming allegories and fables and interesting stories of old which induced men towards the " paths of Religion, Honour and Virtue." As I have already observed, Wilkins was the first to try his hand at Sanskrit Grammar, but owing to his dwelling-house with all its goods and effects having been burnt and destroyed by fire, he could not bring out his work as early as he had expected, so that, as a matter of fact, Colebrooke's work on the same subject appeared first. But not only did Wilkins help Haileybury students by writing a Sanskrit Grammar for their use, he also did them some good service by superintending through the press a new edition of Richardson's "Dictionary of the Persian, Arabic and English languages," and looked over each sheet of the book before it was finally printed off. He revised and enlarged the work by more than twenty thousand pure Persian words drawn from original dictionaries. The work received second revision in 1829 at the hands of Mr. Francis Johnson,* who was Professor of

* Speaking of this well-known Professor, Sir Monier Williams, after stating that, like his namesake the great lexicographer, he was author of a Persian and Arabic Dictionary, goes on to say: "He had never been at a university, had taken no degree anywhere and conld write no letters of any kind after his name, but he was one of the best, kindest and most single-minded and simple-hearted of men endowed with a marvellous power of acquiring languages, an infinite capacity for work, a vice-like tenacity of memory and indomitable industry. Unhappily he was at the same time so humble and so distressingly diffident and shy that he was wholly incapacitated for maintaining

Sanskrit, Bengali and Telugu at the Haileybury College, and who was succeeded in that Chair by Professor Monier Williams so well-known to fame in 1844.

The inscription on the Sanskrit gold medals awarded to successful students at Haileybury College was attributed to his authorship. The words round the margin were: *Atma-buddhi-Prasada-jam-tat-sukham sat-tvikam-proktam.*"—" That pleasure which is derived from the favour (or cultivation ?) of one's own intellect is called true,"—an apothegm (based on a phrase in the *Bhagvat Gita* which, from its being difficult to translate, had the merit of appearing to be pregnant with some occult meaning. In the centre of the medal were the words,—*Sri-Vidya-varah*—the exact meaning of which, too, was obscure.† Wilkins also compiled in 1796 a catalogue of Sir William Jones' manuscripts.

In the memorable Waterloo year, Wilkins published for use at the Company's College a list of the roots of the Sanskrit language—*Sri Dhatu-Manjari*—" the Radicals of the Sans-

---

order in a class-room . . . Speaking for myself I may say that it is impossible for me to exaggerate my debt of gratitude to him for the effectual help which he cheerfully gave me in my efforts to acquire at least five Oriental languages, Sanskrit, Arabic, Persian, Bengali and Telugu." (See " Memorials of old Haileybury College," pp. 71, 72.)

† See " Memorials of old Haileybury College, p. 208

krit language." This vocabulary was compiled from original manuscripts, of which the principal was the *Dhatu Manjari* of Kasinath. When this work was found to be defective, other texts were consulted, more specially the *Kavi Kalpadurma* of Vopadeva, whose grammer called *Mukdhabodha* is quite a favourite with the Bengal Pandits. In fact, no foreigner of that time did so much for Sanskrit learning as Wilkins did. Although Jones, Colebrooke and Wilson subsequently won brighter laurels, it was Wilkins who paved the way and showed them how best to achieve such splendid successes. Sir William Jones was candid enough to say that, but for Wilkins' aid, he would never have learnt Sanskrit. The fame of Wilkins was not confined within the narrow limits of his own country, its fragrance had spread very far indeed. All Europe rang with his praise, and European scholars were acquainted with his works as familiarly as Englishmen with those of their own worthies. He was made an *Associate of the Institute De France.* But greater honours were done him by the land where he has first seen the light of Heaven. Two years after his arrival in England, that is, in 1788, he was elected a Fellow of the Royal Society; and on the 25th June, 1805, the University of Oxford conferred on him the honorary degree of D. C. L. Twenty years after, the Royal Society of Literature awarded him one of their Royal medals as *Princepo Riteratorœ Sanscritœ.* Even His Majesty was not slow to do him the honour he so richly deserved. William IV, commonly known as the Sailor Prince, created him a Knight of the Guelphic Order in 1833. To say sooth, Wilkins' lot was enviable and marked him out as one of the favourites of Heaven. Health, competence, fame, the affection of family and friends—nothing was wanting to render him exceptionally happy; and to these causes may be attributed the advanced age of six and eighty which he had attained. Like David Hume, the famous historian and philosopher, he knew not what ailment was, and it is said that during the whole course of his long life he had only one attack of influenza which gave him a deal of trouble, and probably led to his leaving India for good when he was only twenty-six or twenty-seven years of age. Sir Charles departed from this world on the 15th May, 1836, and was interred at 'the Chapel in Portland town.' His portrait was painted later in life by J. C. Middleton, and a mezzotint by J. Sarton was engraved in 1880.

Wilkins was twice married and left three daughters, one of whom was married to the numismatist, William Marsden. This gentleman was also author of a *History of Sumatra,* and some other works. The father-in-law and the son-in-law were about the same age and died in the same year.

Sir Charles Wilkins occupies a very high place in the domain of Oriental learning. True it is, there have since appeared brighter names in it; but in point of priority none can approach him. He might be called the Morning Star of Oriental lore. Sanskrit was all but unknown to Europeans, and it was Wilkins who, for the first time, opened the rich inexhaustible mines of its untold treasures before their wondering eyes. He knew many Indian languages and had a thorough mastery over some of them. As for his knowledge of Sanskrit, it was simply wonderful at least for the time in which he flourished. He was justly esteemed (as may be seen in extant correspondence) by Sir Williams Jones, who, as he himself said, owed him "a debt immense of endless gratitude." In Indian Epigraphy he was specially the pioneer, being the first European to study Sanskrit Inscriptions, which were unintelligible to the Pundits of his time. Of the five articles by him—in the earlier volumes of the "Asiatic Researches,"—four are on this subject, one of primary importance to the real history of Bengal which has to be written. But the act for which his memory is fondly cherished, and his name regarded with a respect almost bordering on affection, is his introduction of the art of printing in this country. By this noble act he has built for himself a temple in the Indian heart, where he receives daily worship in the shape of prayer and praise from thousands, and will, it is to be hoped, continue to receive it for times unnumbered and through ages without end.

Henry T. Colebrooke

IN the long list of those who have laboured for the cause of Sanskrit learning and Indian research, no name is held with greater veneration than that of Henry Thomas Colebrooke succeeding immediately to the work done by that illustrious Orientalist, Sir William Jones. Colebrooke, by his writings and discourses, had placed the Indian public as well as the Government under a deep debt of gratitude. If those who had held high offices in this country during the past generation had but been inspired by the ideals and feelings of Colebrooke even to a small extent, if they had entered into sympathy with the people as he did, and tried to understand their culture as he had succeeded in doing, the history of Indian political agitation would have been quite different. The first to reveal to the European world India's ancient culture, Colebrooke has done greater services to our country than the array of distinguished proconsuls who sat on the Viceregal Throne.

Colebrooke was born in London in 1765 and his father was Sir George Colebrooke, Bart., One of the most influential man of the times and for several years Chairman of the East India Company, young Colebrooke was of a retiring disposition, and quite early in life had acquired a taste and fondness for study. Educated privately at home, Colebrooke at the age of 17 possessed as much knowledge as might be expected of a graduate of a university. Being of a religious bent of mind he had hoped for an ecclesiastical order but his father had persuaded him to accept a writership in the Civil Service of Bengal. His official career in India, both as a subordinate and a high servant of the Company having had to shape the internal policies of the Government, has been as brilliant as his learning and scholarship. Not that he fell in love at once with all that he saw in this country. On the other hand, his early letters to his father indicate that he was rather disgusted with his stay in India of which he spoke in even contemptuous terms. When, at this time, parliamentarians were also talking of a change in the Indian constitution with a view to end the political supremacy of the East India Company, Colebrooke was yearning to return home. "India is no longer a mine of gold" "Every body here is disgusted with it,"— It was in this strain that he was writing to his father, but a change soon came over him and in the plenitude of his love and regard for Indian culture, he retracted all these remarks. The first important appoinment held by him was that of an Assistant Collector of Revenue at Tirhat. Here he stayed for 9 years spending most of his spare time in sports. But a shrewd father was perisistently demanding from his son full. information about the religion and literature of the people amidst whom he had to live and whose salt he was eating. Colebrooke not only played the truant but practically bamboozled the aged parent by making the latter believe that there was nothing worth learning in this land of the hot sun. According to him Charles Wilkins was "Sanskrit-mad," " 'Asiatic miscellany' was a repository of nonsense " and ' the Institutes of Akbar ' a dunghill in which, perhaps, a pearl or two might be found" There is a tide in the affairs of men and the time had not yet arrived for Colebrooke to taste the beauties of Sanskrit literature. Neverthess, he continued to discharge his duties as Assistant Collector evincing great sympathy for the people. In 1789, while he was Revenue Officer at Purnea, he was deputed in connection with the Permanent Settlement question. After finishing his investigations, he put down his results in the shape of a work on the Agriculture of Bengal. This book of Colebrooke deserves to be studied by all Indian economists. Though a servant of the Company, he has dared to pass severe strictures on its commercial policy. He saw clearly enough the ruin of the cottage industries of Bengal as a result of English competition. The export of cotton-wool was highly injurious to the prosperity of the country and he pleads eloquently in his book on behalf of the poor whose trade had been ruined by the monopolist policy of the Government.

"To a Government enlightened as that is by which British India is administered, it cannot be a trifling consideration to provide employment for the poorest classes. No public provision now exists in these provinces to relieve the wants of the poor and helpless. The only employment in which widows and female orphans incapacitated for field-labour by sickness or by their rank, can earn a subsitence is by spinning and it is the only employment to which the females of a family can apply themselves to maintain the men, if these be disqualified for labour by infirmity or by any other cause. To all it is a resource which, even though it may not be absolutely necessary for the subsistence, contributes at least to relieve the distress of the poor. Their distresses are certainly great and among none greater than among the many decayed families which once enjoyed the comforts of life. These are numerous in India and whether they be entitled to the particular consideration of Government or not, they have certainly a claim on its humanity." Colebrooke, continuing suggests that cotton yarn instead of cotton wool be imported to England as that would mean employment for the poor in India. Citing the example of Ireland which was allowed to import duty free into England linen and wollen yarn, he asks, why not India? Why discourage that of cotton yarn from Bengal by a heavy duty besides all other impediments which we have occasion to notice so often. That is plain speaking and Colebrooke hesitated long before he could be persuaded to publish his book on the agriculture of Bengal.

Colebrooke's first introduction to the study of Sanskrit took place in the 11th year of his residence in India. He realised more and more that, for a proper and intelligent administration of the country, a knowledge of Sanskrit was absolutely essential. He encountered great difficulties in mastering the language and twice abandoned the attempt. In the end he succeeded and continued his studies down to the time of his death. The knowledge that he had gained already was soon utilized. Under the direction of Sir William Jones, a digest of Hindu Law was being prepared and Colebrooke translated it from Sanskrit. This might be said to be his earliest attempt in ancient learning and his fame as a Sanskrit scholar soon spread. In 1798, he was despatched to Nagpur on a special mission and though nothing came out of it, Colebrooke took advantage of his leisured stay there for two years by pursuing a varied and extensive course of study in Oriental Literature and natural sciences. The results of his studies are set forth in a series of articles contributed to "Asiatic Researches." Most of these articles were subsequently collected and published in two volumes by his son, Sir Thomas Edward Colebrooke, Baronet. We shall revert to the subject later on.

In 1801, Colebrooke was appointed to the office of the Chief Judge of the High Court of Appeal at Calcutta and in this congenial atmosphere passed on for several years, studying Civil and Hindu Law. Chief Judgeship in those days implied more leisure than now and Colebrooke found time to act as the unsalaried professor of Sanskrit, in the College established for Civil Servants at Fort William in Calcutta. As a professor he did not deliver lectures but did more useful work by publishing a Sanskrit Grammar, editing a Sanskrit Dictionary, Amarakosha (1808), besides other works, such as Hitopadesa in 1804. This is quite in accord with his educational ideals. He was strongly in favour of the method of instruction by translations and ever anxious that study should be based on systematic principles. In 1805 Colebrooke was elevated to the situation to which he had looked during the past 10 years with alternate hope and indifference—to wit, membership of the Supreme Council. In this position, he remained for 5 years without losing his Chief-judgeship. At the end of the period he vacated his seat in the Supreme Council and having more leisure he once again took to literary pursuits. In 1810, he published his translations of the two celebrated treatises on the Hindu Law of Inheritance. Mention has already been made of Colebrooke's share in the publication of the Digest of Hindu Law. This work, however, did not supersede the necessity of further aid to the study of the Hindu Law of Inheritance. With the sanction of the Government of Bengal he prepared his new treatise. It comprehended the celebrated treatise of Jimutavahana on succession which was cited frequently by Bengal lawyers by the emphatic title of Dayabhaga but included extracts from the still-more celebrated Mitakshara, so much of the work as relates to inheritance. At the time of its publication Colebrooke was disappointed that this work which cost him more labour and time than any he was engaged in, did not get such reception at the hands of the public as it should; excepting a few statements of facts, Colebrooke's work has stood the test of time and is to-day respectfully quoted by jurists of eminence all over the Empire. Colebrooke, as will be seen from a review of his works, was a keen mathematician and a versatile genius. During the last few years' stay in India he interested himself in the question of the height of the Himalayas. Experts cast doubts as regards the claim of the Himalayas as the highest mountain in the world. Colebrooke thought differently and for 10 years had been gathering evidences—judges nowadays have to handle evidences of a different nature—that would strengthen his conclusions. He took a living interest in the investigations of specialists and, when the fame of the Himalayas was established finally, it was a constant source of satisfaction and delight to him. Colebrooke retired from India in 1815 and finally settled near London that he might follow better his literary and scientific pursuits. He contributed frequently on scientific subjects to the Quarterly Journal of Science and though getting old and worn out, maintained his intellectual vitality to the full. A man of strong memory, he had in his library a splendid collection of rare books and MSS; every one of which he had studied. This library which cost him £10,000 he subsequently presented to the East India Company deeming it more likely to be beneficial to Oriental science than it would if it were to remain in the hands of an individual. Owing to constant reading, he became totally blind and died in 1836.

Colebrooke's fame as an Orientalist of the first rank is an abiding and undying one. His miscellaneous essays (2 Vols) published in 1872 by his son would alone entitle him to be considered the foremost Sanskrit scholar. It will be absurd to judge Colebrooke by the fulness of knowledge that we now possess or by the standard of literary and historic criticism that those who have been nurtured in the school of Colebrooke have, in later times, laid for us. At a time when, even among English scholars, literary criticism was unknown and when Indians naturally felt shy and refused to be communicative, Colebrooke was able to astonish the European world by his masterly and, what is even now considered, accurate exposition of Indian religious thought and philosophy. Nor the articles collected deal only with one branch of our national activities. Philology, Astronomy, Law and Mathematics claimed his equal attention. Of those articles dealing with the Indian systems of philosophy, says a French writer:—

"If ever memoirs deserved a complete and faithful translation, they are assuredly those of Mr. Colebrooke, that Indianist, so learned and conscientious, that *Vir nungnam Satis Landandus*, as he has been so justly styled by Dr. Stenzler in the preface to his recent beautiful edition of Raghuvamsa: for we do not hesitate to say that, without the excellent works of Mr. Colebrooke on the Sanskrit language and the most abstruse science of India—where he lived 30 years as a member of the administration, the knowledge so far complete of the language of these sciences and of the sciences themselves, might have been almost independently retarded in Europe. For only to speak of the essays on the philosophy of the Hindus, Mr. Colebrooke had read all the numerous works on that philosophy he had succeeded in procuring and it is from the methodical extracts and resumes from the works that he has composed his memoirs—precious models of exposition and philosophical analysis in which the European scholar withdraws himself to allow us almost constantly to converse with the Indian writers, which secures for these abridged expositions of the philosophical systems of India the highest amount of confidence and accuracy possible."

Nor did Colebrooke rest content with the mere exposition of well-known systems such as the Sankya, Nyaya, Vaisheshika, Mimamsa and Vedanta systems. Thorough in his methods and systems of study, he was the first to give us on an enlarged scale an account of the various minor sects of India —a subject which, in our own day, has been admirably handled by Sir R. G. Bhandharkar. Colebrooke and Col. Mackenzie were the first to notice, in the pages of the Asiatic Researches, the existence and the tenets of the Jains. To their labours enthusiastically assisted later on by Buhler, Jacobi and Hoernle, Jainism owes its rehabilitation as one of the earliest home religions of India. These essays of Colebrooke then are justly considered as standards of reference on matters to which they relate. His essay on the Vedas published in 1805 made the Europeans acquainted for the first time with this most ancient work of the Hindus and the Aryan world. But the effect and importance of the discovery was unhappily marred by Colebrooke's assertion that the study of the Vedas "would hardly reward the labour of the reader, much less that of the translator." Colebrooke was the first European writer again, as has been pointed out by R. C. Dutt, who thoroughly inquired into the subject of Hindu algebra, arithmetic and astronomy and it is feared he is the last European to write on that topic with the confidence and authority of an erudite Sanskrit scholar. His dissertation on the algebra of the Hindus (1817) possesses, therefore, more than the usual interest. In this he has striven to show that the mathematical science was in a state of high development long before the Europeans first learnt the mere rudiments of it either from the Arabs or the Greeks. Every student knows that the first general Hindu writer on algebra and astronomy was Aryabatta who flourished in what R. C. Dutt calls the Puranic age (476). The next great Hindu who wrote on mathematical as well as other natural sciences was Varahamihira, a true born son of Avanti (505-587). After him came Brahmagupta the 12th and 18th chapters of whose book, Sphuta Siddhanta, Colebrooke translated. Then set in the dark age ; political revolutions convulsed the land and finally the Rajput power was established. This was the period of the renowned Bhaskaracharya who completed his great work Siddhanta Siromani (1150). Colebrooke's dissertation is based on the preliminary portions of this work viz. Vijaganita (algebra)and the Lilavathi (arithmetic) both of which had been translated by him. The general view of Colebrooke as regards Hindu knowledge of mathematical science may be stated in his own words.

"The Hindus had certainly made distinquished progress in the science so early as the century immediately following that in which the Grecians taught the rudiments of it. The Hindus had the benefit of a good arithmetical notation, the Greeks, the disadvantage of a bad one. Nearly allied as algebra is to arithmetic the invention of algebraic calculus was more easy and natural where arithmetic was best handled. No such marked identity of the Hindu and diophantive systems is observed as to demonstrate communication. They are sufficiently distinct to justify the presumption that both might be invented independently of each other. If, however, it will be insisted that a hint or suggestion that the seed of their knowledge may have reached the Hindu mathematicians immediately from the Greeks of Alexandria or mediately through those of Bactria, it must at the same time be confessed that a slender germ grew and fructified rapidly and soon attained an approved state of maturity in Indian soil."

Of his other essays we shall but mention their names. In 1795 he published in the IV volume of the Asiatic Researches an essay on the duties of a faithful Hindu widow, containing an exposition of the principles underlying the Sati, that was even then fast disappearing. Between 1795 and 1801 he wrote three essays on the religious ceremonies of the Hindus and of the Brahmans about which owing to imperfect accounts that appeared in the press, wild notions were entertained. Colebrooke's account of the minor sects, the Charvakas and Locayaticas, Maheswaras and Pasupatas, the Pancharatras or Bhagavatas led Oriental scholars to a new branch of research in the religious history of the Indian people. In his "observations on the sect of the Jains, 1807, Colebrooke citing extensively from the writings of Greek authors had successfully established the priority of Jainism over Budhism whose offshoot it was popularly conceived to be. Mr. Colebrooke was equally interested in the inscriptional history of our country. Five of his articles in the miscellaneous essays, Vol. II, are devoted to the study and interpretation of inscriptions found in the rocks of South Bihar, Delhi and other places. In the field of epigraphy, however, Dr. Fleet transcends other European Scholars. One of the founders of the Astronomical Society, Mr. Colebrooke from early days was assiduous in his mathematical studies and he gives further proofs of his excellence in these branches of learning in his articles on "Indian and Arabian division of Zodiac and Hindu astronomy," contributed, of course, to the Asiatic researches.

Both as president of the Asiatic Society of Bengal & Director of the Royal Asiatic Society which he helped to found in 1823, Colebrooke has always placed only one ideal before the members, and that may be seen from the extract of a discourse which he made before a meeting af the R. A. S. in March 1823.

"To those countries of Asia in which civilization may be justly considered to have had its origin or to have attained its earliest growth, the rest of the civilized world owes a large debt of gratitude which it cannot but be solicitous to repay and England, as most advanced in refinement, is for that very cause the most beholden and by acquisition of dominion in the East is bound by a yet closer tie. As Englishmen we participate in the earnest wish that this duty may be fulfilled and that obligation requited and we share in the anxious desire of contributing to such a happy result; by promoting an interchange of benefits and returning in an improved state that which was received in a cruder form."

An illustrious pioneer in the field of Sanskrit learning, a great mathematician, a zealous astronomer, Henry Thomas Colebrooke's writings will ever remain sources of information to those engaged in the same field.

Horace Hayman Wilson.

Birth and Boyhood.

WILSON was born on 26th September, 1786. It is not known for certain where the future scholar and Orientalist first saw the light of heaven, but it is very probable that that event took place somewhere near London, and this we infer from the circumstance of his being sent in his sixth year to a school in Soho Square. Wilson's school-days were remarkable for the striking proof which he gave of his future greatness. It would seem that Wilson was born with a predilection for the Far East, as appears from the fact of his very first juvenile compositions having been on subjects connected with the two most noted countries in Asia, namely, India and China.

Wilson's thirst for knowledge of all sorts was very great, and he never failed to avail himself of opportunities for gaining it. When the school was closed for the long vacation, he would go and stay with his uncle, who held an appointment in the Assay Department of the Government Mint. Being led by curiosity he would accompany his uncle every day to the Mint, and pick up some knowledge of chemical analysis, the properties of metals, and the processes of assaying. This circumstance did him yeoman service in shaping the course of his subsequent career.

VOYAGE TO INDIA

Curiously enough, though the natural bent of his mind was towards polite learning, more especially Oriental lore, Wilson at an early age had made up his mind to qualify himself for the medical profession; and, in 1804, when he was only eighteen years of age, got himself admitted at St. Thomas' Hospital, and began to take lessons in the healing art. Having prosecuted his studies for three or four years, he became qualified to practice, and on September 17, 1808, was appointed Assistant Surgeon in the East India Company's service. Not long after, he left England in charge of some troops bound for India. The vessel met with an accident in the way, which delayed the voyage, so that it could not be completed in less than six months. But young Wilson, who knew how to turn his leisure to good advantage, managed to gain some knowledge of Hindustani from an educated Hindu, who happened to be his fellow-passenger on board the ship. This was the initial step which ultimately led to his ascending to the topmost rung in the ladder of Oriental learning and linguistic studies.

Employment in the Calcutta Mint

Wilson reached Calcutta with his troops in March, 1809, but he did not remain with them long. An opportunity soon presented itself for changing the medical, and to take to a more congenial profession. It so happened that, shortly after his arrival in Calcutta, a new hand was required by the officials at the Local Mint. Wilson at once offered himself, and as he was not a perfect novice, found no difficulty in getting himself employed there. In 1810, Dr. John Leyden * so well known for his scholarly attainments, was appointed Assay Master at the Calcutta Mint; and Mr. Wilson was appointed to act as Assistant Assay Master.

---

* John Leyden, the son of a Scotchman of the shepherd class, is distinguished as a poet and Oriental scholar. He was a friend of Sir Walter Scott, whom he assisted in the collection of materials for his *Border Minstrelsy*. He was, also, a linguist of no mean order. Having served in India in various capacities for some years, he died in 1811. Scott mourned him in some feeling lines introduced into the *Lord of the Isles*. Leyden's principal poem, *Scenes from Infancy*, appeared in 1802, and his *Poetical Remains* were published posthumously in 1821. Some of his verses have found place in D. L. R's once popular *Selections from the British Poets*. Leyden's translation of the Memoirs of Baber was completed by Erskine.

At about the same time he was also appointed Secretary to the Mint Committee. It would seem that the two offices were allied to each other, so that whoever was Assay Master, also became, as a matter of course, the Secretary. These two offices, important as they were, placed Wilson in a position of pecuniary independence; and although they made great demands on his, time and attention, still he managed to find leisure for the cultivation of his taste for linguistic studies. In this way he laboured hard to learn some Indian languages. But though a man of a literary turn of mind, Wilson never neglected the duties of the important offices which he held under Government. In fact, he worked remarkably well as a Government servant, and became a general favourite with his official superiors, who were candid enough to appreciate his valuable services, and to state in so many words that they were deeply indebted to him for many useful reforms in the coinage. His work at the Mint had this importance attached to it that it led him to turn his attention to Numismatics, and the subject got such a firm hold on his mind that he continued its study with due care and diligence, and succeeded, in after years, in producing a very valuable work on that subject. Need we say that we refer to his

Ariana Antiqua which deals with the coins of Afghanistan.

His Study of Sanskrit

While studying the subject of coins and coinage, the labours of Mr. Colebrooke in the field of Sanskrit learning held out quite a charm to him, and it was not surprising that he was led to try his hand in the same sphere. Indeed, the study of Sanskrit, though difficult, has a value of its own, and a man like Wilson could not avoid the temptation of being induced to it as if by the force of instinct. Mr. Colebroke finding in young Wilson an apt and intelligent student, gladly gave him all the help which he could possibly afford, and thus, initiated him into the study for which he had already made himself famous, and for which his name has become a household word in India. Wilson began his study of Sanskrit with his usual zeal and earnestness, and as the bent of his mind naturally tended in that direction, he, in a comparatively short time, got together a fair knowledge of that venerable parent of languages. But with all his efforts Wilson could not attain to the greatness of his master and patron; Colebrooke, who was the ablest and most accurate scholar of his time. In fact, accuracy of scholarship was not Wilson's strong point. True it is he wrote a

Sanskrit Grammar which was largely used in the Haileybury College, but, as a matter of fact, it was not well executed, and its introduction into the curriculum of study in that College was owing principally to the good offices of the well-known Professor Francis Johnson than whom a better grammarian, and a more generous friend in placing his own stores of learning at the disposal of other scholars, never existed.

"In reality," says Professor Monier Williams, "Wilson owed his celebrity to his boldness in entering upon investigations which no one had before attempted, to his excellence as a writer, to his faculty of lucid exposition, to the unusual versatility of his genius, including as it did, poetical, dramatic and musical powers of a high order, and perhaps, more than anything else, to his untiring industry and the wide range of his contributions to almost every branch of Oriental research."

All these are very good qualities, and no wonder that by their aid Wilson rose to a very high position in the world of letters. His boldness was remarkable. No work, however hard and difficult, daunted him: he was up to anything and such was his tact and intelligence that he generally acquitted himself well of it. As for the excellence and quickness of his pen they are best proved by the voluminous nature of his works, none of which, however, is below the average. In fact, one and all of them are worth reading.

His genius was cosmopolitan. He was a poet of no mean order. True it is that his original poems are only few and far between; but his translations of Indian dramas are very many and they testify to his powers as an ardent and skilful wooer of the Muse.* He was himself an accomplished actor, and was especially noted for his impersonations of old men. And not only did he possess musical voice, he also knew to play well on some musical instruments. Thus he was an all-round man, and was in a position to play almost any part that might be given him. As for his industry it was simply wonderful. He was a miracle of labour and diligence, and found pleasure in work,—incessant work,—work without ceasing. In fact, work was delight as well as worship with him. His contributions to Oriental learning were all but marvellous and covered quite a field of subjects. His essays which were on a variety of matters were collected and edited by Dr. Renhold Rost, Chief Librarian at the India Office, in five superb volumes. Though appointed Secretary to the Asiatic Society of Bengal early in 1811, Wilson did not commence to contribute articles to the organ of that Society until

* Some of his verses have found place in D. L. Richardson's once popular *Selections from the British Poets*.

1825. In point of fact, the bulk of his works was written after he had retired from the Indian service.

HIS STAY IN BENARES

At the end of 1819, Wilson was sent by the Government of India to Benares, and he remained in that famous seat of Sanskrit learning and Hindu religion for a year, re-organising the Sanskrit College there, collecting materials for his *Hindu Theatre*,—a monumental work, and adding to and improving his knowledge of Sanskrit by intercourse with the ablest and most erudite Pandits then living in Hindustan. Wilson, though a true-born Briton, was such a warm lover of Oriental learning as to have almost identified himself with it. So that it was only natural that, in the fierce controversy which had been raging for some time at Calcutta between the Anglicists and the Orientalists, as to whether education should be imparted to the natives through English or through their own vernaculars, he took the side of the latter.

With a view to give some idea of the great versatility of Wilson's talents, we cannot do better than give the following extract from the biographical notice in the Report of the Royal Asiatic Society for 1860, referred to at the outset of this Memoir,—a notice which, considering that Wilson was for many years both Director and President of that Society, and an incessant contributor to the pages of its journal, might well have been made more complete. Says the Report :—

> Neither official duties nor literary pursuits nor these combined, were sufficient for the active mind of our late Director (while he was resident at Calcutta). As a member of Society he joined with ardour in every scheme of public amusement; and was, besides, the originator and promoter of many measures for the permanent improvement of the people among whom his lot was cast. The theatre at Chowringhee owed for many years its success to his management and histrionic talents; while his musical skill and proficiency gave him a place in every concert. But his name will live in India, and especially in Bengal, for the part he took in promoting useful instruction. H. H. Wilson was the first person who introduced the study of European science and English literature into the education of the native population whose knowledge of English had hitherto been confined to qualification for situation of an office clerk. For many consecutive years Wilson was the Secretary of Public Instruction at Calcutta, and he devoted himself especially to directing the studies of the Hindu College from the date of its establishment.

THE BODEN PROFESSORSHIP

Wilson lived and worked in Calcutta till the close of the year 1832.

When the intelligence of his election to the Boden Professorship reached India, Wilson lost no time in resigning his appointment at the Mint, and made the necessary preparations for his return to England. On the eve of his departure from this country, the

Pandits met to bid him farewell, and one of them, who was more enthusiastic than the others, addressed him in a Sanskrit *Sloka* which being rendered into English would run thus :—

> The Pandit swans, who dwell in this lake of the Sanskrit College, are deprived of their wings by the influence of malignant fate when thou art gone away for good.

It was said that this flattering *Sloka* moved Wilson's serious face to tears.

WILSON AND BODEN PROFESSOR

Wilson left Calcutta in January 1833,—the very year in which Macaulay arrived at it,—and on landing in England went direct to Oxford, where he took a house in St. Giles' Street. His inaugural lecture was delivered some time in the summer term of the year. He chose for his subject, "The General Principles of Sanskrit Grammar,"—a subject which he thought likely to interest classical scholars from the point of view of its bearing on Comparative Philology,—a subject which had come to receive special attention at the hands of European savants of the day. It is not known for certain whether he gave any other lecture on the same subject; but there is no doubt that he delivered two public lectures at Oxford before general audiences on "The Religious and Philosophical System of the Hindus." These lectures were written to help candidates for a prize of £200 given by Mr. John Muir,*—a well-known old Haileybury man and great Sanskrit scholar, —for the best refutation of the Hindu Religious system. The prize was obtained by one Mr. Mullons.

His usual lectures were given to classes of one or two, and rarely more than four University men. But the audience, though few, were select. Mr. Monier Williams was a regular attendant, and so was Mr. E. B. Cowell, both well-known names in this country. Mr. Cowell was candid enough to say that when he was an Oxford graduate, he learned Sanskrit from Professor Wilson; and he, also, said that the good Professor was always ready to give lectures, three times a week to one person alone on any book he liked to choose. Thus, it is clear that Wilson was not only anxious to store his own mind with knowledge of all kinds, he was equally ready to impart it to others. Mr. Monier Williams, to whom we are mainly indebted for our information on the subject, has observed that it was, perhaps, more by the ardour or the enthusiasm for Oriental

* This gentleman was Judge of Fatehpore, and retired from service in 1853. He must not be confounded with Dr. Muir, who was Lieutenant-Governor of the N. W. Provinces and is well known in Anglo-Oriental literature for his "Sanskrit Texts."

studies,—an ardour which, though outwardly suppressed, occasionally burst forth to kindle sympathetic fire in his pupils,—than by any striking excellence in the matter or method of his lectures that he promoted the cultivation of Sanskrit at the University. Verily, therefore, was Mr. Monier Williams justified in comparing him,—which he did in one of his Calcutta speeches in the Asiatic Society's rooms,—to the vedic Aruni.* It must have been about this time that he was elected a fellow of the Royal Society, which was followed, a few years after, by his being appointed both Director and President thereof,—an honour which fell to the lot of only a select few among Oriental scholars.

The India House Librarianship

Professor Wilson resided at Oxford for about three years; but inasmuch as the climate of the place did not agree with his family, and as in August, 1836 shortly after

* Aruni was a pupil of the great Rishi, Dhauma, and was so very devotedly attached to him that he always tried his level best to bide his biddings, however hard and risky. Once he was directed by his "Guru" to stop an opening in a certain field, but not being able to do so, he laid himself down at the opening in order to prevent water from coming out. By comparing Wilson to Aruni, Mr. Monier Williams meant to say that the Professor was a devoted student of Sanskrit, and spared no pains to promote its study and cultivation.

the death of Sir Charles Wilkins, he was appointed his successor in the post of Librarian at the India House,—an office which carried with it the duties of Oriental Visitor at Haileybury,—he removed in that year to a house in London, merely visiting Oxford for his lectures, which only occupied three weeks three times a year. He used to go to the East Indian College for the Oriental examinations twice a year. He, also, attended regularly at the terminal visitation of the Directors, and always wrote a Report of the result of the Oriental examinations, which was incorporated in the Principal's general report.

His Knowledge of Languages

The versatility of Wilson's powers was best shown by the wide range of his acquirements in Indian languages. He knew Sanskrit, Bengali, Persian, Hindustani, Hindi, Telugu, Tamil and Marathi. Of course, his knowledge of some of these languages was all but scanty.

As for his knowledge of Sanskrit, it was of a very high order; and what is very remarkable in a foreigner, he could pronounce it with the ease and accuracy of a true-born Hindu. Bengali, Hindustani and Persian, also, he had a fair mastery of. He had good knowledge, too, of Telugu, which Madras officials were required to learn in lieu of Persian. But with all his scholarship he fell considerably short of the old Haileybury Professor, Mr. Francis Johnson, than whom a better Oriental scholar has not existed.

His Works

Professor Wilson's literary works are so many that a bare list of them would fill several pages of an ordinary book. Some of these works were written while he was in India; but most of them issued from his fertile pen after he had returned to England on being appointed Boden Professor of Sanskrit at Oxford. Of the books which were written in this country there was one which proved exceptionally useful to Europeans who were then learning Sanskrit. This was his Sanskrit English Dictionary, which first appeared in 1819. A second edition was brought out in the very year the author was appointed Boden Professor. By this excellent lexicon Wilson laid the earliest European Sanskritists under a deep debt of gratitude, so much so that without the aid of such a guide they would have hesitated to venture on the thorny field of Sanskrit learning.

Another useful work of Wilson's is his well-known treatise on the Religious Sects of the Hindus. This gives a more or less detailed account of Hindus of different eligious persuasions, and forms, as it were, a companion volume to Colebrooke's valuable essay on the Religious Ceremonies of the Hindus. He quotes with approval Colebrooke's view that "the real doctrine of the Indian Scripture is the unity of the Deity, in whom the universe is comprehended and the seeming polytheism which it exhibits offers the elements, and the stars and planets as gods." Though the work is not all that could be wished, still it contains a mine of information which is not accessible to the ordinary run of writers on the religions of the world, and if the learned author of the religions of antiquity could get hold of this important work he might have added considerably to the account which he has been able to give of the Hindu religion. It is noticeable that Professor Wilson has laid under an immense debt of gratitude the excellent Bengali writer, Babu Akshay Kumar Datta, who largely drew upon his work in the preparation of his *Upasaka Sampradaya*,—a work upon which his fame as a Bengali writer principally rests, and which is justly regarded as a classic of a very high order in the whole range of Bengali literature. It is true that Wilson's work contains some errors and inaccuracies, but they were almost inevitable and fairly excusable in a foreigner. With all its defects and shortcomings Wilson's "Religious Sects of the Hindus" is a valuable contribution to Hindu religion and theology.

WILSON ON HINDU LITERATURE

Wilson has given us a summary of the Puranas and of the Kathasaritsagara. In his introduction to the *Dasakumara Charita* he points out how it is "in a highly cultivated style, but entirely in prose." In his introduction to the *Mahabharata* he says:—

> "By these means, the merit, both poetical and historical, of the Mahabharata are becoming more extensively known; but in the amplitude of it, extant in the numerous traditions. legends and tales which it contains, and in its many didactic and philosophical paragraphs, it offers an accumulation of materials adopted to different tastes, and auxiliary to diverging researches, which must long advantageously engage the attention, and reward the industry, of Sanskrit scholars."

In regard to Hindu medicine he observes:—

> "That in medicine, or the astronomy and metaphysics, the Hindus have kept pace with the most enlightened nations of the world; and that they attained as thorough a proficiency in medicine and surgery, as any people whose acquisitions are recorded."

He says further: "It would easily be supposed that their patient attention and national shrewdness would render the Hindus excellent observers."

Wilson's translation of the *Rig Veda* is another work for which he is deservedly famous. It is a very creditable performance and appears to have done yeoman's service to those subsequent Sanskritists who made their attempts in the same direction. The learned Professor had commenced to translate that great work before he left India. In the last letter which he wrote to Mr. E. B. Cowell in India, he stated that he had finished the rough draft of the translation; but it is very much to be regretted that he did not live to publish the whole of it. The publication commenced in 1850, and had advanced only barely half when in 1860 he died. The work was taken in hand by Dr. Ballantyne, his successor in the Library of the India Office; but his failing health prevented him from carrying the remainder through the press. In fact, he had been able to do only a little when in the early part of 1864 he departed from this world. Dr. Goldstucker, so well known to fame as a deep Sanskrit scholar, had just undertaken to finish the volume, when finding Mr. E. B. Cowell returning from India he made over the unfinished thing to him, who partly in consequence of the interest which he took in Vedic studies, and partly because he was an old pupil of the Professor, took up the work with great pleasure and in right good earnest.

The translation of the Rig Veda was the last literary work undertaken by Wilson. It had greatly occupied his thoughts, and he had set his heart on its completion. His translation was mainly based on the very excellent commentary of *Sayana*, a very able and erudite Pundit of Southern India. This commentator, as Professor Cowell justly observes, stands to the Veda as Eustathius does to the Homeric poems. Professor Wilson has, with his usual candour, said that, were it not for Sayana's commentary, he could not have finished that most ancient and most difficult of Sanskrit works. As it is, Wilson's translation of the Rig Veda is a splendid performance and has secured for him a high place among Orientalists.

Wilson's essays, which Dr. R. Rost brought out in three big volumes, testify to the variety of his knowledge. They are a very rich storehouse of useful information and are very largely read and highly valued. But his *Hindu Theatre* is a more useful work in one respect, consisting, as it does, of translations of most of the Sanskrit dramas, and places him in addition to his other merits among poets worthy of the name. Indeed, Professor Wilson was a wonderful man, and there have been very few, indeed, who would bear to be compared with him in the domain of of Oriental learning.

ILLNESS AND DEATH

Professor Wilson had been suffering from stone for years. As the disease could hardly be cured without operation, one would have wished that he had submitted to it in time; but for some reason or other, it was deferred till after he had completed the Psalmist's cycle of three-score and ten. Unhappily, at that time there had been no successful application of the science of antiseptic surgery to the saving of life in such cases; and, as a matter of fact, the operation, done as it was late in life, did him more harm than good. The Professor died on the 18th March, 1860.

George Turnour

THE value of George Turnour's contribution to the study of Oriental languages and history cannot be exaggerated. He was one of the great pioneers who had to contend against not only prejudice and ignorance, but also many other difficulties, in the pursuit of a branch of learning that was then considered to be fruitless and unprofitable. Turnour's contribution to the study of Oriental languages and history lay in his undaunted pursuit of the study of Pali. Pali, as is well-known, closely resembles Sanskrit and is the old language in which the scriptures of the Southern Buddhism have been written. The Buddhist scriptures were brought to Ceylon during the reign of Asoka, the great Buddhist Emperor of India, some three hundred years before the birth of Christ. Since then Pali language was cultivated in the numerous monasteries that sprang up in all parts of the Island. A huge mass of exegetical literature in the form of commentaries on the elucidation of the texts grew up and added force and impetus to the study of Pali which in time became the language of the learned, as Latin became during the mediæval times in Europe. Consequently a number of historical works dealing with the fortunes of religion and of kings and reigns and royal dynasties came to be compiled in Pali. So we find two great historical epics, Dipawamsa and Mahawamsa, written in stately and smooth Pali verse, besides other minor poems dealing with a variety of subjects. These facts go to indicate that, during the time of Sinhalese Kings, Pali was studied both as a means to facilitate the understanding of religion and as a branch of national culture.

To appreciate the real value of Turnour's work in this connection one must try to get a glimpse, however inadequately, into the state of Pali learning in Ceylon at the commencement of the nineteenth century. The maritime provinces of Ceylon, after being successively exploited by the Portuguese and the Dutch for nearly three hundred years, were captured by the British in 1796. In 1815 the last King of the Sinhalese was dethroned and the whole Island was ceded to the British Government under a solemn treaty. When these events took place the torch of national culture of the Sinhalese had been practically extinguished. The constant warfare that had to be maintained for centuries against the ruthless foreigners had forced the people of the country to give up the cultivation of arts and sciences and, instead, to grasp the weapons of war and recede to the comparative security of the mountain fastnesses. All studies had perforce to be neglected and utterly neglected they were. The consequent religious and intellectual decline reduced the people to a state of comparative barbarism. Only a very few leaders of culture and learning preserved here and there the embers of the past intellectual greatness fanning in the vain attempt to produce the flame. A few Buddhist priests living far apart in various places possessed some knowledge of Pali, but, ignorant as they were of any foreign tongue, they could hardly communicate with the world outside.

It was at this time that the British rule commenced in Ceylon. The Britishers who came out to rule in Ceylon possessed such an exaggerated notion of their own superiority that they generally looked down upon native languages and literatures which in their opinion consisted of nothing but myths, fables and fanciful stories of a vanished greatness. So the native annals deserved no attention whatever, much less any laborious study. Owing to this snug assumption no European thought it worth while paying serious attention to the mass of literature that existed in the Island. Any attempt on the part of a more scientific student would only meet with scorn and derisive contempt. In the midst of all this prejudice and ignorance George Turnour was a noble and solitary example.

In spite of these hardships and obstacles Mr. George Turnour, one of the early officials of the British Government in Ceylon, deliberately set about to study the Pali language and make his inestimable researches into the ancient history of the Island. The difficulties he had to contend against were many. But the enthusiastic and persevering student in him overcame every obstacle until his labours were amply and more than adequately rewarded. The following extract from a biographical note added by Sir Emerson Tennent to his own monumental work on Ceylon published in 1859, besides giving some important facts about Turnour's life, will enable the reader to understand the nature of hardships that he had to overcome at the commencement :—

"George Turnour was the eldest son of the Hon. George Turnour, son of the first Earl of Winterton; his mother being Emilie, niece to the Cardinal Duc de Bossuet ?. He was born in Ceylon in 1799, and having being educated in England under the guardianship of the Right Hon. Sir Thomas Maitland, then Governor of the island, he entered the Civil Service in 1818, in which he rose to the highest rank. He was distinguished equally by his abilities and his modest display of them. Interpreting in its largest sense the duty enjoined on him, as a public officer, of acquiring a knowledge of the native languages, he extended his studies from the vernacular and written Singhalese to Pali, the great root and original of both known only to the Buddhist priesthood and imperfectly and even rarely amongst them. No dictionaries then existed to assist in defining the meaning of Pali terms which no teacher could be found capable of rendering into English, so that Mr. Turnour was entirely dependent on his knowledge of Sinhalese as a medium for translating them. To an ordinary mind such obstructions would have proved insurmountable, aggravated as they were by discouragements arising from the assumed barrenness of the field, and the absence of all sympathy with his pursuits, on the part of those around him, who reserved their applause and encouragement till success had rendered him indifferent to either."

The services rendered by Turnour to Oriental learning were unparalled in his day. As soon as he could adequately understand the Pali language he commenced the translation of the Mahawamsa, the Island Chronicle of Ceylon, written in verses and in a style somewhat obscure but stately. He was at the time in charge of the district of Sabaragamuwa and staying at Ratnapura, the historic town near Adam's Peak. The inquisitive student that he was, he was always in touch with Buddhist priests who were the only persons considered to be learned in Pali. It was with the ungrudging and kindly assistance of the Buddhist priests that Turnour was enabled to attain his ambition of acquiring a working knowledge of Pali. And whilst at Ratnapura he was also fortunate enough to come by a copy of the old commentary on the text, through the help of a friendly Buddhist priest He translated the first thirty-eight chapters of the Mahawamsa covering the period from 543 B. C. to 304 A. C. and published at Colombo in 1837. The appearance of this volume was an epoch-making event. It was a great surprise to the Oriental scholars in Europe, who hailed it with infinite joy and pleasure. It proved to be the light towards which they were groping. The mass of facts and accurate information that the Mahawamsa contained was so important that even an age of blind faith in its own superior wisdom dared not assail its authenticity. But to dispel all doubts Turnour, immediately after the appearance of his English translation, issued a reprint of the original Pali Mahawamsa in Roman characters. The Mahawamsa contains so much of information about the early history of India, that Turnour's translation turned out to be of great value in reconstructing Indian history. It created a revolution among the learned circles in so far as it affected the opinion hitherto accepted about the early history of India. The Chandragupta of the Mahawamsa was identified with Sandrakottus of the famous Greek Ambassador, Megasthenes.

Its publication led to very happy results in another direction too. Prinsep was at the time engaged in deciphering the inscriptions of Asoka, without the least knowledge of their authorship. Between the two, Prinsep and Turnour, there followed a series of correspondence with the result that Piyadasi of the inscriptions was identified with the Buddhist Emperor Asoka of the Mahawamsa. We can now hardly realize what this discovery meant at that time. It was a great triumph to the patient scholarship of Turnour and of his friend Prinsep.

With the help of both Pali and Sinhalese books Turnour also compiled "An Epitome of the History of Ceylon," fixing the dates of different reigns and principal events with such accuracy that after well-nigh a century of fresh study and research, his scheme of dates holds good with hardly any material alterations. He also contributed in the mean-time many able articles on Buddhist History, Indian Chronology and on other Oriental subjects to the Journal of the Bengal Asiatic Society. Some of his notes on Indian inscriptions were equally valuable and found always to be illuminating. It is said that Turnour had also entertained the idea of translating the whole Buddhist canon into English from the original Pali text, but unfortunately his premature death, which occurred in 1843 at Naples, put a stop to all his plans.

The scholars who were at that time engaged in investigating the Budddist records of Tibet and Nepal found helpful clues in the Mahawamsa in unravelling many obscure points.

Turnour after a long spell of trying duties in Ceylon, conscientiously carried out in his case, found his health fast declining and returned to Europe in 1842, the year before his death. The fact that he had imposed upon himself the severe task of studying Pali and Sinhalese in addition to his arduous duties as an official might possibly have told on his health. Although he died early, he had already achieved much and had created a world-wide reputation as an eminent Orientalist.

Before the beginning of the nineteenth century the European scholars had been coolly affirming that the ancient writings of the Sinhalese and those of the Hindus had no historical value. Happily that time passed away long ago. Students like Turnour and a few others who possessed vision and broad sympathy worked hard to vindicate the general authenticity of our histories. Let us remember with a proper sense of gratitude the names of that noble band of scholars of whom one of the most illustrious was George Turnour.

James Fergusson

IT is a well-known fact that since the foundation of the Asiatic Society of Bengal by Sir William Jones, a group of distinguished European scholars were, by their systematic and organised work, revealing to the Western world the rich culture and sublime philosophy buried in the sacred literature of the Hindus. Long is the list of those who patiently laboured for years together, under not very favourable circumstances, collecting sacred texts and critically editing them, deciphering inscriptions containing strange and obsolete characters, with a view, if possible, to construct, on scientific lines, a history of Hindu religion and philosophy. The names of Buchanan, Wilson, Sykes, Colebrooke, Mackenzie, and Prinsep—not to mention others nearly as great, are therefore household words to those who, in these days of political stress and turmoil, have cared to estimate, after careful study, the value of their contribution to the rich and fruitful stream of Indian culture. Though they have established the claims of India to an old and high civilization, yet material evidences were wanting which, if obtained, would place India side by side with Egypt, Assyria, and Greece, whose fame as centres of ancient civilization rested on the discovery of archaeological remains. It was reserved for James Fergusson to furnish such independent proofs and evidences as served to illustrate still further the antiquity of Indian religion, art and literature. Leaving the limited field of more or less provincial enquiry, he undertook, at great trouble and expenditure to himself, to explore the vast area of Indian architecture, an unknown land into which no traveller had yet set his foot.

James Fergusson was the younger of the two sons of Dr. William Fergusson and was born at Ayr in Scotland in January, 1808. There is nothing remarkable in his early life and career. Educated in a private school at Hounslow, Mr. Fergusson was soon to leave it as he was destined for an employment in Fairlie Fergusson & Co., of Calcutta, of which firm his elder brother was a partner. His early education was neither academical nor classical—a wonderful thing, when one reads his works where a classical ring is noted in almost everyone of the books he has written. His career as merchant's clerk in Calcutta was cut short as his brother's firm failed soon after his arrival. He then became an indigo merchant starting an independent house of business in conjunction with his brother. It was here in his indigo factory that Mr. Fergusson was laying the foundations of his special knowledge as one of the world's leading architects. Unconnected with any department of the Government and hence unfettered in his methods and activities, the young merchant in India, possessed of a fair amount of aesthetic taste and still more of shrewd philosophy, was amusing himself with the curious manifestations that surrounded him. Attracted by the majestic remains of ancient buildings, he soon began to contemplate on the ancient history of this land. The more he thought, the more fascinated he grew by the venerable repose of oriental antiquity. Soon he learnt to dislike the counting house and indigo factory. Instead he devoted his ample leisure to study and study provoked travel and these two shaped his future career as a philosophical explorer of the old architecture of the East.

During the years 1835—1842, he went on long tours visiting various localities in India containing or reputed to contain architectural remains and gathering materials for his forthcoming works on the Art and Architecture of India. At the close of his tour he returned to England. Having been already elected a member of the Royal Asiatic Society in 1840, he began to initiate a small group of friends there into the mysteries of Indian architecture, at the same time creating a special interest in the members of the Royal Asiatic Society, by the learned papers that he read at its meetings. Thus, in 1843, he read a paper on "The Rock-cut temples of South India." This is epoch-making for it is only after Fergusson's learned exposition of Indian sculpture that a critical appreciation of the value of Indian temple sculpture began to be evinced by scholars. At the same time, the Council of the R. A. S. presented a memorial to the Court of Directors of the East India Company requesting them to take a better care of and interest in the ancient remains of India. The East India Company, in its turn, issued orders to the Governors of the various Presidencies asking them to employ competent persons to measure and draw the various antiquities remaining in their provinces. It was a result very pleasing to Mr. Fergusson for he notes in a reprint of his paper: "We may thus escape the hitherto too-well merited reproach of having so long possessed that noble country and done so little to illustrate its history or antiquities."

Early in 1845, Mr. Fergusson returned to Bombay a second time and this was his last visit to India as the acknowledged historian of Indian and Eastern architecture. His surveys this time were much more exhaustive than the previous ones and he was able to obtain more accurate details regarding the various styles of architecture in vogue in the 5th, 6th and 7th centuries of the Christian era, materials which he utilised for his famous "History of Indian and Eastern Architecture." Returning home soon after the death of his father in 1846, he busied himself by publishing the results of his recent study. In 1848 appeared in the Transactions of the R. A. S. his article on "Ancient Buddhist Architecture in India" which was soon followed by an independent publication of "An Historical Enquiry into the True Principles of Beauty in Art, more specially with reference to Architecture." Unfortunately owing to the highly technical nature of the subject only four copies seem to have been sold; but nevertheless Fergusson thought that it was his best production. The following extract from the preface to that book of his will be of more than personal interest.

"In the first place, few men have either from education or the professional pursuits of their life been less prepared for such a work as this. From boyhood I was destined to the desk. From school I passed to the counting-house, from that to an indigo-factory—of all places in the world perhaps the one least suited for a cultivation of any knowledge of the fine arts.

From this to become an acting and active partner in a large mercantile establishment, from the trammels of which, in spite of every endeavour, I have never been able to free myself and during the time this work has been in my hand, I have written and perhaps also thought more about the state of the money market, indigo, sugar, silk and such like articles than I have, regarding architecture, painting or sculpture. This, in ordinary times, would only have delayed the work and rendered its completion less speedy but the last 18 months have been times of anxiety and distress to everyone connected with mercantile pursuits and more specially to those connected with the East. All those with whom I was formerly connected have succumbed one after the other. The whole edifice under whose shade I have passed my life has been swept away and there has been nothing but ruin and misery around me.'.

Mr. Fergusson was not a slave to existing theories. On the other hand, he cut new paths for himself and when he was convinced he was right he put forth his views strongly and courageously which perhaps accounted for some of the animosities he encountered particularly among archaeologists. The following may be taken as a specimen of the manner in which Fergusson forces his "harsh and unfashionable doctrines" into unwilling ears.

"I have also had the good fortune to spend the best years of my life in countries, where art though old and decrepit, still follows the same path that led it towards perfection in the days of its youth and vigour and, though it may be effete, it is not insane. In the East men still use their reason in speaking of Art and their commonsense in carrying their views into effect. They do not, as in modern

Europe, adopt strange hallucinations that can only lead to brilliant failures and in consequence though we may feel inclined to despise results, they are perfection itself compared with what we do, when we take into account the relative,-physical and moral means of the Asiatic and the Anglo-Saxon. * * * * * A course of study pursued among the products of Arts themselves in this manner, I have found far more instructive than books of theories are or perhaps can ever be; and I believe all would find it so if they could follow it in such circumstances as would prevent them being influenced by the errors of bad education or free them from the trammels of the stereotyped opinions of the age. The belief that it has been so to me induces me now to publish the result of my experience. I believe I see the path which other and cleverer men have mistaken and as the veriest cripple who progresses in the right direction will beat the strongest pedestrian who chooses a wrong path, I trust to being able to instruct even those before whose superior knowledge and abilities I would otherwise bow in silence."

During this period questions of a different kind engaged his attention. Europe was in the throes of a revolution and every state was busy strengthening its frontiers. Fergusson had no faith in masonry as an efficient means of protection and suggested earthworks as cheaper and more durable. This doctrine was not fashionable at all in those days and when he published in 1849 his "Proposed New System of Fortification," his suggestions were treated with contempt and scorn. But Fergusson continued to din into the ears of the Government the same view through his pamphlets "The Perils of Portsmouth or French Fleets and English Forts" and " Portsmouth Protected etc." The views of Government changed and Fergusson was appointed a member of the Royal Commission for the defences of the United Kingdom. He was also elected at the same time, a member of the Royal Institute of the British Architects and quite a number of articles appeared from his pen in the Transactions of that body. In these he discusses the history of the Pointed Arch, the Architecture of Nineveh and other points of great interest in the history of the Saracenic style.

In 1855 his great work, " Illustrated Handbook of Architecture' was undertaken at the request of Mr. John Murray. This was afterwards enlarged into four closely printed, profusely illustrated octavo volumes containing the History of Ancient and Medieval Architecture in 2 volumes, the History of the Modern Styles of Architecture and the History of Eastern and Indian Architecture in 2 Vols, the last bearing the date of 1876. It may be of interest to note that those are the only works undertaken by James Fergusson for which he was decently remunerated. All his previous writings were brought out at his own cost and needless to say he suffered from the financial-point of view, heavily, as the number of readers of such subjects as were treated was necessarily small. In all his writings, especially, in his History of Modern

Architecture he has sought to impress upon the minds of the readers his idea of an architect.

> "He was neither classic dilettante nor Gothic ecclesiologist, neither plodding prosaic nor dreaming mystic but a scholarly crafts-man devoting his best energies to the honest and manly exercise of ripened judgment in practical designing, self-taught in the studio and self-made on the building rather than drilled in the academy, relying much upon intelligent reflection and very little upon pedantic controversy, trusting to insight rather than precedent and to aptitude more than rule and so thinking out for himself with every care and every confidence the pleasant problems of his long descended and admirable Art for the sake of its acknowledged graciousness and his own continual joy."

To us Indians, Fergusson's Indian and Eastern Architecture is of more permanent interest than any of his works. Originally published in 1885, it has been vastly improved in its second Edition of 1876. It is a titanic operation requiring for its success a full knowledge of the main results achieved in the various branches of research conducted during the previous half century, philological, ethnological and mythological. It further requires a personal acquaintance with the objects described involving extensive travels in a country then insufficiently supplied with means of communication. The success of the book has been great and the verdict was at once proclaimed that Fergusson had laid both the Government and the public under a deep debt of gratitude to him. The main feature of the whole work is that he has been able to achieve important results single-handed and without Government help. This work of Fergusson not merely satisfies the reader who takes it up with a view to satisfy his aesthetic tastes but it aims at the broader and deeper task of illustrating and explaining in the full spirit of modern architectural enquiry the entire body of Indian history and progress.

It will be a mistake to suppose that Fergusson confined his attention only to Indian Architecture. Every ancient monument or work of art either in the East or in the West claimed his attention, though he loved to write more about Indian sculpture. Thus between the years 1860-68 he devoted his spare time and energy to the exposition of the ancient remains in the Holy Land. The theories that he had enunciated regarding these were not widely approved. He was subjected to considerable criticism but Fergusson would not change them. When it was pointed out to him that his views regarding the holy places were those of one 'who had never been there, he retorted in effect, 'Very well, now that I have been there what is the result? I have nothing to retract and nothing to add."

One of Fergusson's greatest contributions to the realm of thought was his "Tree and Serpent Worship," a monumental work prepared under the authority of the Secretary of State for India and published by the India Office in 1868. The Asiatic Society of Bengal was founded in 1784 and since then it had published hundreds of volumes but not one of them treated about this subject. Fergusson was therefore the first to point out that the serpent played an important part in the mythology of India and that its worship not only prevailed but considerably influenced such faiths as Jainism, Buddhism, and Vaishnavaism. Illustrating from the sculptures at Sanchi and Amravati, Fergusson discourses in a learned manner and proves what a great part the snake played in the religious history of India. That the worship of the tree and the serpent portrayed in the illustration of his work might not be considered as a mere local superstition, Fergusson explains in the introductory chapters of the work how far that form of faith had prevailed in other countries and to what extent it influenced other forms of faith. According to him, serpent worship, if not the oldest, ranks at least among the earliest forms through which the human intellect sought to propitiate the known powers. Traces of the worship were found in the Old and the New Worlds. Everywhere the snake was considered as the bringer of health and good fortune. He is the teacher of wisdom, the oracle of future events. Love and admiration more than fear and dread were the main features of the faith and these being common to it all the world over indicate a common origin. Coming from the mud of the lower Euphrates among a people of Turanian origin, it soon spread thence as from a centre, to every country or land of the Old World in which a Turanian people settled. No Semitic or people of Aryan race ever adopted it as a form of faith. The essence of snake worship is opposed to the spirit of the Veda and the Bible but with varying degrees of dilution the spirit of these two pervades in a greater or less extent all the forms of religions of the Aryan or Semetic races. The publication of Fergusson's Tree and Snake Worship evoked much sympathetic comment from scholars and his reputation was greatly enhanced. Next year, 1869, he was appointed "Secretary of Works and Buildings." Yet in the midst of official duties Fergusson found time to publish more books on the subject of architecture so dear to his heart and answer unfriendly critics in the pages of journals. Writing of Fergusson's relation with other scholars we are reminded of that unfortunate book he published in 1884, Archaeology in India.' To the circumstances of its publication we shall immediately advert. Babu Rajendralal Mitra was attached to an archaeological mission which, in 1869, visited the Katak Caves which were hurriedly examined by Fergusson in 1837. The conclusions arrived at by Mitra were not satisfactory to Fergusson and he therefore urged the despatch of another mission to the same place under *European* guidance and offered to pay the expenses himself if the Government should decline to bear them. This led to an acrimonious controversy in which Fergusson used strong, nay, even violent language regarding Rajendralal. Not satisfied with that, Fergusson long after the incident published a pamphlet, 'Archaeology in India', which was nothing but a peg on which to hang his not very pleasant remarks on Rajendralal Mitra's works. Even the European friends of Mr. James Fergusson did not like it; but at the same time it must be remembered that Fergusson was terribly outspoken when his feelings were roused.

The last contribution of Fergusson was his "Restoration of Westminster Hall" published in the November issue of "The XIX Century and After" in 1885. He died in 1886, loved and respected by all who knew him intimately. A remarkable figure, a versatile genius, one of the most prominent writers of the day upon the recondite subject of

Architecture, Mr. James Fergusson will ever be remembered, in spite of serious drawbacks, for the signal services he has rendered to the cause of pure historical studies. Self educated but somewhat strong-willed, hitting hard in controversy but ever ready to open the matchless stores of his knowledge to co-workers, more sinned against than sinning, Mr. Fergusson's death has caused a void which it has been difficult to fill, in the realm of Indian Architecture.

Rajendralal Mitra

EARLY LIFE AND CAREER.

BABU Rajendralal Mitra belonged to a respectable Kayastha family and was born at Soora in 1824. Besides Rajendralal, his father Janmajay had five other sons and the family resources were too slender to enable the boys to receive any education worth the name. Happily for Janmajay, his widowed and childless sister at Calcutta undertook to educate the most promising of six sons, Rajendra, who was soon made over to her protection. The foundations of his knowledge of English were therefore laid in one of those petty adventure schools that were then springing up all over the country in Bengal. Rajendralal's stay in Calcutta was however short, for his aunt soon died and the youth, who was full of hopes about his future, had to return disappointed to the coarse living and poor accommodation of Soora. The parents however were anxious to do their utmost for the boy and the suggestion was made by friends that he should undergo the course in the Medical College. That was the only course left open for the aspiring poor in those days, for a medical education could be had for the mere asking. In November 1839, he got himself enrolled as a stipendiary student, a position somewhat humiliating to the family pride. At the Medical School Rajendralal distinguished himself by supplying to the Principal useful information on the indigenous systems of medicine. Babu Dwarkanath Tagore was so struck with the ability of Rajendralal that he was prepared to send him to England to complete his education. But caste scruples prevailed and the family not willing to break the rules of the Hindu society, Rajendralal had to decline the offer. His career had to be shaped in a different way. One interesting feature regarding his early career may be pointed out. A few students of the Medical College seriously misbehaved, and even though Rajendralal knew all particulars, he refused, as a point of honour, to accuse any of his fellows at the trial. For this he was rusticated from the College along with others and in disgust Rajendralal turned his attention to law. But misfortune awaited him even here. He diligently studied and sat for the examination. When he was hoping to hear of his success, it was notified that the whole examination was cancelled as the questions had all oozed out. This was a blow to him and in despair, he was prepared to accept any job in any public department or private establishment. He was now in his 22nd year and during this time had mastered the various vernaculars of India, Sanskrit, Persian and Latin with a working facility in French, German and Greek. It was the Asiatic Society of Bengal that discerned the genius in the young man and at once appointed him as its Librarian and Assistant Secretary. As an official of the Society, Rajendralal proved himself very useful and efficient, besides getting for himself that training and study which he lacked owing to his deficient early education. The duties of an official of such a learned body as the Asiatic Society of Bengal were multifarious requiring not merely intelligence and industry but a sound knowledge of the various branches of research conducted by the Society. By laborious study he soon acquired a taste for antiquarian research and began to contribute and fill the pages of the Society's journal. Altogether he contributed nearly 114 papers to the *Journal* of the Asiatic Society of Bengal, every one of which has been admired by European and Indian scholars. A man of inexhaustible energy Rajendralal started in 1850, the 'Bibidhartha Sangraha' an illustrated Bengali magazine devoted to science and literature which he conducted for nearly 7 years. In

1856, he was appointed Director of Wards' College, an institution for State wards and orphans. In this congenial position he passed for several years branching out into various forms of activities. Contemporary opinion seems to be harsh in its judgment of the work done by Rajendralal as Director of Wards' College. The boys, most of them wealthy Zemindars, with enough of money and little inclination for study, were surrounded by all the temptations of a great metropolis and they seem to have been left much to themselves free from the disciplinary control of the Director. This roused much comment from the press and when the whole thing became a scandal, the Government very wisely closed the institution and the good Director was pensioned. This incident does not mean that the Government had no faith in the abilities of Rajendralal. On the other hand he was frequently consulted by the Government on various points. Only two years previous to the closing of the Wards' College, Mr. Mitra was made a C. I. E. The Calcutta University honoured him by conferring on him the honorary degree of D. L. On this occasion, the then Vice Chancellor, the Hon'ble Sir Arthur Hobhouse spoke of the doctor thus:

"There is no European Society of oriental scholarship to whom he is not honourably known and there are many who have been glad to admit him as member and colleague. He has thrown light on many a dark corner of the history, antiquities and languages of the country."

For many years he was an active member of the Calcutta University and the Municipal Corporation. As a wise and honoured leader of the Landholder's Association in Bengal, he was rightly held with great veneration by the land owning class for whose amelioration he strived hard using his influence and pen freely. He also took an active and intelligent interest in the Indian National Congress, an institution which, in those days, represented the quintessence of political wisdom found in this country. In the Welcome Address to the second Congress, he said :

It has been the dream of my life that the scattered units of my race may some day coalesce and come together ; that, instead of living merely as individuals, we may some day so combine as to be able to live as a nation. In this meeting I behold the commencement of such coalescence. I hope the union will not be very distant. It may not be left to me to realise the sight, but it is highly gratifying to me that we are here assembled together, delegates from the North and from the South, from the East and from the West, all anxious to join as members of one nation for the good of our country.

Diverse we are in origin, in religion, in language, and in our manners and customs, but we are not the less members of the same nation. We live in the same country, we are subjects of the same sovereign, and our good and evil depends entirely on the state of the Government and the laws passed in this country. Whatever is beneficial to the Hindus is equally beneficial to the Mahomedans and whatever is injurious to the Hindus is equally injurious to the followers of Mahomed. Nations are not made of sects but of tribes bound together in one political bond. We are all bound by the same political bond, and therefore we constitute one nation.

A young Hindu of a clever and worldly type and possessed of an abundant stock of knowledge, Rajendralal was quite willing to push his fortunes by means of it. Exploration was his hobby and his leisure hours were devoted to this. But unfortunately he overworked himself which in the end brought his death much too soon. He took charge of the paper *The Hindu Patriot* after the death of his friend Kristodas, put all his money into the enterprise and was so unsparing of himself that he succumbed in 1891 after a short period of accute suffering from paralysis. Contemporary estimate of his character, was not always very complimentary. Revered as a scholar he was yet feared as a man of strong emotions.

An example of perseverance in the pursuit of knowledge under difficulties, he was haughty and quarrelsome, more feared than loved. He was an able critic : he had a trenchant pen and his command of the English Language was wonderful."

LITERARY ACTIVITIES.

Rajendralal's literary activities are almost coeval with his connection with the Asiatic

Society of Bengal. For more than 40 years he had been contributing to that Journal on a variety of topics. The more important of these, numbering as many as 114, had been collected and published in book-form. His earliest contribution was an interesting article entitled "On some Græco-Bactrian relics from Rawalpindi" (1862). In 1868, a new impulse was given to the cause of Indian historical research and it came from an altogether unexpected quarter. In that year the Royal Society of Arts suggested to the Government of India that casts of some of the more important sculptures of ancient India should be obtained and for that purpose placed a large sum of money at its disposal. A portion of this grant was made over to the Government of Bengal and the then Lieut.-Governor, Sir William Grey, at once started making the necessary enquiries regarding the existence of ancient sculptures. It was then that the suggestion was made by Rajendralal Mitra that the party of modellers and moulders which the Government was then about to send to Orissa, should proceed to Bhuvaneswara where it would find the oldest and most interesting specimens of Hindu architectural ornament. Mitra's suggestion was at once approved and he himself was selected to conduct the operations which he cheerfully undertook during the winter of

1868—69. The results of his work are embodied in two large volumes, "Antiquities of Orissa," profusely illustrated. In this, by no means an easy task, Mitra had two objects in view (1) to carry out the directions of the late Lord Canning as embodied in a Government of India Resolution *i e.*, to secure an accurate description, illustrated by plans, measurements, photographs and by copies of inscriptions, of such remains as most deserve notice with the history of them so far as it may be traceable and (2) to notice prominently such points in them as were calculated to throw any special light on the social history of the ages to which they referred. Thanks to Sir Gardner Wilkin's learned work on the "Ancient Egyptians" which served as a model, Rajendralal was able to realise in a full measure the objects he had in view. Mitra's "Antiquities of Orissa" (2 Vols.,) in spite of adverse criticisms from interested sources, even to-day serve as an important source-book and throw a flood of light on one of the most sequestered corners of Indian history. Putting together all the information regarding Orissa from available ancient authors he had presented in a readable form and charming style, the architectural, religious and social history of Orissa, treating under separate heads the history of particular localities. The chapter dealing with the history of several systems of religion that had influenced the growth of Orissan art is at once enchanting and provocative of great thought and one desires that a similar enquiry should be conducted by Tamil scholars regarding their country which had seen strange vicissitudes of religion and which is studded with temples and sculptural monuments of hoary antiquity. As has been remarked, this work of Mitra alone would have raised him to a very high rank among Indian scholars second only to those who, like Bhagawanlal Indraji, had acquired the methods of true historical criticism. Equally learned and exhaustive was his other work "Buddha Gaya-the Hermitage of Sakyamuni." His visit to this holy place inspired him to fresh efforts and eventually he translated several important Buddistic works pertaining to the country of Nepal of which mention will be made later on. In 1875, he wrote on 'The Greek Art and leprosy in India', which attracted wide attention. His next important article was on "the representation of foreigners in the Ajanta frescoes," the value of which can never be over-estimated. The neighbourhood of Ajanta was first known to Europeans during the battle of Assay which broke down the Mahratta power. Since then the Ajanta Caves were not visited till at last in 1819, an officer of the Madras Army much struck at the beauty of Ajanta designs gave a short notice of them in Mr. Erskin's "Remains of Buddhists in India." Many other accounts of the caves and the frescoes appeared from time to time but they were meagre and inaccurate. In the meantime Fergusson's epoch-making book "Rock-cut Temples of India" (1843) laid the foundation for a critical study of these remarkable works of art. The Court of Directors whose attention was drawn to this subject requested Captain Gills to write an account of these but his description subserved only to whet the desire for further information. The illustrious Bombay scholar, Dr. Bhau Daji also visited Ajanta in 1865 and took fascimiles of inscriptions which yielded but few points of historic interest. He was of opinion that, though it could not be asserted that the Bactrian Greeks were the authors of the Caves, the influence of the Bactrians could be traced in the paintings. Of the beauty and style of these remarkable Art treasures, thus speaks Mr. Griffiths, Principal of the Art School in Bombay, who then took copies of the paintings :—

"For the purpose of art-education no better example could be placed before an Indian art-student than those to be found in the Caves of Ajanta. Here we have art with life in it, human faces full of expression, limbs drawn with grace end action, flowers which bloom, birds which soar and beasts that spring or fight or patiently carry burdens:—all are taken from Nature's book-growing after her pattern and in this respect differing entirely from Mahomedan art, which is unreal, unnatural and incapable of development."

Such is the beauty of the Ajanta designs which Rajendralal Mitra, following the lines of Messrs Ralph and Grisley, who were the first to notice the existence of foreigners in those frescoes, describes in his learned article. His conclusion was that the various scenes depicted represented phases of Indian life from 1800 to 2000 years ago. To read this article side by side with Fergusson's illustrated book on the same subject is an education by itself.

Rajendralal's next work is the "Indo-Aryans," in 2 vols. As has been already stated this is merely a reprint of the more important of his articles contributed to various research journals. In their collected form they serve as source materials for the elucidation of the ancient and medieval history of the Indo-Aryans—a subject to which the attention of European scholars was just then being drawn. The reprints, 21 in number, deal with Indian architecture, manners and customs of Indian society, history of the dynasties of Bengal and Behar and one or two articles are devoted to philology. The vastness of the knowledge he exhibits, the perfect accuracy of details and the mastery of North Indian vernaculars show the author to be a versatile genius. The articles of Indian architecture have got some melancholy interest attached to them, for they at once recall to our minds the unseemly and acrimonious controversy carried on in the press by Mitra and Fergusson. It was a wordy strife between two strong men who would both remain in a state of inconvincibility and would yet carry on agitation against each other. In this war of pamphleteering Fergusson seems to have been worsted as is evident from his further abuses of Mitra in his book 'Archeology in India'. In his article on Indian Architecture (1870), Rajendralal Mitra had strongly controverted the opinion held by some that the Hindus had first learnt the art of building in stone from their Greek conquerors. Fergusson criticised it in 1871 in the pages of the Indian Antiquary. But Mitra was persistent and published the same article as the first chapter in his "Antiquities of Orissa." A second criticism of it soon appeared in Fergusson's History of Indian and Eastern Architecture. But Mr. Mitra was irrepressible and a rejoinder was printed in his work on 'Buddha Gaya.'

"Fergusson's remarks have not been of a comprehensive character dealing with the subject in all its bearings. He seems to overlook if not to ignore and repudiate, historical evidence and to confine himself exclusively to the interpretation of lithic remains."

It is with reference to this controversy, unseemly because of the needlessly violent language indulged in by Fergusson, that Dr. Peterson remarked:

"Rajendralal in my opinion did not always receive from English critics the courtesy and consideration to which his honesty of purpose and his devotion to learning entitled him."

But Mitra bore the abuse with dignity and that was enough to explode the fantastic theories of archaeologists.In the end Rajendralal's view that Indian Architecture was self-evolved and self-sustained was admitted by all scholars who have read and thought about the subject. Space forbids the review of his other equally interesting articles. But mention must be made of article No. 7 in the collections, "Spirituous Drinks in Ancient India". Here the learned author traces the history of spirit-drinking in India. The earliest Brahman settlers were a spirit-drinking race, both soma-beer and strong spirits being used by them. Wine was sold publicly both for the use of the God and the community. Strong arrack formed a prominent feature of Santramani and the Vajapaya rites. But there soon came a revulsion of feeling against wine. Spiritual threats were held out and wine was prohibited by Sukra Acharya, Krishna and also the Smrithis.

Not to spoil a movement by imposing excessive punishments, expiatory ceremonies were laid down. But this movement against intoxication failed. For we find copious references to wine drinking in the literature of later times from which Rajendralal quotes extensively to prove his statements. The moral is obvious and those who to day are attempting to close arrack shops with a view to diminish the Government income may well do to read this learned article of Mitra and draw their own inferences. As the great historian Gibbon has expressed it "the wines of Shiraz have always prevailed over the laws of Mahomed."

Besides publishing books that helped to reconstruct the ancient history of India, Rajendralal distinguished himself in another sphere—collection of Sanskrit munuscripts for the Government. For this purpose he travelled extensively and his reports in connection with the search for Mss. are as illuminating as those of Dr. Peterson and Sir R. G. Bhandarkar. He had, besides, an important share in the publication of that extremely useful series, Bibliotheca Indica, undertaken by the Asiatic Society of Bengal. The object of this series was to disseminate a knowledge of the most standard works on Religion and History, in Sanskrit, Persian, Arabian and Urdu. A versatile genius and well-versed in

North Indian Vernaculars, no one is better fitted for the task than Dr. Rajendra Lal Mitter. He also edited several important Buddhistic texts. Thus he edited and translated into English important portions of the Lalitha-Visthara, and began to edit the Prajna-Paranitha, another of the standard works of the Nepalese Buddhists. His work in this direction may not be perfect but there is absolutely no doubt that he has rendered accessible to scholars the contents of many recondite works. The following testimony of that great friend of India, Prof. Max Muller clearly indicates with wnat great regard he was held by European scholars.

"He (Mitra) is a pundit by profession, but he is at the same time a scholar and a critic in our sense of the word. He has edited Sanskrit Texts after a careful collation of MSS and in his various contributions to the Journal of A. S. of Bengal, he has proved himself completely above the prejudices of his class, freed from the erroneous views on the history and literature of India in which every Brahman is brought up and thoroughly imbued with those principles of criticism which men, like Colebrooke, Lassen, and Bernont, have followed in their researches into the literary treasures of his country. His English is remarkably clear and simple and his arguments would do credit to any Sanskrit scholar in England. * * * Our Sanskrit scholars in Europe will have to pull hard if, with such men as Raja Rajendra Lala in the field, they are not to be distanced in the race of scholarship."

Kashinath Telang

EARLY YEARS AND EDUCATION.

TELANG* was born on August 30th 1850. He belonged to a middle-class Hindu family. His family was one of the twelve Saraswat families that had left their native home in Goa early in the last century, to seek their fortune, in the busy and commercially growing city of Bombay. His father and mother were quite uneducated as we understood education now. But they were characterized by mother wit, were pious and frugal, with noble traditions of respectability and steady virtue behind them. His mother was gentle and amiable. These traits of a sweet and amiable disposition, Telang shared in no small degree.

It was early in life that Telang was sent to school to learn his vernacular. Even at that early age he seems to have been very studious. He finished his vernacular studies in due

---

* Condensed from "Kashinath Trimbak Telang. The Man and His Times" by Vasant N. Naick, M. A. Price Re. 1. G. A. Natesan & Co., Madras.

course winning prizes from the Deputy Educational Inspector, Rao Saheb Viswanath Narayan Mandlik, with whom in later life he was destined to rub shoulders on a common platform. He was sent to learn English at the Elphinstone School. In the Middle School he won a prize in English in 1861 and he was selected on the occasion of the prize distribution to recite the poem on the death of Sir John Moore. He won another prize in 1862. It was at this time that his attention was drawn towards Marathi poetry, and to appreciate its spirit he began the study of Sanskrit under a Shastri. His fellow-student was the famous linguist and the first Indian Civilian, Shripad Babaji Thakore. He was now promoted to the Matriculation class where his fellow-students were Jamsetji Ardesir Dalal, Gajanan Krishna Bhatavdekar, Rao Shaeb Tullo, Thakore, and Nadkarni. All of them rose to distinction in their respective walks of life.

In his secondary course Mr. Telang proved himself an apt pupil, with a special bias for languages. His tutors marked him out as a promising lad, took special care to cultivate his tastes, not however at the sacrifice of subjects absolutely needed for the University Examination. The late N. M. Parmanand who was his teacher in the school and who became afterwards his trusted friend and a revered and sage guide in all public matters, guided him in getting up his Mathematics thus making his path smooth for success at the University. Under the able guidance of Parmanand, his proficiency in Mathematics was so marked that he secured a prize in that subject and in English in 1863. He passed the Matriculation in 1864 with Sanskrit for his second language. At this time he got from his Principal, as a prize, MaxMuller's "History of Sanskrit Literature." It was also during this period that he became an ardent student of Marathi poetry, the love for which he retained through life. Mr. Telang was known in after life to be a brilliant conversationalist. He would quote often from his favourite English poets. This trait of his manifested itself also at this time in connection with Marathi poetry, the choicest couplets of which he would quote on occasions to the delight of his friends and teachers. Mr. Telang passed his Matriculation at the age of fourteen. While at college he showed the same deligence and passion for general reading that marked him out at school. He won the junior scholarship in 1865; and senior scholarship in April 1866; passed his F. A. in December, won another scholarship in 1867 and secured the Raja of Dhar prize and Ganpatrao Vithal prize in English.

At seventeen, he took his B. A. degree, at

nineteen , he passed the M. A. examination in languages. Six months later he obtained the Bhagwandass scholarship in Sanskrit which then meant a separate and a severer test than at present. The same year he passed his LL.B. examination. Three years later he passed the Advocate's examination. Thus at twenty-two he qualified himself for the legal profession. From seventeen to twenty-two he was a fellow at his college. It was during this period that he formed the habit of strenuous application and laid the foundation of that accurate, deep and extensive knowledge which made him the versatile scholar that he was known to be.

Early in life, again, he had resolved to throw himself whole-heartedly in the public life of his country.

Men like Dadabhai Nowroji, Nowroji Furdoonji, Sorabji Shapurjee Bengali, Dr Bhau Dajee, Sir Manguldass Nathubhoy had already chalked out a path for others to follow and young aspirants readily followed. The struggle of life was not so keen ; problems had not become so complex ; paths had not diverged ; the future was not overcast with a leaden hue. There was the zest of youth in the indulgence of its own energetic life. The men of those times saw glorious prospects, but they did not discern the fatal barriers that closed the approach. A youth of brilliant parts like Mr. Telang readily fell into the way of his predecessors and soon attained a conspicuous position.

On the completion of his College course Telang betook himself to the practice of law. In those days the profession was not quite so over-crowded as now though the best minds of the University were naturally attached to that career, so full of opportunities for acquiring wealth and reputation. Telang belonged to the second generation of graduates turned out by the University. Mehta and Tyabji were already on the road to fame and fortune and Telang followed the path of law with his transcendent gifts of scholarship.

In six months' time, it became plain to all that Telang was marked for success. As Sir Raymond West puts it, in virtue of that sympathetic faculty which Telang possessed in quite an unusual degree, he almost at once acquired the "English tone of the bar and moved morally and dialectically on a platform absolutely the same as that of his learned friends" from Europe. Success at the bar was but a prelude to further preferments and distinction. The way to the Bench lay open: and the Government were so impressed by his learning and judicial wisdom, that the offer of a judgeship was almost inevitable. The more fortune smiled upon him, the more keenly was he awakened to his own responsibility. Thus at the age of 39 he attained that far shining eminence that was a marvel to all. At that age when judgeship was offered to him, he accepted it because he thought it would afford him rest and seclusion to carry on his literary pursuits.

It would be out of place in this short sketch to give a resume of his decisions and rulings which have become so familiar to every practising lawyer in India. Both as a lawyer and a judge he helped a great deal to formulate aright the canons of Hindu Law and it is to be regretted that a man of such parts and such special knowledge should have been cut off too soon to leave behind a monumental work on the subject. No one was better fitted for the undertaking both by his Sanskrit scholarship, his broad general culture and above all his literary gift of luminous treatment.

This is not the place to discuss his many-sided activities, social, educational and political. Suffice it to say that Mr. Telang was a versatile scholar accomplished in various spheres of learning. His public services would, in themselves, require a special volume for adequate treatment and it would take us far afield to recount however briefly his contributions to the cultural aspect of Hindu civilization. Here we confine ourselves rigorously to his Oriental researches—his elucidation of difficult Sanskrit texts.

LITERARY WORK.

We are now turning to perhaps the most inward phase of Mr. Telang's life, the work which he cherished most and to which he would fain have devoted all his energies if circumstances had so shaped his career. In India, men of superior talents cannot, without great loss to the country, adopt the life of the literary recluse. Our condition in that respect somewhat resembles that of France at the time of Diderot, Voltaire and Rousseau. Literary work of an abiding character has to be postponed before the more imperative need of what Mr. Gokhale has called "the liberation of the Indian mind from the thraldom of old world ideas and the assimilation of all that is highest and best in the life, thought and character of the West." Hence it is that the actual literary output of our countrymen falls so short of expectation.

Telang's literary work may be divided under three heads. 1. The books he translated or annotated. 2. The various essays on antiquarian topics contributed either to the Journal of the Bombay Branch of the Royal Asiatic Society or to the Indian Antiquary. And 3. His miscellaneous essays on varied topics read either before the Student's Literary and Scientific Society, of which he was for many years the Secretary, or before the Hindu Union Club. The purpose of the last was to give an incentive and stimulus to correct thinking on the topics of the day.

His labours in vernacular and English literature and Mahratta history form no negligible part of his contribution to scholarship. He was deeply interested in Philosophy and social science.

He read two papers in Marathi before the Hindu Union Club, one in 1886 called "The Relative Importance of Shastra and Custom" and the other in 1889 on "Compromise in Social Matters," which was an application to Hindu social reform of some of the principles enunciated in John Morley's great work. These two papers embody what may be called Telang's method of social reform. In the first Telang quotes texts from the different Smritis, some in favour of custom and others in favour of the Shastras and next turns to the Epics to note therein the conduct of the high-souled, like Drona and others, to show that they introduced changes in the canons of the Shastras to suit the exigencies of the hour. Therefrom Telang deduces the proposition that there is a precedent in our past history to introduce change in our manners and customs and in the rulings of the Shastras to suit time, place and circumstance.

If we do not restore, he says, to our Smritis the life and elasticity which they possessed in the palmiest days of Hindu Society, our religion will cease to be a living force, a state of things which is undesirable as it is bound to lead to moral chaos.

In the second lecture he examines the application of the principles of compromise to (1) thought, (2) speech and (3) action. In the first he advocates absolute freedom. He warns his people against the tendency of the human mind to find out arguments in justification of conduct rather than mould conduct, according to convictions. He deprecates such a course as altogether unworthy of a human being and in the end ruinous both to himself and to the society of which he forms an integral part. Right thought will impart seriousness to our conduct and will enable us to avoid the prevailing attitude of the people in our midst which is "to compound for the sins we are inclined to, by damning those you have no mind to."

The translation of Lessing's 'Nathan the Wise' was undertaken with the purpose of directing the taste of Marathi readers to healthy, instructive, elevating, first rate foreign literature. The translation of Reynolds and Boccacio threatened to poison the spring of pure literature. Telang wanted to stem the tide. The Drama was translated also to inculcate the principle of toleration in the minds of its readers.

Another essay of his deals with the social and religious aspects of the history of the Marathas as gathered from the examination of original documents. It was delivered as a lecture before the Deccan College in 1892. "Mr. Telang's paper represents" writes Justice Ranade in his preface to the "Rise of the Maratha Power," "the true spirit in which native historians should treat the past history of their country." It has also a melancholy interest attached to it. It was a sort of prelude to the more comprehensive work on the History of the Marathas which he had undertaken to write for the Longmans.

We now turn to the labours of Telang in the advancement of Sanskrit scholarship and original research. Dr. Bhandarkar has laid down three qualifications for the man who would fruitfully devote himself to this field of enquiry.

> One who enters into that field is required to be a man of exceptional intelligence, a man with a clear head and with very acute and keen reasoning powers. The next requisite and a very essential requisite is that there must be curiosity in him: and the third requisite is there must be a freedom from bias and thorough impartiality in forming an opinion on any question that comes forward.

All these qualities were found in combination in Mr. Telang and he could therefore leave behind him a legacy of materials "enough to make the society distinguished for generations to come." Telang was endowed by nature with a transcendent intellect, which he had further strengthened and disciplined by the studies to which he had subjected it in the early years of his life. Speaking of Mr. Telang's work as an Oriental scholar, Justice Chandavarkar said :—

> Trained in the school of Mill, Huxley, Spencer and Strauss and disciplined in the severe logic and close dialectics of Shri Shankaracharya, Telang had more of the critical than the constructive talent and was at his best when he strove to detect the flaws and fallacies in opinions advanced and theories contributed by scholars. He approached all these questions on antiquarian subjects with a complete freedom from bias or preconceived theories and rigidly held with Emerson that a scholar at all events must take into himself "all the ability of the time, the contributions of the past, all the hopes of the future". There was no point however small, which he did not take into account and to which he did not strive to do justice, in determining some knotty point in antiquarian research.

We cannot do more than barely chronicle the many papers he contributed to the Bombay Branch of the Royal Asiatic Society's *Journal* and to the *Indian Antiquary*. It was after finishing his studies and qualifying for the profession, that he turned his attention to "antiquarian work and the work of making researches into the history of India, and the development of Indian thought." It was in 1872 that the *Indian*

Antiquary was started by Dr. Burgess. Its first volume contained two essays, by Telang, one is on the 'Date of Nyayakusumanjali, and the other is a short note pointing out "that however right Dr. Rajendralal Mitra might be in holding that there was a time in historic memory, when the ancestors of the Hindoos ate beef freely that time came to an end sometime before Christ." In the same volume appeared Rev. Boyd's translation of Weber's paper in which the latter had set himself to shaking the tradition of the extreme antiquity of the Ramayana. Weber sought to show that "the great Hindu Epic really dates from the third or the fourth century A. D. and that it contains clear internal evidence of an acquaintance with the Homeric Saga-cycle." Telang answered the arguments of Weber in an essay called "Was the Ramayana copied from Homer"? He was not a pseudo patriot who thought that shaking the antiquity of the Ramayana was belittling to national glory. He was induced to reply to the contentions of Dr. Weber because he thought first and foremost that they were based on an insufficient and one sided evidence. Telang was a fair critic. He was a disciple of Mill in that respect. He knew how to weigh evidence. He used to regret that "among us there was a disposition to accept much as a proof which hardly rested on any good basis and to consider something as history merely because people believed it to be history. Telang from the beginning trained his mind to get rid of this popular cant. Before writing his well known paper in answer to Prof. Weber he went through a course of study in Biblical criticism and read some works on the "Proofs of Historical Criticism." Mr. Weber based his argument on the ground that the source of the Ramayana was to be found in a Buddhistic myth borrowed from Homer. Telang meets the argument by saying that

> the Buddhistic story may just as likely have been borrowed from the Ramayana as have been the origin of it. Secondly he says that concidences, so far as they are coincidences, are but slight and probably casual. In the folklore of Northern India there was for the Brahminical and for the Buddhist author an ample store to draw upon. It was in the highest degree improbable that a Buddhist should be adopted as a Brahmanical hero. On the other hand the Buddhists parting from Brahmanism would still carry with them many of the earlier myths and traditions of their race, but the orthodox already amply supplied with legendary materials would be slow indeed to find in a Buddhist hero, a subject for adoration and adoption as their own.
>
> That there was a Homeric poem in Sanskrit might be true, the Ramayana would in a manner justify the assertion, but that there was an Indian translation of Homer as stated by Dio Chrysostom and others appears wholly erroneous.

This was in substance Telang's second argument. "The whole mental and moral atmosphere in which the Ramayana is steeped is so fundamentally different from that of the Homeric poems that no substantial influence of the latter can be traced in the Indian Epic."

The geographical and astronomical references and the literary notices of the poem on which Dr. Weber relied for the late production are handled by Telang with fairness and ability. Telang adds several affirmative indications which support his own view that the composition of the Ramayana must be referred to a period several centuries before the Christian era and before the date assigned as probable by Weber. The criticisms of the young Hindu scholar have been confirmed by subsequent investigations both in India and Europe.

The publication of this critical essay gave Telang a place of acknowledged prominence amongst Sanskrit scholars. The essay was subsequently published in the pamphlet form and was highly praised by the academy.

The essay refuting the contentions of Dr. Weber was read in 1873. Early in 1870 he had read a paper before the Students' Literary and Scientific Society on the life of Shankaracharya. The same year he contributed a criticism on Dr. Kielhorn's Sanskrit Grammar to the columns of the *Native Opinion.* In 1871 he had read an essay before the Students' Society on Muktikopanished. The Essay on Ramayana has already been noted. The same year he wrote an essay on the date of Shri Harsha for the *Indian Antiquary.*

In 1874 he read a paper before the Students' Literary Society contesting the theory of Lorringer as regards the Bhagwadgita, that it was copied from the Bible. The Essay was afterwards embodied as an introduction to the metrical translation of the "Divine Lay" published in 1875.

In the same year he contributed four essays to the Indian Antiquary (1) on the Drama of Bana called Parvati Parinaya: (2) on Kalidas, Shri Harsha and Chand; (3) The Ramayana older than Patanjal: (4) Note on the Ramayana. The same year he read two learned papers before the Bombay Branch of the Royal Asiatic Society, (1) on the Chalukya Copper-Plates (2) the Date of Madhusudhan Saraswati, the author of Gita Gudhartha Dipika. In this paper he combated the views of Lassen and Burnouf that Madhusudhan lived in the XVI century A. C. Telang came to the conclusion that he flourished in the reign of Aurangazeb either at the end of the fifteenth or beginning of the sixteenth century.

In 1876 he wrote a note in the Indian Antiquary on Anandgiri's Shankarvijaya and read an essay on "Three Copper-Plates of the Kudamba Dynasty" before theBombay Branch of Royal Asiatic Society. In 1880 he wrote a note on the useful Marathi Serial, the Kavyetihas Sangraha, in the *Indian Antiquary*, recommending it to public attention as the work devoted to the publication of original sources of Maratha History. The same year he wrote an essay on the Silhar Copperplate for the same monthly. In 1881, he contributed a review of Mandlik's Hindu Law to the pages of *Indian Antiquary*. About Mandlik's Hindu law and Telang's review on it Sir Raymond West writes as follows :—

> Mandlik's Hindu law has added materially to our means of forming a true comprehension of the Hindu law as a living system, but it rests on an insufficient collection of the manuscripts of the Mayukha. It presents defects of scholarship ane doubtful speculations which invite criticism. Telang's observations may be deemed an almost necessary pendant to the work, for the purpose of the lawyer who wishes to stand on a sure ground.

In 1884 he read another essay on the Date of Shankaracharya before the Students' Literary and Scientific Society. He also read an essay on Purnavarma and Shankaracharya and another on the Gleanings from the Sharia Bhashya of Shankaracharya before the Bombay Branch of the Royal Asiatic Society. Of his many papers on Shankaracharya it is said as follows :—

> The most important of his contributions were those devoted to determining the age of Shri Shankaracharya, his opinion being that he flourished in the

reign of the Buddhistic King Purnavarma who is mentioned by Hiueu-thsang as having been the ruler of West Magadha. In Telang's opinion Purnavarma must have reigned at the latest in about 590 A. D. In 1885 he read before the Bombay Branch of the Royal Asiatic Society an essay on the Date of Badarayana, the author of Bharam Sutras. He pointed out that these BramahSutras dated back to a remoter age than 400 or 500A. D. assigned by Weber. This closes the chronicling of his contributions to Oriental Research. It is said about them that they reveal his "vigorous style and fertile imagination." Mr. Telang was unequalled among his countrymen as an exponent of the treasures to be found in the "rich mine of Oriental literature". Mr. Telang's opinion about the fixing of the chronology of Sanskrit writers is expressed thus. He says in one place, "It is almost impossible to accept any one line of reasoning or any single group of facts as conclusive about the precise date of any book in Sanskrit literature, at all events in the present state of Sanskrit Chronology when it is almost literelly true that, as an American Sanskritist puts it, "Indian literary dates are for the most part only so many pins set up to be bowled down again."

He edited two Sanskrit works for the Bombay Sanskrit Series, (1) Bhartrihari's Niti and Vairagya Shataka,(2)The Mudrarakshasa of Vishakhadatta. His metrical translation of the Bhagwat Gita to which is prefixed his reply to Dr. Lorringer and his prose translation of the same work for MaxMuller's Sacred Books of the East Series complete his work in the field of Sanskrit literature.

We have now brought to a close this brief record of Telang's literary work. Learning with him was not a mere source of intense delight nor was it only an intellectual pastime. He found in it "lamp for his feet." It was not a miser's hoard to gloat on with pleasure, but a treasure readily placed at the disposal of others, for guidance, instruction and to serve as an inspiration to similar endeavour.

The highest pleasure of his life was to live the life of culture and rectitude. His inner nature, says Sir Raymond West, was that of a meditative saint. Telang became an evangelist to a large section of his countrymen because, as the ripest fruit of his scholarship, he furnished them with fertile ideas on many of the questions that agitated their minds and perplexed their souls. Telang's greatness, says Sir Raymond West, was at bottom a Hindu greatness, the greatness of a scholar, of a contemplative spirit, of a man of thought diffusing light in many directions, and widening the area of human interest for the people whom he represented.

THE END.

Telang's period of active work covered only twenty years. Considering that the last years of his life were passed away in the trammels of office and in a very precarious and poor state of health, it betrays marvellous precocity of talent to find so much sterling work, so much earnest endeavour compressed within such a small span. The honours that come to a man at the very end of his career were showered upon him in the very prime of life and the position he won in the hearts of the people would have constituted for any other man a sufficient reward for the last days of a long life spent in the service of his country. Mr. Telang's career was meteoric ; but it left permanent traces on the generation that followed him. To this day his words carry conviction and are pregnant with sage counsel. He died in the prime of life at the age of 43 when others begin their public career and yet his scholarship, insight, and foresight invest his utterances with the breadth and penetiation that come only from the riper experience of life and its stern discipline.

Telang embodies for modern India a type of culture and enlightenment in which currents of opposite kind had commingled to constitute the light, wisdom and the sobriety of his opinions. He was a great Sanskrit scholar, a deep student of Marathi literature and history, at the same time that he had thoroughly imbibed the spirit of Western thought as reflected in its literature, history and philosophy.

Bhau Daji and Indraji

THESE two names together cover a period of more than half a century of active work in the field of Indian Archæology, and stand out prominently as those of two pioneer Indian scholars in this somewhat novel line of work for Indians. Dr. Bhau Daji, the elder of the two, came of humble parentage from South Bombay from the confines of Goa and Sawantvadi. After receiving general education in the Maratha Central School and later in the Elphinstone Institution, he entered life as a teacher in the Elphinstone Institution itself. He began soon after to study Sanskrit privately and undertake those tours, for the study of antiquarian remains, which remained through life the holiday that he gave himself from his regular work. The first such journey he undertook with the then Chief Justice of Bombay, Sir. E. Perry. Soon afterwards the Medical College, that is now Grant Medical College, was established. Young Bhau Daji was one of its pupils and soon he became a favourite with Dr. Morehead and the professors. At the end of his course he became a graduate in medicine and obtained the position of an Assistant Professor in the Grant Medical College itself. He soon gave up this position and set up private practice which in time exceeded all his expectations and put him beyond need, notwithstanding the fact that he dispensed medical advice and even medicines to the poor without remuneration. Having become a medical man with a considerable extent of practice, he found the opportunity to carry on investigations into works on Hindu medicine. Thus, before reaching middle age, he became a man of means with varied interests which enabled him to carry on his investigations covering a vast range of subjects from the treatment for leprosy on the one end to the interpretations of the "cave-numerals" at the other.

In the society of Bombay he came to occupy an acknowledged position comparatively early in his life. He was the first representative of the Elphinstone Institution and of the Board of Education before the establishment of the University, of which he was one of the Fellows mentioned in the Act of Incorporation. He was the first Indian President of the Students' Literary and Scientific Society and played a prominent part in the social, educational and humanitarian activities of the time. He was a great deal responsible for the establishment of the Bombay Association and the Bombay Branch of the East Indian Association. He was twice Sheriff of Bombay and a Member of the Bombay Branch of the Royal Asiatic Society. He became a Member of its Committee of Management in 1859 and five years after, one of its Vice-Presidents, which position he kept till his death. His reputation as an antiquarian was so great that, when Lord Northbrook visited the caves of Ellora, he invited Dr. Bhau Daji to be his guide.

Dr. Bhau Daji's work as an antiquarian and scholar extends to every branch of Archæology. In the field of Sanskrit literature, he tried to estimate the age of the Sanskrit poet, Kalidasa and exhibited such a wealth of learning for the time in which he carried on his investigation that all the advance that has since been made only heightens our admiration for his penetrating insight and sound critical acumen. It was he that was responsible for the bringing out of the Jain story of Kalakacharya into connection with the Saka invasions—a problem that remains still unsolved. He first brought to the notice of scholars the succession of pontiffs according to the *Satrunjaya* and tried to settle the chronology of the Jain Pattavalis. A great deal of advance has since been made in this subject by other scholars among whom the late

Dr. Hoernle deserves prominent mention. He published a note on the 'Age of Hemadri', the famous minister of the Yadava King, Mahadeva, and of his successor whose foreign minister he was. He fixed his age "as at the end of the twelfth and the commencement of the thirteenth century" which remains more or less his age as yet. He wrote short notes on the Mukundaraja, the old Maratha scholar, Hemachandra, Madhava and Sayana.

A slightly different branch of work, but still coming under the same general head, were the brief notes he contributed on the age and authenticity of the great astronomers of India, Aryabhatta, Varahamihira, Bhattothpala and Bhaskaracharya.

In the department of Epigraphy Dr. Bhau Daji interpreted the Girnar Inscription of Rudradaman as also the Gupta Inscription on the same rock. By a misreading he called the first the Sah Inscription, which is now known as the Saka Inscription of the famous Saka Satrap Rudradaman. His reading and interpretation of the other inscription has been productive of more important consequences. It was in the course of the reading of this, that he discovered the prevalence of the Gupta Era and inscriptions being dated in this era. He was able to proceed on this and formulate the thesis in regard to Saka, Gupta, and Vallabha eras and dynasties which remains substantially sound in spite of great advances. More remarkable than this is his collection and translation of the Ajanta Inscriptions. His work in this line included also the interpretation of the Jasdan Inscription, a short inscription at Amranath, near Kalyan, some inscriptions from Dharwar and Mysore and the inscription of Prataparudra I at Anamakonda and the inscriptions on the Bhitari Lat and the Kutb Minar.

The most important branch of it all was his interpretation of the numerals in the Cave inscription which have come to be called the "Cave Numerals". But, according to the competent authority of the late Dr. Buhler, the credit of this remarkable achievement ought to be shared by him with Bhagavan Lal Indraji, his collaborator. Dr. Buhler's remarks are worth quoting in this connection:

> "In the interest of truth I cannot suppress the remark that Pundit Bhagavan Lal's name ought to have been mentioned by Bhau Daji in his article on 'the cave numerals.' I have strong reasons for the belief that at least a considerable share of the results at which Dr. Bhau Daji arrived is due to Pandit Bhagavan Lal's industry and ingenuity."

Dr. Bhau Daji's interest did not exclude Numismatics and his works in this line are embodied in two papers,—' Report on some Hindu coins," and " The making out of the numerals of the 'Sah' coins." Taking the period of his work in the early stages of Indian archæological research and considering his achievement as a whole, he well deserved the praise of two such scholars as the late Professor Max-Muller who said, "I always look upon Bhau Daji as a man who has done excellent work in his life—and though he has written little, the little he has written is worth thousands of pages written by others"; and Sir. R. G. Bhandarkar who recorded it as his opinion that "No one who wishes to write a paper on the antiquities of the last two thousand years can do so without referring to Dr. Bhau's writing."

Busy man as Dr. Bhau Daji was, he engaged a number of assistants to help him in this self-imposed, but laudable department of his activities. The most conspicuous of his lieutenants was a Gujarati Brahmin, Pandit Bhagavan Lal Indraji, for whom Dr. Bhau had high regard bordering upon affection, as an incident in the life of both puts beyond doubt. When Dr. Bhau himself was seriously ill in bed, information reached him that this indomitable assistant of his contracted Terai fever in the course of one of his tours to Nepal on behalf of his master. He summoned a European friend to his bed-side and through him conveyed a pressing message to the Resident in Nepal requesting his good offices on behalf of Bhagavan Lal; till information was received from the Resident to say that Bhagavan Lal was well-looked after, Dr. Bhau was restless, and on receipt of the news he showed himself considerably relieved, although he died before Bhagavan Lal returned from this tour to Nepal. This clearly indicates the affection of Dr. Bhau Daji to Bhagavan Lal Indraji.

Bhagavan Lal came of a highly respectable Brahman family of Junagadh and was the younger brother of the head of the Sanskrit school maintained by the Durbar of that State. He had undergone the early Sanskrit education due to his station in life and acquired a fair knowledge of Sanskrit classical literature. He soon got into an aversion for the traditional Shastraic studies and was attracted by the historical traditions of his native province of which the Girnar mountain is a standing monument. By his own efforts as a boy, he early picked up sufficient knowledge of Indian Palæography to read the edicts of Asoka, the inscriptions of Rudradaman and Skandagupta on the face of the Girnar rock. A little later he made further advances in the study of Palæography and came to the notice of Mr. Kinloch Forbes, through whose good offices he became introduced to Dr. Bhau Daji in 1861. He threw himself into the work of Dr. Bhau

Daji whole-heartedly and copied inscriptions and took out transcripts for him sometimes with the assistance of a colleague, often without. These were interpreted by Dr. Bhau Daji and his Pandit, Gopal Pandurang Padhye. On doubtful passages, the inscriptions had to be verified again with the originals, some times new copies had to be made and occasionally new emendations had to be studied on the spot. The travelling work involved in all this and the taking out of transcripts devolved on Pandit Bhagavan Lal, which had sometimes to be repeated in the light of Dr. Bhau Daji's second line of criticism owing to information available from other sources of evidence. All this proved such a good training for young Bhagavan Lal that Dr. Bhau Daji confided to him, all his inscriptional work, namely, the copying of all land grants and the preparation of transcripts of inscriptions all over the country. Bhagavan Lal had to travel, therefore, through Gujarat and Kathiawar, Ujjain, Vidisa, Allahabad, Behar, Sarnath and Nepal. His travels for this purpose embrace the Northern half of the Bombay Presidency, a considerable part of Rajputana and Central India, the Southern half of the United Provinces, the whole of Bihar including Orissa, Nepal and considerable portions of the Punjab and the Frontier Province. He toured through these parts of the country mainly to take copies, mostly ink impressions and paper rubbings of all the more important known inscriptions. He made use of the occasion thus offered for collecting hundreds of coins and manuscripts. These copies were carefully translated and indexed by him. In the course of this work he picked up a little English and studied Prakrit as well.

When he had done about twelve to thirteen years of this kind of work to Dr. Bhau Daji, the latter died in May, 1874. Owing to the somewhat adverse circumstances of the family, Pundit Bhagavan Lal was given possession of the Mss. and transcripts that he had himself collected. Notwithstanding all these advantages together with the training he had had and in spite of the fact that archæological work was just then being organised in Western India by Dr. Burgess, Bhagavan Lal had no opportunity to find employment suitable to his taste and training, as he had not acquired enough English. He had to remain quiet for two years before he could publish a first article to the *Indian Antiquary* through the good offices of the late Dr. Buhler. His work on the "Cave Numerals" was published in the *Indian Antiquary* for 1877 and thereafter he was in a better position for work by the access he had acquired to the Library of the Bombay Branch of the Royal Asiatic Society which elected him an Honorary Member in 1877, since which date his contributions to the journal were many and valuable. His published articles were twenty-eight exclusive of the large contributions he made to some volumes of the Bombay Gazetteer and smaller ones to the archæological works published by Sir. A. Cunningham. These contain in them many discoveries of permanent value and his name will remain as that of a most successful student of Indian epigraphy and history.

Apart from his contributions to the study of the 'cave numerals' he is responsible for the discovery of many letters which had never hitherto been recognised. It was to his skill we owe the best facsimiles we have of the Nasik Inscriptions. He discovered a fragment of Asoka's 8th Rock Edict at Sopara on the Konkan Coast. He was the first to take out a copy and interpret the famous Udayagiri Inscription of Kharavela and discover therein a reference to the Mauryan Era. Much work has since been done upon this famous inscription during the last ten years, though without very substantial advance in point of results beyond those achieved by Pandit Bhagavan Lal Indraji, contributed to the International Congress of Orientalists. We are indebted to Pundit Bhagavan Lal for much valuable information regarding the Andhras which he made available to us by his work on the Nana Ghat Inscriptions and in the Andhra coins. He was responsible for twenty-one inscriptions bearing on the dynasties of Nepal and for this service Buhler aptly described him as the 'path-finder in the history of Nepal.' His discovery of the Elura Inscription makes a substantial contribution to the history of the Rashtrakutas of the Dekhan. The existence of the once powerful Traikutaka dynasty and of its connection with the Chedi Era and the Haihayas have become possible through the efforts of this untiring scholar. His attempt at explaining the occurrence of the Chedi Era in Gujarat by ascribing its introduction to the Abhira King, Isvaradatta, and his identification of the Abhiras of Gujarat and Nasik, with the Traikutakas and Haihayas of Chedi are illuminating and are being gradually confirmed by further research. At the time of his death he was engaged on a history of Gujarat.

His contributions in other directions were not inconsiderable and he held opinions which were very considerably in advance of his times such as that 'the religious movements in India did not consist of successive developement of what he sometimes called Vedism, Brahmanism and Buddhism.' Even his epigraphical contributions indicate considerable knowledge of ancient geography and make distinct contributions to archæology. The achievements of this eminent savant received public recognition first of all from the University of Leyden, which, on the recommendation of Prof Kern, conferred on him the honorary degree of Doctor of Philosophy. Shortly afterwards the Dutch Oriental Society of Netherlands and the Royal Asiatic Society of Great Britain and Ireland made him an Honorary Member. He enjoyed the esteem and privilege of many an Orientalist both in India and Europe, the most conspicuous of the latter being E. Senart and G. Buhler.

At the death of Dr. Bhau Daji, his worldly circumstances were unsatisfactory and notwithstanding generous contributions from the chiefs of Kathiawad and occasional remuneration from Drs. Campbell and Burgess, he died in very straitened circumstances in January 1888 in his forty-ninth year. It must be placed on record to the credit of the great scholar that it was on his death-bed that he, for the first time, complained of his straitened circumstances to the late Dr. Buhler whose friendship he had enjoyed for fourteen years at the time.

Dr. Buhler

WHEN, on the 16th of April, 1898, the cold and cruel waves of the Lakeof Constance closed over the remains of Hofrath Dr. J. G. Buhler,it was at once recognised that a great and remarkable career of Oriental scholarship had come to an untimely end. An Indianist of a very wide range of acquirements and the very centre and chief promoter of Indological studies in Europe, Dr. Buhler was one whose activity has decidedly determined the progress of Indian research.

The son of a clergyman and born at Borstel, 19th July 1837, in the then kingdom of Hanover, Dr. Buhler received his early education in the public school at Hanover. In 1855 he entered the University of Gottingen. Here he came in intimate contact with one of his professors, the famous linguist and folklorist, Theodor Benfey, of whom it is recorded that 'his inspirations were more wonderful than his science.' It was through Benfey that Buhler first learnt that the true foundation of Sanskrit scholarship must be laid on the study of the Vedas. It is needless to say that, instructed on sound lines to start with, Buhler more than fulfilled the expectations that were formed of him by his beloved master, whose writings connected with Sanskrit literature and philology, like those of his famous pupil, still remain as useful and important as when they were first published. Buhler took his Doctor's Degree in 1858 and then went to Paris, Oxford and London with a view to work in the Oriental section of the big libraries in these centres of learning and, if possible, to copy and collate Vedic manuscripts. At London he became acquainted with Prof. Max Muller and the acquaintance soon ripened into intimate friendship. While in England, Buhler held the post of Assistant Librarian at the Royal Library at Windsor. Three years after he quitted the office to hold a similar one in his own university of Gottingen. But firmly convinced that no real progress can be made in Oriental scholarship unless one went to India and sat at the feet of the Pandits, he resolved to find his way to India, even as a merchants' agent. However, through the kindness of his good friend, Prof. Max Muller, an appointment was promised him in the Bombay Educational Service by Mr. Howard, the then Director of Public Instruction. Buhler came to India with great hopes but the moment he landed he was told that Mr. Howard was absent and that there was no vacancy in the Department. Considerably distressed, Dr. Buhler sought the help of another friend of Max Muller's, Sir Alexander Grant, the Principal of the Elphinston College, Bombay who, in the end, got for him an appointment in that institution as Professor of Oriental languages (1863). From 1863 to 1880, he remained in the Educational Service of the Government of Bombay, serving in various capacities as Professor, Educational Inspector and officer in charge of the search for Sanskrit manuscripts. Both as a teacher and Inspector, Buhler was warmly praised by the Principal of the Elphinston College and the Director of Public Instruction. His strenuous efforts in the field of Sanskrit learning and Oriental research and generally his zeal for the cause of Indian Education won the following encomium from the D. P. I. who thus refers to Dr. Buhler's services on the eve of the latter's retirement :—

"His Excellency in Council will take this opportunity of expressing his great regret at the loss which the Department has sustained by the retirement from service of Dr. Buhler whose zealous labours have done so much to lay the foundation of a sound popular education in Guzaret; while he has no less distinguished himself by his successful exertion in the collection of some thousands of manuscripts in Central India, Rajputana and the Punjab, Kashmir etc. as well as in this Presidency, in the preparation of standard works on Hindu Law and literature, and in adding to the stock of philological and archæ-logical lore. By his influence as a teacher in Government Colleges and Examiner in the University of Bombay, he has not only kept alive an interest in Sanskrit but has extended the study of that language and raised the standard of Oriental scholarship throughout the West India."

These words were not mere official platitudes, pæans of praise sung in regard to every person that is relinquishing power. That every one of the services mentioned above is strictly true will be seen from the following review of Buhler's activity.

The Indian climate had considerably affected Buhler's health rendered poorer owing to hard work and incessant travel across a country ill-equipped with good roads and means of conveyance; and he retired somewhat early in 1880. When the news of his retirement reached Europe, he was at once appointed to the Chair of Sanskrit and Indology in the University of Vienna. It was the desire of Buhler to make the Austrian capital a centre of Oriental studies and, with this object in view, he founded in 1886 the Oriental Institute of Vienna University and when, as an auxiliary to it, the *Vienna Oriental Journal* was started, he frequently contributed to it many original articles on Indian History, Paleography, and Epigraphy. As a member of the Imperial Academy of Sciences at Vienna, he took every occasion to urge the management to devote its money and energies more and more to the cause of Sanskrit studies. As the Vienna University Representative to the International Congress of Orientalists he took such an active part that he was by tacit consent recognised as the leader of European Sanskritists. He very often presided over the Indian section and his opinions always received the greatest consideration at the hands of the Government of India and this has been of great help to workers in this country. It was amidst the congenial atmosphere of the Vienna University that he planned and partly completed the Encyclopedia of Indo-Aryan Research, the greatest enterprise yet undertaken in the field of Oriental scholarship. More about this later on.

Dr. Buhler, on account of his learning and scholarship, was naturally invited to join many learned societies in Europe and elsewhere. Thus he was corresponding member of the German Oriental Society (1871), of the American Oriental Society (1873), of the Berlin Academy of Sciences (1878), of the Royal Society of Sciences at Gottingen(1883), of the Imperial Academy of Sciences in Vienna (1883), of the Petersburg Academy (1893), of the Institut de France (1887), and of the Ecole des Langues Orientales Vivantes at Paris. In India he was an Honorary Member of the Gujerat Vernacular Society, of the Asiatic Society of Bengal and of the Anjuman-i-Punjab. Nor were the respective Governments with which he was closely connected slow to honour him. The Indian Government with its characteristic generosity towards all learned men made him a C. I. E. in 1878. Earlier, however, he was appointed a Knight of the Prussian Order of the Crown. Buhler was also the proud possesser of the titles : Comthur of the Order of Franz-Josef and was nominated K.H. Hofrath in 1889. The Edinburgh University honoured itself by conferring on him the Doctor's Degree.

On the 5th of April 1898, Dr. Buhler started from Vienna with a view to spend the Easter vacation with his wife and child at Zurich. But tempted by fine weather he broke his journey at Lindaw on Lake Constance to enjoy two days rowing. On the 8th April while out alone in a small boat, he lost one of his oars and in trying to recover it, over balanced himself and he was drowned. It was suspected by some that Dr. Buhler committed suicide from ethical or philosophical motives but those who were his nearest friends at Vienna promptly denied it.

Literary Activity.

Dr. Buhler's literary activity commences from the time when he passed out of the University. His earliest articles were all concerned with comparative philology and Vedic Mythology and these were contributed to '*Orient and Occident*' edited by Buhler's own master, Prof. Benfey. While at London working in the Library, he prepared, at the request of Prof. Max Muller, an index to the latter's *History of Sanskrit Literature*. Soon after coming to India he fell in love with the Indians, particularly with that class of much-ridiculed men—the Pundits, for whom Buhler had nothing but profound respect. "The Shastris," he says, in one of his reports, "are the representatives of the traditional knowledge of Sanskrit and in the present state of Sanskrit studies their services are by no means to be underrated." In conclusion he requests the Government to appoint 'one of the thorough-bred Shastris'of the old School both as a help to the advanced students and as an assistance to the Professor. Yet he was not unmindful of the serious drawback in the pundit of the old type, lack of critical scholar ship. It was his earnest endeavour to combine the advantages of classical European education with those of the traditional Hindu methods of teaching. If Sanskrit education in other parts of India had but followed the lines chalked out by Buhler, the rest of India would have seen the rising into prominence of Buhler school of Orientalists, the illustrious Indian representatives of which are Bhandarkar, Telang, Shamkar Pandit, Apte and others. As it was, this New Shool of Scholars was confined, owing to various reasons, to the geographical limits of the Presidency of Bombay. Contact with orthodox pundits and the crude materials they possessed for imparting instruction led Dr. Buhler in conjunction with Prof. Keilhorn who was then in Poona, to found the *Bombay Sanskrit Series* "The object of the Series was to give young native scholars an opportunity of learning European methods of criticism in editing texts and to procure cheap and good editions of Sanskrit standard works for use in Indian schools and colleges." Dr. Buhler himself was responsible for the publication of several books in the series. Besides editing the four books of *Panchatantra*, he brought out for the same series the first part of Dandin's *Dasakumaracharita.* In 1875 he edited the historical romance of Bilhana, *Vikramarkadeva Charita* which he himself had discovered.

Quite early in his Indian career in 1867 in co-operation with Sir Raymond West, he produced the famous *Digest of Hindu Law.* Not much was known before Buhler about the oldest legal literature of India and Judges had to depend mainly on the interpretation of the Shastris. As the work of the Judiciary increased with the increase in business prosperity of the people, a keen necessity was felt for a proper *Digest of the Hindu Law of Inheritance—Partition and Adoption.* The services of Buhler were readily available and he contributed the famous introduction to Wests' *Digest* on the sources of the Hindu Law, which contains a concise but full survey of Hindu Law Literature. Buhler's first introduction to this Branch of Sanskrit Literature tempted him to explore the regions of Ancient Hindu Law as embodied in the sacred literature of the Hindus and the publication, in 1871, of *Aphorisms on the Sacred Laws of the Hindus by Apastamba* was the result. For Prof. Max-Muller he translated two Volumes of the *Sacred Books of the East* (Vols. II and XIV). In regard to the circumstance of Dr. Buhler's share in the well-known series and the merits of his production, thus writes Max-Muller himself:— "When at a much later time I conferred with him on the plan of publishing a series of translations of the Sacred Books of the

East, he was ready and prepared to undertake the translation of these Sutras so far as they had been preserved in Manuscripts. Some of these manuscripts, the importance of which I had pointed out as early as 1859 in my *History of Ancient Sanskrit Literature*, I handed over to him: others he had collected himself in India. The two Volumes in which his translation of the legal Sutras of Apastamba, Gautama, Vasishta and Baudhayana are contained have been among the most popular of the series * * * * In 1886 followed his translation of *the Laws of Manu* * * * These were substantial works sufficient to establish the reputation of any scholar but with him they were a by-work merely undertaken in order to oblige a friend and fellow-worker."

Writing of Buhler's connection with Prof. Max-Muller one is reminded of the famous controversy regarding the age of *Alankara* literature in Sanskrit. In one of his Cambridge lectures Prof. Max-Muller propounded the theory of a 'literary interregnum' in India and boldly suggested that the whole of the Indian literature so far as it was not Vedic or Buddistic was written sometime after the Indo-Scythian invasion. Many were carried away by the somewhat fascinating arguments of Max-Muller till at last Buhler took up the question for re-examination of evidence and in a learned paper on *Indian Inscriptions and Kavya Literature* (Sitzungsberichte der Wiener Akademic, 1890) conclusively proved that specimens of ornate poetry occurred again and again in the pre-Gupta inscriptions and that there was no literary interregnum at all. This brilliant discovery was acknowledged by Max-Muller and though it was a question mainly affecting Sanskrit Kavya literature, in which Dr. Buhler was perfectly at home, it greatly helped to fix the chronology of Hindu India. Never carried away by mere sentiment nor at any time obsessed like other Western Scholars by the idea that Oriental literature and culture were founded on the bed-rock of Greek civilisation, Buhler was always inclined to give a higher antiquity to the sacred books of the Hindus than that assigned by the most well-meaning of Western savants.

The necessity to fix mile-stones in the long history of Sanskrit literature led Dr. Buhler to a critical study of inscriptions which, in turn resulted in the elucidation of the Hindu period of Indian History. His 85 articles in the *Indian Antiquary* mostly bear on the interpretation of Indian historical documents and it may safely be asserted that, during his time, no one has done more in this branch of Indian Research.

Buhler's interest in Indian Inscriptions are

not merely historical but paleographical. The results of his epigraphic studies are to be found in two of his masterly treatises, *on Indian Brahma Alphabet* and *on Indian Palaeography* (with 9 tables)—works not yet superseded or supplemented.

Unlike the generality of Orientalists who are specialists in particular branches of research, Dr. Buhler was an all-round genius. There is hardly any branch of Indian research, Archaelogy, Epigraphy, Philology, Literature etc., which has not yielded important results to his patient study and penetrating sagacity. While labouring in the field of Sanskrit and Prakrit philology, he had not kept out of his mind the importance of monuments. Thus he took a profound interest in the archaelogical investigations of Doctors Hultzsch, Fuhrer, Waddell and others. According to one of his distinguished pupils, Dr. Winternitz, all his Indian studies are intended as a kind of preliminary work for the great scheme which he had in view for years —the publication of a connected history of ancient India. What a great loss to India that this learned German did not live sufficiently long to realise his aspirations! A good early history of India we now have but Buhler's would have been much more exhaustive and trustworthy. Dr. Buhler's claim to world-wide renown rests, however, on his special qualifications as a successful discoverer and zealous collector of manuscripts. In this respect he not only equals Rask, Wright and Hodgson and Chambers who were makers of Oriental schools of learning in Copenhagen, Cambridge, Paris and Berlin respectively but far surpasses them all. Writing on manuscripts collection in general and of Buhler's activity in this direction in particular, Prof. Leumann says :—"Well-written books, like fragrant flowers, chiefly attract the general attention and also in a titanic publication (like Murray's or Littre's or Grimn's Dictionary) which looks like a majestic oak in the park of literary and scientific productions. But who thinks of the roots hidden in the ground, which furnish the elementary materials for stems, branches, and blossoms?" Few among scholars, even in recent times, realise the importance of manuscripts collection. It will be recalled that Dr. Buhler entered the educational service of Bombay in 1863. Between 1863 and 1866, on his own private account he collected some 200 manuscripts of the Brahmanical literature. The Bombay Government, soon realising the importance of such a collection, deputed Dr. Buhler between 1866—1868 to explore Indian libraries in South Maharatta and North Canara countries. Consistent with the time and labour spent, Dr. Buhler was able to get 200 more manuscripts which were deposited in the Elphinston College. In 1868, chiefly through the exertion of Buhler, a regular search for Sanskrit manuscripts was instituted by the Government and Dr. Buhler, of course, became the head of the organization. We have not space to mention the various arts he employed before he could persuade heads of Jain Mutts to open their rich manuscript treasures to him. His familiarity with the Indian vernaculars, his genuine love for the people, his tact and skill, his respect for native prejudices and superstitions, ultimately got for Buhler what no other European scholar could have obtained, a splendid collection of rare texts and manuscripts, the subsequent critical editions of which alone are responsible for what little knowledge we now possess on Indian Sanskrit Literature and History. When Buhlerleft India, more than 2300 manuscripts were deposited in Government archives. It is not that Buhler was 'lucky' infinding them. Many of these were the brilliant discoveries of the great Doctor, due entirely to his profound knowledge of Sanskrit. Many branches of the sacred literature of the Indians have been rescued from oblivion *e.g.*, the Kashmir branch comprising Vedic and Sanskrit Texts and the extensive Prakrit and Sanskrit Texts of the Svetambara Jains.

This leads us to another of the great services rendered by Buhler to the cause of Indian Religious History. European and Modern Indian interest regarding one of the earliest religious systems of India, Jainism, dates from Buhler's discovery of manuscripts pertaining to that faith. More than 500 texts and Jaina Prakrit manuscripts were discovered and purchased by Buhler and these were promptly despatched to the University of Berlin where it had the effect of awakening German scholars to almost unprecedented literary activity. But for this act of Buhler, the learned world would not have known of the brilliant treatises of Prof. Weber, Klatt and Leumann. In fact Berlin became a centre of German Jain Philology. Another direct result of Dr. Buhler's search for Jain manuscripts may be briefiy adverted to. That illustrious scholar Prof. Jacobi accompanied the Doctor in the course of his tours to Rajputana and other Jaina centres. This spurred him on to undertake the critical examination of Jain texts. Prof. Jacobi's edition and translation of the *Acharanga Sutras* and his learned commentaries on the *Kalpa Sutras* have cleared up the mystery surrounding the early history of the Jain sect. Dr. Buhler's own services to the cause of Jain religious history are immeasurable. Besides inducing other competent scholars to pursue studies in Jaina history and religion, he himself published, in 1887, in German, *The Indian Sec of the Jainas.* The Jain community in India is greatly indebted to him. By a systematic study of the famous Mathura Inscriptions and those of Karavela he successfully and incontrovertibly established the priority of Jainism over Buddhism. To the great benefit of Indian scholars, this booklet of Buhler has been translated into English.

Buhler's last great service to the world of science was the editing of the *Encyclopedia of Indo-Aryan Research,* which, as has been stated in the beginning, is the greatest enterprise yet undertaken in the field of Oriental scholarship. A man of vast influence, friend of all and enemy to none, Buhler soon enlisted for his work, the co-operation of 30 different scholars in various parts of the world and the work was pushed through rapidly enough. The series contemplates to furnish *all* knowledge about the Indo-Aryans —their history, religion, philosophy etc. Unfortunately Buhler was not destined to see the completion of the task. Under his editorship nine parts appeared including his own contribution on Indian Paleography (Vol. i Part ii). Most of the series were written in German but Dr. Buhler had always urged the necessity of contributors expressing themselves in English for the benefit of scholars in India. We have thus reviewed the most important aspect of Buhler's literary activities. None the less useful and important are the many learned articles he contributed to the *Indian Antiquary, Epigraphia Indica, Journal of the Royal Asiatic Society* and to various continental journals.

Of the man, of his character, of the qualities of head and heart that he possessed let his intimate friends, all distinguished professors of Oriental learning speak :—

" Buhler's clear-sightedness in questions of detail, his far-sightedness in dealing with great historical problems will be missed for years to come. We shall miss again and again, his noble character, his great and influential personality, his inspiration, his advice and help. And all that he might still have produced, is lost,—irretrievably lost! He who has been a leader of men, a trusty guide, has been taken from us! He is gone, and it merely remains for us to cherish his memory by continuing the work which he had so much at heart, to the best of our power and by building on the solid foundations which he has laid, for though he is no longer with us, his life-work will remain for ever,—*na hi Karmakshiyate*" :—Prof. M. Winternith Pz. D.

" Buhler had the true nature ot a scholar —accurate, incisive, critical in his own work, helpful, kindly and stimulating to others.

His tact and *Savoir-faire* made him a natural leader of men on occasions like Congresses of Orientalists * * *. His genial, hearty manner made him equally popular and influential with scholars and with men of the world. In all senses he made the best of both worlds":—C. H. Tawney C.I.E.

" His mind was of an unceasing activity and ever awake. His learning, admirably suggestive, was never taken unawares. A rich fulness of culture, a wide shore of remembrances animated his conversation which was at once solid and lively. All those who have had the good fortune to know Buhler personally will retain a faithful memory of a man, obliging without any display—who softened by unvarying uprightness and true benovolence the commanding authority of a vast science and of a very decided turn of mind ":—Emile Senart.

Sir Monier Williams.

INTRODUCTION.

THE commingling of the great civilisation of Ancient India and the great civilisation of western Europe is the greatest event of the world since the French Revolution. The French Revolution shattered many illusions of the past. The shock of the contact between the two great civilisations of the world is destined to shatter many illusions and superstitions which are believed to-day as if they are gospel-truths. The modern worldliness and love of exploitation, the misfits of social life and disharmonies of social feeling, the low aims of literature and art to-day, the ever-crumbling edifices of Western philosophy built on the ever-shifting sands of human speculation, and the ill-concealed helplessness and defect of modern religion loudly call for radical change. The change can and will come only from the authoritative proclamations to be issued from modern India where the greatest civilisations of the world have met. Those select-souls who realise the mingling of the civilisations in the higher planes of life are hence entitled to special respect as the pioneers of the new age, and one of them, despite his limitations of scholarship and sympathy, was Sir Monier Monier Williams.

His Life.

Sir Monier Monier Williams was born in 1819 at Bombay. He was educated in England and received a writership in the East India Company's Civil Service in 1839. He studied at Hailebury in 1840 but abandoned his idea of going to India and entered the University College, Oxford. He studied Sanskrit and became Boden Scholar in 1843. From 1844 to 1858 he was Professor of Sanskrit and Persian and Hindustani at Hailebury. In 1860 he became Boden Professor of Sanskrit at Oxford in 1860. He helped at the foundation of the Indian Institute at Oxford in 1883. He was a Fellow of Balliol College from 1882—1888 and a honorary fellow of University College, Oxford, in 1892. The degree of D. C. L. was conferred on him in 1875 by the Oxford University. He was knighted in 1886 and was made a K.C.I.E., in 1887. He died in 1899.

His Dictionaries.

His *Sanskrit-English Dictionary* is a monumental work displaying considerable and patient research. In his introduction to the work he says: "In some subjects too, specially in poetical descriptions of nature and domestic affection, Indian works do not suffer by a comparison with the best specimens of Greece and Rome while in wisdom, depth and shrewdness of their moral apothegms they are unrivalled. More than this, learned Hindus had probably made great advances in astronomy, algebra, arithmetic, botany, and medicine, not to mention their admitted superiority in grammar, long before any of these sciences were cultivated by the most ancient nations of Europe." Equally valuable is his "*Dictionary, English and Sanskrit.*"

Sir Monier Williams on Buddhism.

His book on *Buddhism* is of great value and displays considerable research and learning. He says of Buddha: "He always maintained that the only revelation he had received was an illumination from within—due entirely to his own intuitions, assisted by his reasoning powers and by severe purgatorial discipline protracted through countless previous births in every variety of bodily form."

He describes in his work Buddha's life and successful search of self-enlightenment. He points out that "in fact Gautama's Doctrine of a universal brotherhood, open to all, constituted the corner-stone of his popularity."

He further describes in his work the later history of Buddhism and also the Buddhist institutions of *Sangha*, and *Dhamma*. Though he well contrasts the Hindu conception of the threefold path of Karma, Bhakti and Jnana with the Buddhist conception of salvation through knowledge, he errs in holding Hindu philosophy also to be pessimistic like Buddhist philosophy. A system of thought asserting the soul to be *Sachidananda* and showing how this truth can be realised can certainly not be called a pessimist philosophy. His bias is clear when he says: " In India, on the contrary, the Upanishads and systems of philosophy which followed on them all harped on the same string. They all dwelt on the same minor keynote. Their real object was not to investigate truth, but to devise a scheme for removing the misery believed to result from repeated bodily existence and from all action, good or bad, in the present, previous, and future births." He says at the same time about Western philosophic thought: "Happily the general tone of European philosophic thought is in another key, and the admirers of Aristotle still constitute a majority in Europe. The great Stagirite described God as Energy." It is clear that Sir Monier Williams had no clear idea of the Vedanta and had no real knowledge of the true significance of the Shakti cult.

He shows how Buddhism had no belief in a Creator and could not and did not inculcate piety. But his Christian bias is again apparent when he contrasts Buddhist morality and Christian morality. He says: "Buddhist morality is like a showy edifice built on the sand. It is a thoroughly fair-weather structure, incapable of standing against flood, storm, and tempest. For every Buddhist is like a trader who keeps a ledger, with a regular debtor and creditor account, and a daily entry of profit and loss. He must not take, make, or hoard money. He is forbidden to store up a money-balance in a worldly bank, but he is urged to be constantly accumulating merit-balance in the bank of Karma.'

He shows clearly how Buddhism got degraded later on. It advocated celibacy; yet even monks had children in later times. It denied supernatural Power; yet the Dhamma and the Buddha were actually worshipped as God. It denied the efficacy of prayer; yet prayers multiplied in unknown forms and were invested with mystical powers and became mechanical. It denied the efficacy of image worship; yet Buddha's relics and images were worshipped. Sir Monier Williams shows how Buddhism lost itself in Vaishnavaism and Saivism.

In later times a theistic Buddhism was sought to be evolved. When Buddha attained Nirvana, it was alleged that he transferred his Bodhisattwaship to Maitreya, who dwells in the *Tushita* heaven and who is to appear as the fifth Buddha of the present age, five thousand years after the Nirvana of Gautama. We can well realise what inspiration is responsible for the recent advertisements in India about the forthcoming advent of Maitreya.

Sir Monier Williams deals in his work also with mystical Buddhism, hierarchical Buddhism and ceremonial and ritualistic Buddhism.

"Religious Thought in India."

This work is "an account of the religions of the Indian peoples based on a life's study of their literature and on personal investigations in their own country"—to use his own words. It contains much valuable matter and shows considerable study and research but shows traces of his defective sympathy which is now and then responsible for lack of vision and insight and errors of statement and interpretation. His classification into Vedism, ritualistic Brahmanism, philosophic Brahmanism, mythological Brahmanism, and nomistic Brahmanism has more symmetry than truth. The work describes also Saivism, Vaishnavism, Saktism etc., and various ceremonies performed by Hindus.

HIS INDIAN WISDOM.

This is the work on which his chief title to fame rests to-day. It is a brief and well-written sketch of various departments of Sanskrit literature. He accepts uncritically the view that the vedic religion is only deification of natural forces. This is one of the erroneous declarations of Western scholarship which we have to combat and replace by sounder ideas. The *Veda* always realised the infinite God amidst the manifoldness of His creations and His manifestations. The worship of the Aryan heart was always offered to the Infinite in and through the Finite. It was proclaimed and realised that He was one and supreme though called by various names एकं सद्विप्राबहुधावदंति ।

The lack of real vision which make the labours of Western savants so often fruitless and valueless is seen in Sir Monier Williams when he speaks of " the labyrinth of mystic language, fanciful etymologies, far-fetched analogies, and puerile conceits which bewilder the reader of the Upanishads." The twin guides through this labyrinth are vision and sympathy and he was unfortunately largely lacking in both. Complaints are more often due to the deficiencies of the complainant than those of what is complained against.

He then proceeds to describe briefly the six systems of Hindu philosophy, the Sutras, the Smritis, and the Vedangas, as also the two great poems of the Ramayana and the Mahabharata and the later Sanskrit literature. The following passages from the book are noteworthy for their beauty and for their insight :—

"It must be admitted, however, that, in exhibiting pictures of domestic life and manners, the Sanskrit epics are even more true and real than the Greek and Roman. In the delineation of women the Hindu poet throws aside all exaggerated colouring and drawn from nature—Kaikeyi, Kausalya, Mandodari (the favour—wife of Ravana), and even the hump-backed Manthara are all drawn to the very life, Sita, Draupadi, and Damayanti engage our affections and our interest for more than Helen or even Penelope. Indeed, Hindu wives are generally perfect patterns of conjugal fidelity; can it be doubted that, in these delightful portraits of the *Pativrata* or devoted wife, we have true representations of the purity and simplicity of Hindu domestic manners in early times." * *

Indeed, in depicting scenes of domestic affection, and expressing those universal feelings and emotions which belong to human nature in all time and in all places, Sanskrit epic poetry is unrivalled even by Greek Epics. . . . . In the Indian epics, such passages abound, and besides giving a very high idea of the purity and happiness of domestic life in ancient India, indicate a capacity in Hindu women for the discharge of the most sacred and important social duties." * *

"Yet there are not wanting indications in the Indian Epics of a higher degree of civilization than that represented in the Homeric poems. The battlefields of the Ramayana and Mahabharata, though spoiled by childish exaggerations and the use of supernatural weapons, are not made barbarously wanton cruelties; and the descriptions of Ayodhya and Lanka imply far greater luxury and refinement than those of Sparta and Troy."

"He (Rama) is the type of a perfect husband, son, and brother. Sita also rises in character far above Helen, and even above Penelope, both in her sublime devotion and loyalty to her husband, and her indomitable patience and endurance under suffering and temptation. As for Bharata and Lakshmana, they are models of paternal duty; Kausalya of maternal tenderness; Dasaratha of paternal love; and it may be affirmed generally that the whole moral tone of the *Ramayana* is certainly above that of the Iliad." "No one too can read either the Ramayana or Mahabharata without feeling that they rise above the Homeric poems in this—that a deep religious meaning appears to underlie all the narrative, and that the wildest allegory may be intended to conceal a sublime moral, symbolizing the conflict between good and evil, and teaching the hopelessness of victory in so terrible a content without purity of soul, self-abnegation, and subjugation of the passions,"

Sir Monier Williams then proceeds to discuss the later poems and plays in Sanskrit literature. He says about the great drama of *Mrichakatika*.

"The dexterity with which the plot is arranged, the ingenuity with which the incidents are connected, the skill with which the characters are delineated and contrasted, the boldness and felicity of the diction are scarcely unworthy of our own great dramatists. Nor does the parallel fail in the management of the stage business, in minute directions to the actors and various scenic artifices. The asides and aparts, the exits and the entrances, the manner, attitude, and gait of the speakers, their tones of voice, tears, smiles, and laughter are as regularly indicated as in a modern drama."

About the *Niti Sastras* he says:

"Anyone who studies the best Hindu writings cannot but be struck by the noral tone which everywhere pervades them. Indian writers, although they do not trouble themselves much about the history of past generations, constantly represent the present condition of human life as the result of actions in previous existences. Hence a right course of present conduct becomes an all-important consideration as bearing on future happiness; and we need not be surprised if, to satisfy a constant longing for *Niti* or guidance and instruction in practual wisdom. nearly all departments of Sanskrit literature—Brahmanas, Upanishads, Law books, Epic poems, and Puranas—are more or less didactic, nearly all delight in moralizing and philosophizing, nearly all abound in wise saying and prudential rules.

On Hinduism.

This is a brief manual of Hinduism. It surveys a wide and varied ground and is important as giving a *resume* of the historical development of the Hindu religion, though in it also his Christian bias intrudes often. He says in it:—

"Starting from the Veda, Hinduism has ended in embracing something from all religions, and in presenting phases suited to all minds. It is all-tolerant all-compliant, all-comprehensive, all-absorbing."

He says further:

"India, though it has, as we have seen, more than five hundred spoken dialects, has only one sacred language and only one sacred literature, accepted and revered by all adherents of Hinduism alike, however diverse in race, dialect, rank, and creed. That language is Sanskrit, and that literature is Sanskrit literature—the only repositary of the Veda or 'knowledge' in its widest sense, the only Vehicle of Hindu theology, philosophy, law, and mythology; the only mirror in which all creeds, opinions. customs, and usages of the Hindus are faithfully reflected; and (if we may be allowed to use a fourth metaphor) the only quarry whence the requisite materials may be obtained for improving the vernaculars, or for expressing important religious and scientific ideas."

HIS NALOPAKYANA.

He published the Nalopakhyana (the story of Nala), an episode in the Mahabharata, with a copious vocabulary, grammatical analysis, and an introduction. As usual with his works generally it shows considerable scholarship and assiduous research. In the introduction he says :—

"We live in an age of competition, when the gain of a few minutes may make all the difference between success and failure. Education now is a race of eyes: and he comes in the winner, whose vision can taken in the meaning of a given quantity of printed matter in the shortest space ot time."

HIS TRANSLATION OF SAKUNTALA.

This work has become a classic and is full of real grace and power. He says about the great poet and the great play :—

"No one can read this act (4th Act), nor indeed any act of play, without being struck with the reciness and elevation of its author's genius, the exuberance and glow of his fancy, his ardent love of the beautiful, his deep sympathy with nature and nature's loveliest scenes, his profound knowledge of the human heart, his delicate appreciation of its most refined feelings, his familiarity with its conflicting sentiments and emotions"

I shall quote here only his excellent translation of that great stanza which occurs in

5th act of the play and is one of the finest gems of the world's literature :—

> " Not seldom in our happy hours of ease,
> When thought is still, the right of some fair form,
> Or mournful fall of music breathing low,
> Will stir strange fancies, thrilling all the soul
> With a mysterious sadness, and a sense
> Of vague yet earnest longing, can it be
> That the dim memory of events long past,
> Or friendships formed in other states of being,
> And flits like a passing shadow the spirit ? "

SIR MONIER ON MODERN INDIA

This book is what he calls a series of impressions, notes and essays. He says in it about pandit learning in India: "Their fluency in talking Sanskrit surprises me, and certainly surpasses mine." In regard to modern Indian education he says :—

> "This sort of education is, in some cases, better than nothing, but too often it inflates young men with conceit, unhinges their faith in their own religion without giving them any other, leads them to despise the calling of their fathers, and to look upon knowledge as a mere stepping-stone to Government situations which they cannot all obtain."

He says further :—

> "I submit that in all our Indian colleges and schools we pay too much attention to the linguistic and literary element in education and too little to the practical and scientific............ We do not sufficiently encourage the Vernaculars."

In the same book he says of South India and its people: "Indeed, all the races of South India seem to me to show readiness and aptitude for any work they are required to do, as well as patience, endurance and perseverence in the discharge of the most irksome duties." He says further:—

"At any rate it is certain that men may hinder and men may impede, but the living waters of the river of God's truth will flow on for ever."

HIS MISCELLANEOUS WORKS.

Prominent among these may be mentioned his Sanskrit Manual and his practical Grammar of the Sanskrit Language. These are of great value and show how he was desirous of spreading the culture of India by all the means in his power. Work of such intention and such quality has to be done and in an abundant measure for the spread of a great culture and for the mutual goodwill of the East and the West.

SIR MONIER ON INDIAN CULTURE.

He had always a keen insight into the greatness of Indian culture, though he exhibited often a defective sympathy for it. In his book on *Modern India* he says about Sanskrit: " Let us not forget that Sanskrit is as closely allied as Greek to our mother-tongue, that its symmetrical grammar is the key to all other grammars, that its system of synthesis is as useful to the mind as the study of geometry and that its literature contains models of true poetry and some of the most remarkable treatises on philosophy, science and ethics that the world has ever produced. Above all let those who are preparing for an Indian career bear in mind that Sanskrit is the only source of life, health and vigour to all the spoken languages of the Hindus, the only repositary of Hindu religious creeds, customs, and observances."

Sir Monier Williams on Religion.

He says in his work or Buddhism that a religion must reveal God to man, must reveal man to himself, must reveal the method by which man may communicate with God, and must regenerate man's nature. Unless religion takes up all these fields of activity, its hold on man's inner nature will grow weaker and weaker and will eventually cease altogether. It is in the intensification of the religious consciousness of men that the salvation of humanity here and hereafter can securely rest; and hence religion must know both her duty and her power before she can fulfil her mission.

Conclusion.

Thus, despite his deficiencies of scholarship and sympathy, Sir Monier Monier Williams was a great man and a real friend of India. We want many men of his type and temperament to make Sanskrit well-known among the sons of men, to make Indian culture a living force in life, to bring about a union of the East and the West, and to help humanity to gain and possess one of the richest treasures of human experience.

Max Muller.

IN a letter sent by Max Muller in November, 1886, to one who criticised his views signing himself as a Silesian Horseherd he says:

"I am an old professor, am now seventy-two years old, or as has been often said to me, seventy-two years young. Like yourself I commenced life with nothing, and have laboured till I have become not rich, but independent. Here in wealthy London and in wealthy Oxford I am considered a poor man, but I am quite content, and call that riches. I have been married thirty-seven years, have one son, Secretary to the Embassy at Constantinople, and a happily married daughter, with four grand-children. Of my sorrow, the loss of two daughters. I must remain silent. All my life I have been engaged in investigating the past; I am a philologist and have therefore been also a student of history, have especially studied the historical development of the various religions of mankind, and to this end have had to make a study of ancient languages, particularly Oriental languages."

Such is the beautiful and brief summing up of his life by himself and no other words can be a better introduction to this brief sketch of his life and writings.

"MY AUTOBIOGRAPHY"

In this book he gives us a vivid description of his life and his recollections. His son says of him in the preface to the book: "The real secret of his success lay not in his friends, but in himself;—in the knowledge that his success or failure in life depended entirely on his own efforts; in the fixity of purpose which made him refuse all offers that would lead him from the pathway that he had laid down for himself; and in the unflagging industry with which he strove to reach the goal of his ambition." Max Muller says of himself in it:

"One confession I have to make, and one for which I can hardly hope for absolution, whether from my friends or from my enemies. I have never done anything; I have never been a doer, a canvasser, a wire-puller, a manager, in the ordinary sense of these words.........The only thing of consequence, to my mind, is what we think, what we know, what we believe!"

Deutsche Liebe (German Love.)

In this beautiful book we have Max Muller's re-collections and reminiscences of his early life, though, as pointed out by his son in his "Life of Max Muller," this prose idyll is "pure fiction as far as the characters and circumstances are concerned." He says: "This is what I recollect of my earliest childhood, and amidst it floats a loving mother's face, also a father's kind, earnest eyes, and gardens, and a vine-covered arbour, and green soft turf, and a venerable old picture book; and that is all that I can still discern on the first faded pages of memory. He then gives us the first impact of the world on him. He says: "Would not the child's heart break from anguish when it feels the first cold blast of this unfriendly world, were it not that the warm sunlight of love shines on him from his parents' eyes, like a softened recollection of heavenly light and love?" He then describes his youth and his school and college life and says. "School life was over and the first merry years of college life were over; and many a fair dream of life was over too. But one thing remained: faith in God and man."

His Life.

He was born on 6th December 1823. He was the son of the well-known German lyric poet, Wilhelm Muller. His mother was Adelheid, a daughter of President Von Basedow, Prime-Minister of the Duchy of Dessau. *The Life and Letters of Friedrich Max Muller* by his son are two volumes full of valuable details about his life and reveal a loveable and fascinating personality. The biographer says of him: "Throughout his whole life he took every good thing, every honour that he received, as a gift he had not deserved." He joined the University of Leipzig in 1841. He was an eager and laborious scholar and took to the study of Sanskrit as his life's passion

Every circumstance in his early career helped him in the pursuit of Oriental learning. "Professor Brochaus of the University of Leipzig, where Max Muller matriculated in 1841, induced him to take up Sanskrit; Bopp, at the University of Berlin (1844), made the Sanskrit student a scientific comparative philologist; Schelling at the same University, inspired him with a love for metaphysical speculation, though failing to attract him to his own philosophy; Burnouf, at Paris in the following year, by teaching him *Zend*, started him on the track of inquiry into the science of comparative religion and impelled him to edit the Rig Veda. In 1846 he came to England upon this errand when Bunsen and Prof. H. H. Wilson prevailed on the East India Company to undertake the expense of the publication.

He settled at Oxford in 1848. Bunsen introduced him to the Queen and the Prince Consort who took a lively interest in the German Scholar. Later his introduction to the Oxford University brought him incontact with the best men in the social and intellectual life of England. In 1850 he was appointed Deputy Taylorian Professor of Modern European languages, becoming Professor four years later, and Curator of the Bodleian Library 1856. In the following year he was made M.A. and honorary Fellow of Christ

Church and in 1858 he was elected a Fellow of All souls. How much of unappreciative indifference he had to overcome is clear from a letter of his to Baron Bunsen on 20th October 1849 wherein he wrote :

> "The love of science, of desire, of distinction are often too weak to overcome the *visinertiæ* and the longing for rest and retirement, especially in these days of barbarism of mental poverty and godlessness, where one finds no hearing for research, let alone the hope of starting anything useful."

In 1838 he was elected first Professor of Comparative Philology. He edited the famous *Sacred Books of the East* series. His *Gifford Lectures* are full of valuable ideas about the growth and development of religious ideas. He has said truly about lectures in words that deserve to be remembered:

> "Lectures are not meant to stuff and cram the mind. Lectures are meant to excite an appetite for knowledge, and to show how such knowledge may best be acquired."

Max Muller lived the life of the scholar to his finger tips and though interested in the broad currents of political or social movement of his time, seldom interfered in anything that did not savour of learning. The most remarkable external events of his later years were his delivery of lectures at the restored University of Straasburg in 1872 when he devoted his honorarium to the endowment of a Sanskrit lectureship and his presidency over the International Congress of Orientalists in 1892. Besides these he seldom left Oxford "the city of dreaming spires" of which he became an honoured denizen worthy to be counted amongst some of the wisest and best men of the nineteenth century.

He was made a Privy Councillor in 1896. On 29th October 1900 he died in perfect peace and serenity of spirit. Canon Farrar has summed up his life's work admirably by saying that he introduced and popularised Comparative Philology, that he showed the importance of Sanskrit, that he edited the *Rig Veda*; and that he introduced into England the science of Comparative Religion. Max-Muller has said of himself in beautiful words:

> "Through the whole of my life, I have cared for truth, not for success. And truth is not our own. We may seek truth, serve truth, love truth; but truth takes care of herself, and she inspires her true lovers with the same feeling of perfect trust."

MAX MULLER THE MAN.

His was a sweet and gentle nature, which was sweetened and refined even more by his study of Hindu religion and philosophy. In a letter to his mother on 28th July 1849, he wrote about life:—"It is but a short journey, and on a journey one can do without many things which generally seem necessary to us." In another letter written on 4th October, 1856 he says:

"Let us wait for a little while—and to those whose eyes are turned to God and eternity the longest life is but a little while; let us wait then in faith, hope, and charity; these three abide, but the greatest of these is charity."

In a letter to his wife on 17th June 1864, he wrote:

"It is a perfect sin not to be happy in this world, and how much of the misery which there is, is the work of men, or could be removed by men, if they would but work together for each other's good"

In another letter to his wife he says on 27th August 1867:

"One look up to heaven and all this dust of the high-road of life vanishes. Yes! one look up to heaven and even that dark shadow of death vanishes."

I shall quote here only one more passage which occurs in his letter to Colonel Olcott on 10th June, 1893, wherein he says:

"If I can be of any use, I am always willing to help; and, in spite of many disappointments, I have never lost my faith in man, nor in the final victory of truth."

General Aspects of His Work.

Max Muller's luminous conception of and his devotion to the science of language are among his greatest qualities. In his *Biographical Essays* he points out how the tie of language is the strongest and dearest of ties.

"I say *intellectual kith and kin*, because that kinship is far more important than the mere kinship of blood. Blood may be thicker than water, but language is thicker than blood, at least to beings who, though for a time identifying themselves with flesh and blood. are themselves something very different from mere flesh and blood."

He says in his *India; What Can It Teach Us*:

"The results of the science of language, which, without the aid of Sanskrit, would never have been obtained, form an essential element of what we call a liberal, that is, an historical education."

He was, however, aware that Comparative Philology is only a means to an end. He says in his *Last Essays*:

"And what is that higher purpose which the science of language is meant to serve? It is to discover the secrets of thought in the labyrinth of language, after the dark chambers of that labyrinth have first been lighted up by the torch of comparative philology."

Max Muller's depth and range of vision in regard to the panorama of human development are equally remarkable. He gained the same by his study of the science of language and the science of religion. He says:

"If history is to teach us anything, it must teach us that there is a continuity which binds together the present and the past, the East and the West. And no branch of history teaches that lesson more powerfully than the history of language and the history of religion."

It is but natural that an outside student like Professor Max Muller should have no faith in the Vedas as a revelation. Further, his insight into the excellences and potencies of the Indian genius had strange limitations.

It would be out of place in this sketch to enter upon a detailed criticism of his views.

In spite of certain peculiar views of Hindu pantheism Max Muller had a keen intellectual apprehension of the Hindu conception of God as revealed in the Vedas. He says in *Auld Lang Syne* :

"Even the highest heights and the deepest depths which can be reached by the human mind are lighted up by the omnipresence of Brahman, the Indian name and concept of what we mean by the omnipresent Father, or if you like, of that ineffable Godhead of which even the Father is one person only."

He had also a clear and correct view in regard to the misunderstood doctrine of the noumenon and the phenomenon in the Vedanta philosophy. He says in the same work:

"It is generally supposed that the Vedanta philosophy denies the reality of the whole world. But this is not so; it only declares, and even more consistently than we do, that the world is phenomenal. It is not what it seems to be. but it would not even seem to be, unless it reposed on the Divine, which alone is really real."

In the same work he removes another widely prevalent misconception that the Vedantin has, and describes to have, no touch with God. He says:

"A distant God like the Jewish Jehovah would be no God at all to the Vedantist, he cannot be too near to his God; nay, to be without Him but for one moment would be death and annihilation to Him."

As to the Vedantin's view of the relation of God and man he observes :—

"What seems to us almost blasphemy—a kind of *apotheosis* of man, is with the Vedantist an act of the highest reverence. It is taken as man's *anatheosis*, or return to his true Father, a recovery of his true God—like nature." ("Auld Lang Syne" Vol. II, page 251).

His insight into the Hindu mind does not stop with Hindu philosophy and religion. The following passage in *Auld Lang Syne, Volume II*, shows his deep insight into Hindu customs. He says:

"I deeply sympathise with your *Shraddha* ceremony; nay, I wish we had something like it in our own religion. To keep alive the memory of our parents, to feel their presence during the great trials of our life, to be influenced by what we know they would have wished us to do, and to try to honour their name by showing ourselves not unworthy bearers of it, that is a Shraddha ceremony in which we can all partake, nay, ought to partake whatever our religion may be. There is a real, though unseen bond of union (*tantu*) that connects us through our parents and ancestors with the Great Author of all things; and the same bond will connect ourselves through our children with the most distant generations. If we know that, and are constantly reminded of it by ceremonies like that of your Shraddha, we are not likely to forget that responsibility that rests on every one of us. In that sense your Shraddha is a blessing, on your parents because on yourselves, and whatever the future of your religion may be in India, I hope their communion with the spirits of your ancestors, or *Pitris*, will always form an essential part of it."

Though this does not show a grasp of all that the ceremony implies, it contains ample evidence of his sympathy and insight. Another passage in the same book shows his insight into the character of the Hindus. He says:

"With us philosophy remains always something collateral only. Our mainstay is formed by religion.

and ethics. But with the Hindus, philosophy is life in full earnest, and it is but another name for religion, while morality has a place assigned but as an essential preliminary to all philosophy."

Though his Sanskrit studies lay generally outsite the field of poetry yet he had a wonderful insight into the real and distinctive treasure of thought and emotion contained in Sanskrit poetry proper.

"Some of the most beautiful poetry of ancient and modern India was inspired by that sentiment of unworldliness, the very opposite of that passionate love and attachment which forms the constant theme of European poetry. Love, so far as it means passion and desire, or exclusive attachment to one person, was considered of this world, and everything belonging to this world was perishable and therefore not worthy of our highest affection.........We find it difficult to enter into these ideas, they are so entirely absent from our own literature, particularly from our poetry, but they were quite familiar to the Hindus."

In *Auld Lang Syne* he says in regard to the Indian Student in England:

"Altogether the experiment of sending young Hindus to prepare for the Civil Service Examination in England has not, as far as I have been able to judge, proved a great success.........If the young students from India have money to spend, there is danger of their falling into bad company, and even if they pass their examinations, I am afraid that some of them return to India not much improved by their English exile."

In regard to "Theosophy in India" he says:—

I am afraid that great and lasting mischief has been wrought, for instance, by Madame Blavatsky and her friends who went to India, ignorant of Sanskrit and Sanskrit literature............But what has been the result of all her labours? Indian philosophy has gained some Corybantic followers, but the true teaching of Badarayana and Kapila has been obscured rather than illuminated by being mixed up with poor and contemptible conjuring tricks.........It is difficult, therefore, not to get angry if one sees the elevated views of these ancient philosophers dragged down to the level of cloudy hallucinations, and rendered absurd by being mixed up with vulgar trickeries. *Corruptio optimi pessima*............I feel convinced that no good has ever come from anything that is not perfectly honest and straightforward, and what a lurid light has been thrown on the Theosophist Society at Adyar!"

Max Muller was never weary of impressing on Indians the futility of running after mysterious Mahatmas supposed to be possessed of occult knowledge and powers.

"That there are hermits living in the Himalayan forests, that some of them are extremely learned, and that others are able to perform extraordinary acts of austerity, is well known. But equally well known are the books which they study, and acts of Yoga which they perform, and there is really no kind of mystery about them. They themselves would be the last to claim any mysterious knowledge beyond what the Sastras supply. Nor are such Mahatmas to be found in the Himalayan recessess only. India is full of men who seek retirement, dwell in a small cell or cave, sleep on the skin of a tiger or stag, abstain from flesh, fish, and wine, never touch salt, and live entirely on fruits and roots."

His deep interest in current movements of thought enabled him to give to the world valuable ideas which were due to his having been able to bring to bear on such movements a mind which gained rare vision and power and acumen by its very aloofness and pre-occupation with the past and which was thus able to see things in proper perspective and relate the present to the past wisely and well. In regard to the Darwinian theory he says well in *the Silesian Hcrseherd* :

"Darwin certainly brought much that is beautiful and true to the light of day. He demonstrated that many of the so-called species are not independent creations, but have been developed from other species. ....…That sounds splendid, but everyone who does not quite ignore the past, knows that evolution or development is neither anything very new or very useful.........Here we then found a transition from the animal to man? Certainly not; for man is man, not because he has no tact, but because he speaks, and speech not only communication,—an animal can do that perhaps better than a man,—but it implies thinking, and not only as an animal thinks, but thinking conceptionally."

He then continues:

"We ask, why does the fittest survive? And when we come to Natural Selection, who is the selector that selects? These are nothing but phrases, which have long been known and long since abandoned, and still are always warmed up again.........Neither survival of the fittest nor natural selection could bring order into this confusion; we might as well believe that, if the type in a printing office be thoroughly shaken and mixed, it could produce Goethe's *Faust* by chance. If we insist upon adherence to the theories of natural selection, or survival of the fittest, be it so; we only transfer the choice to a something which can choose, and leave the fitness or adaptability to the judgment of an originator, who can really judge and think.........Darwinisin is a high-sounding, but hollow and unreal word, like most of the names that end in *ism.*"

In his work *Psychological Religion* he puts the matter very clearly and concisely:—

"That certain species were evolved from lower species, even during the short time of which we possess any certain knowledge, is no doubt a great discovery, but it does not touch the deeper question of the origin of all species.........Unless we admit the eternal existence of these ideas in a rational mind, or in the Primal Cause of all things, we cannot account for our seeing them realised in Nature, discovered by human reason, and named by human language."

His works abound in pregnant observations on life which are the result of wide study and mature reflection. He says in *Auld Lang Syne:* "What is ideal is not necessarily unreal, it is only like a landscape seen in sunshine."

"CHIPS FROM A GERMAN WORKSHOP."

One of the most interesting works is his well-known "Chips from a German Workshop" The origin of this work is given by Max Muller himself in his preface to the volumes. After Bunsen got for him the undertaking by the East Indian Company to publish the *Rig Veda,* he told Max Muller: "Now you have got a work for life—a large block that will take years to plane and polish. But mind let us have from time to time some chips from your workshops." The preface contains a valuable idea that should be of special interest to us as bearing upon the question of religion and religious revelation. He says:

"The elements and roots of religion were there, as far back as we can trace the history of man; and the history of religion, like the history of language, shows us throughout a succession of new combinations of the same radical elements. An intuition of God, a sense of human weakness and dependence, a belief in a divine government of the world, a distinction between good and evil, and a hope of a better life, these are some of the radical elements of all religions. Though sometimes hidden, they rise again and again to the surface. Though frequently distorted, they tend again and again to their perfect form. Unless they had formed part of the original dowry of the human soul, religion itself could have remained an impossibility, and the tongues of angels would have been to human ears but as sounding brass or a tinkling cymbal."

In the first lecture contained in Volume I he says; "In no country, I believe, has the theory of revelation been so minutely elaborated as in India." He points out how in *Rig Veda* III, 37, 4. the Rishis speak of their hymns as God-given (*Devadattam*). The second chip "Christ and other Masters" is not of great value and shows Max Muller's limitations as a student of Indian thought and as an interpreter of Hindu religion. The third chapter deals with the Veda and the Zend-Avesta. It says: "It is natural to suppose that, though perhaps the eldest brother, the Hindu, was the last to leave the central home of the Aryan family." It is not possible to deal here with the myth of this Aryan immigration *into* India.

The subsequent chapters deal with the Aitareya Brahmana, the Zend-Avesta, Buddhism, and Semitic monotheism. Subjects so varied as these cannot be discussed adequately in this brief sketch but we shall give here a few extracts showing Max Muller's wide and varied scholarship. He says:

"Ideas grow and change, yet each generation tries to find its own ideas reflected in the sacred pages of their early prophets, and, in addition to the ordinary influences which blur and obscure the sharp features of old words, artificial influences are here at work distorting the natural expression of words which have been invested with a sacred authority."

In regard to Buddhism he points out the real glory and the real weakness of that marvellous world-religion.

In the second volume of the *Chips* we have a long and valuable chapter on *Comparative Mythology*. He says in it:

"*Mythology* is only a dialect, an ancient form of language. Mythology, though chiefly concerned with Nature, and here again mostly with those manifestations which bear the character of law, order, power and wisdom impressed on them, was applicable to all things. Nothing is excluded from mythological expression; neither morals nor philosophy, neither history nor religion, have escaped the spell of that ancient Sybil"

The third volume of *Chips from German Workshop* contains valuable essays on literature, biography, and antiquities. In the first lecture he gives us some of his well known ideas on German Literature. He describes, in a beautiful passage, what is the highest function of the highest poetry.

"Beauty, love, virtue, happiness,—everything, in fact, that moves the heart of the poet, has a hidden reference to something higher than this life; and the highest object of the highest poetry seems to be to transfer the mind to those regions where men feel the presence of a divine power and a divine love and are lost in blissful adoration."

MAX MULLER'S BIOGRAPHICAL WRITINGS.

Max Muller's *Biographical Essays* are of great value not only as dealing with the lives of some great men and as revealing the qualities that made men great but as showing how Max Muller had a nature full of the noblest impulses, generous and loving in his estimates of men, and fired by a genuine passion for understanding and disseminating Vedic thought. His devotion to the study of Comparative Philology also finds ample expression in this volume as in his other works. He says in regard to great men: "Great men, depend upon it, do not come down from the sky like shooting stars. They come in the fulness of time, and if we want to understand their true character, we must try to understand that fulness of time, that is, the time that lay behind and the time that lay before them." It is in this spirit that this volume is conceived. In the biography of *Rajah Ram Mohan Roy* he says: "The Supreme and all-absorbing interest of Ram Mohan Roy's life was religion." The Raja had however but little knowledge of Sanskrit and had a leaning towards Christianity—characteristics that have persisted in all the later stages of the Brahmo movement. Max Muller says that the Raja was a great man as he had unselfishness, honesty and boldness.

The next biography is that of one of the great leaders of Brahmo Samaj—Keshub Chunder Sen. It is pathetic to know that in Keshub's last letter to Max Muller on 20th June 1883 he said:

> "Our affinity is not only ethnic, but in the highest degree spiritual, which often draws you into my heart and makes me enjoy the pleasures of friendly intercourse."

The next biography is that of the founder of the Arya Samaj—Dayanand Saraswathi. The volume deals also with two Buddhist priests, Colebrooke, Dr. Mohl Bunsen, and Kingsley.

Max Muller's *Auld Lang Syne* consists of two volumes of charming reminiscences and give us an intimate knowledge of himself and his many distinguished Indian and European friends. In the first volume he gives us his musical and literary recollections and recollections of royalties. It is full of wit and wisdom. The first volume deals mainly with literary recollections and contains very valuable ideas about the literary art in general and about the Professor's great literary contemporaries. He says:

> "Inspired útterance requires, nay produces, rhythmic movements not only of the voice (song and prosody), but of the body also (dance).........language itself bears witness to the fact that the oldest metres were the steps and movements of dancers. As the old dances consisted of steps, the ancient metres consisted of feet."

"A strophe also was originally a turning, to be followed by the anti-strophe or the return, all ideas derived from dancing." This volume contains many beautiful personal reminiscences of great authors. One of these may be mentioned. Max Muller says that Tennyson was particularly struck with his metaphor in his first Essay on Comparative Mythology to the effect that the sun in his daily passage across the sky had ploughed a a golden furrow through the human brain, where sprang in ancient times the first germs of mythology, and afterwards the rich harvest of religious thought.

The second series of *Auld Lang Syne* are of even greater interest to us as they bear directly on India and on his Indian friends. It describes his impressions of Dwarkanath Tagore, Debendranath Tagore, Radhakhanta Deva, Nilakantha Goreh, Keshub Chunder Sen, Ramtanoo Lahiri, Dayanand Saraswathi, Ramakrishna Paramahamsa, Behramji Malabari, Pandita Ramabhai, Anandibai Joshee, and

Gaurisankar Udayasankar Ojha. It shows his genuine love for them and his appreciation of their worth. When dealing with the lies circulated by traducers of the national character of the Indians, he says: "We appeal to the literatures of other nations as records of their true character, why not in the case of the Hindus." He pays a just and noble tribute to the excellences of Indian character. He shows how Hindu philosophy is really an inspirer of higher activity and not a force leading to quietism and death-in-life.

The Indians, whom Max Muller knew personally, were Hindu protestants or the Brahmos. His book on *Ramakrishna Paramahamsa*, however, deals with one of the finest blossoms of the traditional life and culture of the land. And he goes on to distinguish between saints and reformers: "The people of India evidently distinguish clearly between these professed ascetics and saints on one side, and mere reformers such as Ram Mohan Roy and Keshub Chunder Sen and others. They evidently want to see a complete surrender of the world and its pleasures before they quite believe in the truth and the sincerity of any teachers and reformers." About Sri Ramakrishna himself he says:

"He was a living illustration of the truth that Vedanta, when roperly realised, can become a practical rule of life..........Men possessed of wonderful Yoga powers and great learning came to learn from this illiterate Paramahamsa of Dakshineswara, and in their turn acknowledged him as their spiritual director (Guru), touched as they were by the wonderful purity, the childlike simplicity, the perfect unselfishness, and by the simple language in which he propounded the highest truths of religion and philosophy."

"INDIA: WHAT CAN IT TEACH US."

This famous volume containing Max Muller's lectures delivered before the University of Cambridge is one of great charm and value. The whole of the second chapter is devoted to the proving of the truthful character of the Hindus. The third chapter deals with the great human interest of Sanskrit literature.

Such is the marvellous continuity between the past and the present in India, that in spite of repeated social convulsions, religious reforms, and foreign invasions, Sanskrit may be said to be still the only language that is spoken over the whole extent of that vast country.........But even if Sanskrit were more of a dead language than it really is, all the living languages of India, both Aryan and Dravidian, draw their very life and soul from Sanskrit."

He then points out how religion was the all-absorbing interest of the ancient Hindus.

"Now let us look to the ancient inhabitants of India. With them, first of all, religion was not only one interest by the side of many, it was the all-absorbing interest, it embraced not only worship and prayer, but what we call philosophy, morality, law and government,—all was pervaded by religion."

"Philosophy in India says Max Muller, "is what it ought to be, not the denial, but the fulfilment of religion."

"To the present day India acknowledges no higher authority in matters of religion, ceremonial, customs and law than the Veda, and so long as India is India, nothing will extinguish the ancient spirit of Vedantism which is breathed by every Hindu from his earliest youth, and pervades in various forms the prayers even of the idolater, the speculations of the philosopher, and the proverbs of the beggar."

And then follows a noble passage:

"If I were to look over the whole world to find out the country most richly endowed with all the wealth, power and beauty that Nature can bestow—in some parts a very Paradise on earth—I should point to India. If I were asked under what sky the human mind has most fully developed some of its choicest gifts, has most deeply pondered on the greatest problems of life, and has found solutions of some of them which well deserve the attention even of those who have studied Plato and Kant—I should point to India. And if I were to ask myself from what literature we, here in Europe, we who have been nurtured almost exclusively at the thoughts of Greeks and Romans, and of one Semite race, the Jewish, may draw that corrective which is most wanted in order to make our inner life more perfect, more comprehensive, more universal, in fact more truly human, a life, not for this life only, but a transfigured and eternal life,—again I should point to India."

"HISTORY OF ANCIENT SANSKRIT LITERATURE."

In this valuable book he deals with the Hindu sacred scriptures with insight and learning, "It is impossible" he says, "to find the right point of view for judging of Indian religion, morals, and literature without a knowledge of the literary remains of the Vedic age"—a truth lamentably forgotten even by Hindu Scholars and Pandits to-day. He refers with evident admiration to the beautiful hymn in the Rig Veda which says:

सतो बन्धु म सति निरविंदन् हार्दिप्रतीय्य कुवयो मनीषा ।

(Poets discovered in their heart, through meditation, the bond of the Eternal in the non-eternal.)

But the Professor has read the scriptures with a critical eye. And he finds that "there is a contradiction running throughout the religious life of India from the time of the Ramayana to the present day. The outer form of the worship is Vedic and exclusively so; but the eye of religious adoration is turned upon quite different religions." The fact is that the religious life of India is due to Vedic inspiration as much to day as ever before. But the emphasis on this or that aspect of Vedic doctrine or ceremonial differs from age to age or from individual to individual.

"THE SIX SYSTEMS OF INDIAN PHILOSOPHY."

This is one of his greatest works. In his preface he speaks of the Vedanta philosophy as "a system in which human speculation seems to me to have reached its very acme." His object is "to give a more comprehensive account of the philosophical activity of the Indian nation from the earliest times, and to show how intimately not only their religion, but their philosophy also, was connected with the national character of the inhabitants of India." In the book itself he points out:

"In certain chapters of the Brahmanas and in the Upanishads we see a picture of the social and intellectual life of India at that early time, which seems fully to justify the saying that India has always been a nation of philosophers."

It is impossible in the brief space at our disposal to discuss at length all his philosophical disputations. It is easy enough to pick holes in the work of pioneers who were hampered with great difficulties in understanding and interpreting the spirit of the subtle theology of the East. Doubtless Max Muller had his limitations. But on the whole he has well entered into the spirit of the Vedanta philosophy and the following passage is as faithful to its vital elements as it is beautiful in expression:

"And yet, after lifting the Self above body and soul after uniting heaven and earth, God and man, Brahman and Atman, these Vedanta philosophers have destroyed nothing in the life of the phenomenal beings who have to act and to fulfil their duties in this phenomenal world. On the contrary they have shown that there can be nothing phenomenal without something that is real, and that goodness and virtue, faith and works, are necessary as a preparation, nay, as a *sine qua non*, for the attainment of that highest knowledge which brings the soul back to its source and to its home, and restores it to its true nature, to its true Selfhood in Brahman."

He points out generally in regard to Indian philosophers that they

"have the excellent habit of always explaining the meaning of their technical terms."

"There remains with me" he says, "a strong conviction that Indian philosophers are honest in their reasonings, and never use empty words." He then gives us a brief—too brief and uninforming exposition of Nyaya and Vaisheshika systems."

He sums up the main traits of the six systems thus :

"In this respect all the six systems of philosophy are alike, they always promise to their followers or their believers the attainment of the highest bliss that can be obtained by man. The approaches leading to that bliss vary, and the character also of the promised bliss is not always the same; yet in each of the systems, philosophy is recommended not, as with us, for the sake of knowledge, but for the highest purpose that man can strive after in this life, that is, his own salvation."

His splendid tribute to all of them may fitly be quoted here :—

"To have mounted to such giddy heights, even if we have to descend again frightened and giddy, must have strengthened the muscles of human reason, and will remain in our memory as a sight never to be forgotten even in the lower spheres in which we have to move in our daily life and amidst our daily duties.

Speaking for myself, I am bound to say that I have felt an acquaintance with the general spirit of Indian philosophy as a blessing from my very youth, being strengthened by it against all the antinomies of being and thinking, and nerved in all the encounters with scepticism and materialism of our own ephemeral philosophy."

THREE LECTURES ON VEDANTA.

These valuable lectures were delivered at the Royal Institution in March 1894: In the first lecture he deals with the origin of the Vedanta Philosophy. He says there: "If philosophy is meant to be a preparation for a happy death, or Euthanasia, I know of no better preparation for it than the Vedanta philosophy." He points out that in India philosophy is inseparable from religion and is looked upon "as its most precious flower and fragrance." The second lecture deals with the Soul and God. It is refreshing to read:

"In India the truth was open to all who thirsted for it. Nothing was kept secret, no one was excluded from the temple, or rather the forest, of truth." The *Atman* is not the Ego but lies far beyond it—such is the message of the Vedanta. The Vedanta is not an apotheosis of man but an *anatheosis* as a return of men into the divine nature.'.

The third lecture deals with the similarities and differences between Indian and European Philosophy. The first truth declared and demonstrated in this lecture is the tolerance of Indian religion and philosophy.

"This fact, this perception of a relative truth contained in our phenomenal experience, explains, I believe, why we find in the Vedanta philosophy the same tolerant spirit which we find generally in Indian religion."

As regards the ethics of the Vedanta he says:

"However sceptical we may be on the power of any ethical teaching, and its influence on the practical conduct of men and women, there can be no doubt that this doctrine of Karman (Karman means simply out or dead) has met with the widest acceptance, and has helped to soften the sufferings of millions, and to encourage them *not only in their endurance of present evils, but likewise in their efforts to improve their condition.*"

"With the Vedantists" however, "this feeling of a common interest, nay, of the oneness or solidarity of the human race, was most natural."

"THE SILESIAN HORSEHERD."

This book is valuable as giving us Max Muller's ideas about the relation of language and thought, "in which he had long since recognised the clue to man's knowledge of the relation of his spirit to God," in the words of J. Estlin Carpenter in the preface to the book, Max Muller points out to what power Christianity owed its rapid spread:

"Christianity is especially indebted for its rapid spread to its practical side, to the energy of its love, which was bestowed on all who were weary and heavy-laden."

But to attract men of culture a religion must have a philosophy as well. Max Muller says :—

"The bridge which led across from Greek philosophy to Christianity was the Logos.........It is only needful not to forget that for the Greeks thought and word are inseparable, and that the same term, namely Logos, expressed both, though they distinguished the inner from the outer Logos.........Although it is now the custom to speak slightingly of the later Platonists, we should always recognise that we owe to them the preservation of this, the most precious jewel out of the rich storehouse of Greek philosophy, that the world is the expression and realisation of divine thought, that it is the divine word expressed."

The Scylla and Charybdis of human thought are well pointed out by him in his description of Greek and Jewish philosophies.

"While the Greeks had almost lost sight of the bridge between the world and God by abstaction, the Jews, through mistaken reverence, had so for removed the Creator above His creation that on both sides the need of mediation or a mediator was deeply felt."

The inter-relation of the doctrine of the Logos and the Darwinian theory of the survival of the fittest is thus brought out by him:

"And what is the fittest, if not the rational, the Platonic 'Good,' that is, the Logos? Why, then, turn back to the stone age of human thinking, why again turn Nature into wood, when for thousands of years Greek philosophers and Christian thinkers have recognised her as something spiritual, as a world of eternal ideas?".

This article of Professor Max Muller's was keenly criticised in a letter by a German

American calling himself *The Silesian Horse-herd.* The latter criticised from the point of view of the modern *illuminati* to whom religion is a manifestation of ignorance and who believe that there is nothing beyond this life. Max Muller's reply to him covers a wide ground and discloses his mental sweep and his penetrative power of vision. He emphasises that two factors are always present in religion, *viz.* that the world is the result of thought and that thought is not the outcome of matter but is the *prius* of all things.

He says about the Hindu Philosophy :

"Nowhere is the idea of revelation worked out so carefully as in their literature.........In nearly all religions, God remains far from man. I say in nearly all the religions for in Brahmanism the unity, not the union, of the human soul with Brahman is recognised as the highest aim."

THE SCIENCE OF RELIGION.

Some of Max Muller's finest work consisted in development of the science of religion. The fundamental ideas at the bottom of the science of religion are very well stated by him.

"There is nothing in the idea of revelation that excludes progress, for whatever definition of revelation we may adopt, it always represents a communication between the divine on the one side and the human on the other. Let us grant that the divine element in revelation, that is, whatever of truth there is in revelation is immutable, yet the human element, the recipient, must always be liable to the accidents and infirmities of human nature." (*Natural Religion.*)

But what does this science consist in?

First of all, in a careful collection of all the facts of religion; secondly, in a comparison of religion with a view of bringing to light what is peculiar to each, and what they all share in common; thirdly, in an attempt to discover, on the strength of the evidence thus collected, what is the true nature, the origin, and purpose of all religion."

In his *Natural Religion*, he examines various definitions of religion, the differences of which are due to variations in the angle of vision and says that religion is due to the perception of the Infinite in Nature, in Man, and in Self. This idea is developed in his three other books called *Physical Religion, Anthropological Religion, and Psychological Religion.* He points out that while science as well as religion deals with the Infinite, religious perceptions are those perceptions of the Infinite which influence man's actions and his whole moral nature.

"Religion consists in the perception of the Infinite under such manifestations as are able to influence the moral character of man."

The materials for the study of natural religion are language, myth, customs and laws, and sacred books.

"What we call language is not, as is commonly supposed, thought *plus* sound, but what we call thought is really language *minus* sound."

His book on *Physical Religion* deals with the worship of the powers of Nature. He points out how the three phases of religion above referred to are often contemporaneous. His view that the Vedic Religion is physical religion proceeds on a fundamental error of thought. His idea that the Rig Veda is the only true Veda is equally open to question. The theory of Aryan immigration into India is a similarly erroneous assertion of early Western scholarship and must be revised in the light of the new facts brought to light by modern and specially modern Indian scholarship.

The realisation of an eternal, infinite, or omnipresent, and invisible presence in natural phenomena is not a process of personification or anthropomorphism at all. It is due to

> "That sense sublime
> Of something far more deeply interfused,
> Whose dwelling is the light of setting suns,
> And the round ocean, and the living air,
> And the blue sky, and in the mind of man,
> A motion and a spirit that impels
> All thinking things, all objects of all thought,
> And rolls through all things."

In Max Muller's *Anthropological Religion* he begins by summing up the results reached in the two books above referred to. He says that man conceived that every movement must have a mover and that this was a result of the necessity inherent in language *viz.*, that all roots were expressive of man's own actions.

"We have proved that, given man, such as he is; and given the world, such as it is, a belief in divine beings, and at last, in one Divine Being, is not only a universal, but an *inevitable* fact."

He then deals with Anthropological Religion, the second branch of Natural Religion.

"It is called anthropological, simply and solely in order to comprehend under that name all the attempts which have been made to discover something not merely human, the super-human, then divine and immortal in man. The most interesting parts of this process are the beginning and the end, the first discovery of something different from the body, and the final identification of that something with the Divine."

He shows that, as in the case of physical nature man rose from a conception of agents to the conception of an Infinite Agent, so in the case of the human personality man realised the Infinite in man by beginning with contemplation on the phenomena of sleep and death.

"Real religion, however, requires more than a belief in God, it requires a belief in man also, and in an intimate relation between God and man, at all events in a life to come."

We now come to his *Psychological Religion* dealing with the third of the three discoveries which he describes as "the discovery of God, the discovery of the Soul, and the discovery of the oneness of God and the Soul." He points out that philosophy begins with doubting the evidence of the senses.

> The last result of what I called Physical Religion and Anthropological Religion is the very belief that the human soul will after death enter the realm of light, and stand before the Throne of God, whatever name may have been assigned to him. This seems indeed the highest point that has been reached by natural religion. But we shall see that one religion, at least that of the Vedanta, made a decided step beyond.........The Vedanta, whether we call it a religion or a philosophy, has completely broken with the effete anthropomorphic conception of God and of the soul as approaching the throne of God, and has opened vistas which were unknown to the greatest thinkers of Europe.........I doubt whether Natural Religion can reach or has ever reached a higher point than that reached by Sankara, as an interpreter of the Upanishads."

He gives us a clear and correct idea as to the main doctrines of Sankara and Ramanuja about the relation of the soul to God and about the reality of the world.

We must remember, he says, that what he (Sankara) calls unreal is no more than what we should call phenomenal.

> It is as real as anything presented to our senses ever can be. Nor is the *Vyavaharika* or phenomenal God more unreal than the God whom we ignorantly worship. Avidya or nescience with Sankara produces really the same effect as *Parinama* or evolution with Ramanuja...........Sankara claims for the phenomenal world a reality sufficient for all practical purposes (vyavaharika), sufficient to determine our practical life, our moral obligations, nay even our belief in a manifested or revealed God."

He deals also with the religions which declare that the human and the divine can never be one and says:

"They have first created an unapproachable deity and they are afterwards afraid to approach it; they have made an abyss between the human and the divine and they dare not cross it."

In regard to the Vedanta, he points out that the Hindu thinkers laid down that a life of perfect moral discipline was the sole means of self-realisation. There was no esoterism in the Hindu schools of thought.

"*Esoteric* mysteries seem to me much more of a modern invention than an ancient institution. The more we become familiar with the ancient literature of the East, the less we find of Oriental mysteries, of esoteric wisdom, of Isis veiled or unveiled."

He then describes other aspects of religion which he happily describes as a bridge between the visible and the invisible world and which aims at "uniting these two worlds again, whether by the arches of hope and fear or by the iron chains of logical syllogisms." He then deals with the conception of the Logos and Christian Theosophy. In describing the doctrine of the fatherhood of God he says: "Human language could hardly have supplied a better metaphor for expressing intrinsic oneness and extrinsic difference."

In his *Introduction to the Science of Religion*, published in 1873, he says in his felicitous manner: "There is in man a third faculty, which I call simply the faculty of apprehending the Infinite, not only in religion but in all things; a power independent of sense and reason, a power in a certain sense contradicted by sense and reason, but yet a very real power, which has held its own from the beginning of the world, neither sense nor reason being able to overcome it, while it alone is able to overcome both reason and sense." He says further: "It is language and religion that make a people, but religion is even a more powerful agent than language."

THE SCIENCE OF THOUGHT.

In his valuable book on *The Science of Thought*, he gives us in his inimitably clear manner the distinctive origin and component elements of human thought. He points out that sensation and consciousness of sensation are two different worlds; and that we never in reality perceive anything unless we can distinguish it from other things by means, if not of a word, yet of a sign, that is, till we have passed through the four stages of sensation, perception, conception, and more important than all, of naming. In these four processes four faculties are involved, *viz.*, sense, imagination, intellect, and language. He shows the poverty of the results got from *Menagerie psychology* and *Nursery psychology.* Space, time, and causality are of the essence of the process of thinking. He says further:

"Sensations, once planted on the soil of our mind, grow into percepts and concepts, but the three can as little be torn asunder as a flower can be torn from the stem, or the stem from the seed.' "They (words) are the very limbs, as they may become the very wings of thought. We do not complain that we cannot move on without legs. Why then should it be humiliating that we cannot think without words?"

He says that words are the signs of concepts and not signs of things and that the real historical development of the human mind should be studied in the history of language. He shows that roots are the ultimate elements in the science of language, that they are not interjections or imitations of natural sounds, and that they express concepts.

"I make bold to say that there are few concepts in English or Latin or Greek that could not be expressed with the words derived from Sanskrit roots. I believe, on the contrary, that the number of roots necessary to account for the whole wealth of the English Dictionary, which is said to amount to 250,000 words, is smaller than that of Panini's roots, even after they have been reduced to their proper limits.........There is no sentence in English of which every word cannot be traced back to the 800 roots, and every thought to the 121 fundamental concepts which remained after a careful sifting of the materials supplied to us by Panini."

He finally sums up his view by saying "what we have been in the habit of calling thought is but the reverse of a coin of which the obverse is articulate sound while the current coin is one and indivisible, neither thought nor sound, but word..............the science of thought is to the science of language what Biology is to Anatomy."

"THE SCIENCE OF MYTHOLOGY."

In the introduction to this book Max Muller speaks of "the work of my life as I had planned itmany years ago, namely, an exposition, however imperfect, of the four sciences of Language, Mythology, Religion, and Thought, following each other in natural succession, and comprehending the whole sphere of the activity of the human mind from the earliest period within the reach of our knowledge to the present day." Max Muller's exposition of mythology has many elements of value and truth. His attempt to explain the characteristics and achievements of the Gods in the light of the physical phenomena such as fire, clouds, etc., however, leads him into the most far-fetched explanations and suggestions in regard to which disproof is as impossible as proof.

"THE SACRED BOOKS OF THE EAST."

But by far the most important of his works in Oriental Scholarship was the monumental publication known as "The Sacred Books of the East" which he began to edit since 1875. It was a magnificent conception to bring the whole of Oriental knowledge in a series of encyclopædic volumes. Alike in copiousness and erudition, these volumes bear the impress of a masterly mind. They comprise in all no less than fifty-one volumes including indexes, all but three of which appeared under his superintendence during his life time. "These comprise translations by the most competent scholars of all the really important non-Christian scriptures of Oriental nations which can now be appreciated without a knowledge of the original languages." Max Muller himself wrote on Indian philosophy in his later years and his exertions stimulate search for Oriental manuscripts and inscriptions now rewarded with important discoveries of early Buddhist scriptures, in their Indian form, in Japan.

"LAST ESSAYS."

Melancholy interest attaches to these two volumes as the essays were selected for re-publication by Max Muller shortly before he died. In the first volume we have lectures and essays dealing largely with questions raised in the science of language. He points out that "languages suffer from wealth even more than from poverty." He shows that thought is impossible without words. A previous passage showing the worthlessness of the modern heresy of education without memorising may well be quoted here:

"I have occasionally given expression to my regret that the old system of learning by heart at our public schools should have gone so completely out of fashion. Old men like myself know what a precious treasure for life are the few lines that remain indelibly engraved on our memory from our earliest school days. Whatever else we forget they remain, and they remind us, by their very sound, of happy days, of happy faces, and happy hearts."

In a valuable chapter on *The Savage* he shows the utter untenability of the theory which identifies the modern savage with primitive man. In the chapter on *Kant's Critique of Pure Reason* he clearly lays bare the modern confusion of thought which confounds and even obliterates the bounds of physics and metaphysics.

The second volume of *The Last Essays* deals mostly with religious subjects. It describes forgotten bibles and ancient prayers. In the chapter on *Indian Fables and Esoteric Buddhism* he traces the growth of the epidemic of fraud on the one side and of credulity on the other side in regard to certain recent religious developments in India. He says:

"I am afraid it can no longer be doubted that Dayananda Sarasvati was as deficient in moral straight-forwardness as his American pupil (Madame Blavatsky).........You may ask how educated people could have been deceived by such ordinary jugglery but with some people the power of believing seem to grow with the absurdity of what is to be believed."

Then he pillories M. Notovitch's fraud about the alleged sojourn of Christ in India. Then the points of similarity between Mahomedanism and Christianity are examined in another chapter. The religions of China are dealt with in *extenso* in the next chapter. The next chapter deals with the Parliament of Religions held at Chicago in 1893. He says well therein:

"Practical religion is life, is a new life, a life in the sight of God; and it springs from what may truly be called a new birth."

In the chapter on *Why I am not an Agnostic* he points out that the human mind in its highest functions is not confined to a knowledge of phenomena only."

The last chapter on *Is Man Immortal* deals with the proofs of the immortality of the soul.

MISCELLANEOUS WORKS.

His lectures on *The Science of Language* have been published in two volumes. The historical progress of the Science of Languages can be traced in its three stages, the Empirical, the Classificatory, and the Theoretical. Each physical science begins with analysis, proceeds to classification, and ends with theory. This is as true of the Science of Language as of other sciences. Grammar arose everywhere from the study of sacred or secular literature. Max Muller takes us into the very dawn of language and shows how it is the real barrier between brute and man and how it has evolved with the growth of humanity. His lectures on the *Origin and Growth of Religion* in 1878 are of a high order of merit. Among his other works are *German Classics, Missions*, and innumerable essays on a variety of subjects.

CONCLUSION.

Many and varied as were his works, his character far out-shone even the splendour of his achievements in scholarship or interpretation. His attachment and devotion to friends, his sympathetic and genial enthusiasm for things intellectual, his zeal for all social and liberal movements for the uplift of humanity and his abounding charity were widely appreciated by all who came in contact with him. Years brought him fame and he was acquainted with most of the Royalties in Europe and a special favourite with the English Royal House. His hospitality, says the writer in the *Encyclopædia Britannica*, was ample, especially to visitors from India where he was far better known than any other European Orientalist. Many a distinguished publicist in this country has given testimony to the extraordinary love that Max Muller had for India. The late Mr. Malabari wrote many touching anecdotes of the Professor's attachment to India, her peoples and her civilization. Swami Vivekananda who had a great admiration for Max Muller specially went to his residence in England before returning to India. He has left a beautiful account of his last farewell. Here is the luminous record of the Swami with which we may fittingly close this sketch :—

"What an extraordinary man is Prof, Max Muller! He was first induced to enquire about the power behind, which led to the sudden and momentous changes in the life of the late Keshava Chandra Sen; and since then he has been an earnest student and admirer of the life and teachings of Sri Ramakrishna.* "Ramakrishna is worshipped by thousands to-day, Professor," I said. "To whom else shall worship be accorded, if not to such?" was the answer. The Professor was kindness itself: he asked Mr. Sturdy and myself to lunch with him and showed us several colleges in Oxford and the Bodleian Library. He also accompanied us to the railway station; and all this he did because, as he said: "It is not everyday one meets a disciple of Ramakrishna Paramahamsa." That was really a revelation to me. That nice little house in its setting of a beautiful garden, the silver headed sage, with a face calm and benign, and a forehead smooth as a child's in spite of seventy winters and every line in that face speaking of a deep-seated mine of spirituality somewhere behind: that noble wife, the helpmate of his life through his long and arduous task of exciting interest, over-riding opposition and contempt, and at last creating a respect for the thoughts of the sage of ancient India—the trees. the flowers, the calmness, and clear sky—all these sent me back in imagination to the glorious days of Ancient India, the days of our *Brahmarishis* and

*The great Guru of Swami Vivekananda, one of the greatest of the modern saints.

Rajarishis, the days of the great *Vanaprasthas*, the days of Arundhatis and Vasishtas.

It was neither the Philologist nor the Scholar that I saw, but a soul that is everyday realising its oneness with the *Brahman*, a heart that is every moment expounding, to reach oneness with the universal. Where others lose themselves in the desert of dry details, he has struck a well of life. Indeed his heart-beats have caught the rhythm of the *Upanishads*. "Know *thyself* and leave off all other talk."

Although a world-moving scholar and philosopher, his learning and philosophy have only led him higher and higher to the realization of the spirit; his lower knowledge has, indeed, helped him to reach the higher. This is real learning. Knowledge gives rise to humility. Of what use is knowledge if it does not show us the way to the highest?

And what love he bears towards India! I wish I had a hundredth part of that love for my own motherland. An extraordinary and at the same time intensely active mind has lived and moved in the world of Indian thought for fifty years or more and watched the sharp interchange of light and shade in the interminable forest of Sanskrit literature with keen interest and heart-felt love, till they have all sunk into his whole soul and coloured his whole being.

Max Muller is a Vedantist of Vedantists. He has, indeed, caught the real soul of the melody of the Vedanta in the midst of all its settings of harmonies or discords—the one light that lightens up the sects and creeds of the world, the Vedanta, the one principle of which all religions are only applications. And what was Ramakrishna Paramahamsa? The practical demonstration of this ancient principle, the embodiment of India that is past, and a foreshadowing of the India that is to be, the bearer of spiritual light unto nations. The jeweller alone can understand the worth of jewels: this is an old proverb. Is it a wonder that this Western sage does study and appreciate every new star in the firmament of Indian thoughts before even the Indians themselves realise its magnititude?

"When are you coming to India? Every heart there would welcome one who has done so much to place the thoughts of their ancestors in the true light," I said. The face of the aged sage brightened up—there was almost a tear in his eye, a gentle nodding of the head; and slowly the words came out: "I would not return then, you would have to cremate me there." Further question seemed an unwarrantable intrusion into realms wherein are stored the holy secrets of man's heart.

Who knows but that it was what the Poet has said:—

"He remembers with his mind the friendship of former births, firmly rooted in his heart."

His life has been a blessing to the world; may it be many, many years more, before he changes the present plane of his existence.

John Faithfull Fleet.

MANY a Kanarese peasant still cherishes with revered memory the long summer evenings that he had spent in the camp of Dr. Fleet, as the latter sat amidst the peasantry listening to their many tales of adventure and recording their ballads. A perfect master of Sanskrit literature, Dr. Fleet had a thorough grasp of the Kanarese language in its old and mediæval forms. This enabled him to collect the vast mass of Sanskrit and old Kanarese inscriptions, of which the Bombay Presidency was full and month after month, throughout the 30 years of his stay in India, he was educating the learned world by editing and interpreting these inscriptions. That Indian chronology is firmly fixed, that the science of epigraphy itself has progressed by leaps and bounds is entirely due to him. A prince among Epigraphist-Historians of India, Dr. Fleet occupied during his lifetime the position of the founder and leader of Indian historical studies.

The son of John George Fleet of Roystons, Chiswick, and coming from a typical English stock of the best type, Dr. Fleet was born in 1847. Educated at the Merchant Taylors School, he soon equipped himself with sufficient knowledge to take up the duties pertaining to the Indian Civil Service to which he was appointed in 1865. It was a good rule that prevailed in those days that the young civilian proceeding to India should have a sound knowledge of Sanskrit language and literature. The young Fleet lost therefore no time in sitting at the feet of that eminent Sanskrit Professor, Theodore Goldstücker.

Dr. Fleet's official career may be briefly summarised. He came to Bombay in 1867 and entered at once the graded service of the Revenue and Executive branch of the Government of India. Punctual in his habits and extremely industrious, he was able easily to win the love and approbation of his superiors and soon he was made Assistant Collector and Magistrate, which position he held down to 1872.

As an officer he was eminently popular and deservedly praised by all with whom he came in contact. In 1872 he was appointed Educational Inspector in charge of the southern districts of the Bombay Presidency To us in the high state of the development of the official machinery it may sound strange that a purely revenue officer was asked to preside over the Educational department. But it must be remembered that in those days the Bombay Presidency had the good fortune to possess as revenue officers the best Englishmen that public schools produced. Moreover the duties of an Educational Inspector did not then require such a highly specialised knowledge that one in modern days associates with a similar office. Nevertheless it must be stated in fairness to Dr. Fleet that he was eminently qualified for the post he was selected for not merely because he could speak the language of the country with great fluency but he had a genuine love for the Kanarese whom he desired to elevate in every way open to him. In 1875, Dr. Fleet was transferred as Assistant Political Agent in the South Mahratta country and Kolhapur. His keen and accurate knowledge of men and things, his soft manners and diplomatic skill were thus utilized to the best advantage of the Government. He did not remain in this position for a long time. New activities were shaping themselves. The Government realised the great need for the conservation of ancient monuments and the deciphering of inscriptions that were found in plenty in the South Mahratta country. They created a special department, the Epigraphical Department. In January, 1883, through the influence of General Sir Alexander Cunningham,

K.C.I.E. and Mr. Gibbs, C.S.I., Dr. Fleet was appointed to this specially created post and he was charged with the primary duty of preparing the volume that was to contain the inscriptions of the early Gupta kings. He held this appointment up to June 1886 when it was abolished.

Dr. Fleet subsequently reverted to the Revenue Service as Junior Collector. Since then he was rapidly promoted to the senior ranks of the service. He was Senior Collector in 1889 and in 1891 he held the important post of Commissioner of Southern and Central Divisions. The foreign trade of Bombay was developing enormously and Dr. Fleet was soon appointed as Commissioner of Customs, which post he held down to the time of his retirement in 1897. Proceeding Home in the same year he settled permanently at Ealing. Freed from the pressure and worry of official duties, he continued from thence his favourite Indian epigraphical studies. He was for sometime Honorary Secretary of the Royal Asiatic Society which awarded its Gold Medal to him in 1912. He died in February, 1917, much to the regret of all who knew him. Thus speaks L. D. Barnett in regard to the great qualities of head and heart possessed by the Doctor :—

"Fleet's position is that of a *maestro di color che sanno*, a leader of scientific research. * * * He had a warm humanity and keen interest in the real things of life, which led him to delight in the simple ballads of his sturdy peasantry many of which he collected with loving care, and some of which he published in the *Antiquary* with their music. Allied to this quality was his capacity for friendship. He was a singularly warm and generous friend, endlessly kind and thoughtful and freely lavishing time and labour in order to aid others. There was no trace of selfishness or egoism in his nature. He invited new comers into the domain in which he was acknowledged master and generously helped them with counsel and guidance. He persuaded Frank Kielhorn, the great master of Sanskrit grammar, to turn his attention to Epigraphy and Chronology; and others are still living who can testify to their indebtedness to him for inspiration and help. *Non omnis mortuus est*; to all he has bequeathed a noble example of high achievement and to his friends a dear and gracious memory."

LITERARY ACTIVITY.

Thanks to the excellent Sanskrit education that Dr. Fleet had received at the hands of Prof. Theodore Goldstücker, his writings commenced the very year he arrived in India. Dr. Fleet's early papers were all contributed to the *Journal of the Bombay Branch of the R. A. S.* and these articles on Indian Epigraphical studies shewed the author to be possessed of those qualities essential for the Epigraphist-Historian—a perfect mastery of the classical and vernacular languages, a thorough grasp of details combined with remarkable skill in synthesis, a highly sober and critical judgment based on a pursuit of strictly scientific methods. Dr. Fleet was soon marked as a coming leader of Indian Epigraphy. But his talents were fully drawn out when the *Indian Antiquary* was started in 1872 by that enterprising scholar and Scotchman James Burgess. Dr. Fleet was connected with the Journal from the commencement and for seven years (1885-1892) he was Joint-Editor along with Sir Richard C. Temple.

His first literary undertaking on a large scale was the publication for the India Office of a volume entitled "Pali, Sanskrit and Old Kanarese Inscriptions." The Bombay Presidency in general and the Kanarese districts in particular contained a large number of original records which, if studied carefully, would yield materials for the compilation of an authentic history of the of the Bombay Presidency and the neighbouring parts, from the middle of the 6th to the end of the 16th century A.D. Various attempts were made from time to time to collect these inscriptions and arrange them in chronological order. Thus Sir Walter Elliot K.C.S.I. of the Madras Civil Service, compiled manuscript copies of no less than 595 stone-tablet inscriptions. The results of this scholar's labours were subsequently published in the *Madras Journal of Literature and Science*. Major Dixon in 1865 and Sir Theodore Hope K.C.S.I., in 1866, interested themselves in the collection of Kanarese inscriptions. Their publications, so useful for the reconstruction of the History of Western India, soon went out of print and the Government of India requested Dr. Fleet to utilize the negatives of inscriptions at the India Office and to re-arrange their contents. It was not an easy task to do. But with characteristic energy and promptitude, Dr. Fleet not only re-arranged and re-classified the India Office records but added himself a good deal to the existing stock of information and published in 1878 the volume of Pali, Sanskrit and Old Kanarese inscriptions. It is curious to note that owing to lack of funds only 9 copies of the work were printed.

This useful and scholarly collection was later on followed by the publications of his "*Inscriptions of the Early Gupta Kings and Their Successors.*" This formed Volume III of the *Corpus Inscriptionum Indicarum*, 'a splendid monument of exact scholarship and critical judgment' which by establishing the epoch of the Gupta Dynasty in 319—320 A. D., laid the key-stone of Indian Chronology. Till very recently Indian Chronology remained indeterminate. Records of political events in Ancient India were rarely preserved and when they existed the dates recorded therein could not be understood, owing to the confused systems of

Indian eras. According to Cunningham there were more than a score of systems for the computation of dates. The difficulties of interpreting the Gupta Era were particularly great. A fierce controversy existed in regard to it since 1838, when James Prinsep took up for discussion the Kataumi Pillar inscription of Skanda Gupta. It may be said that Dr. Fleet's determination of the Gupta Era marked a great advance in our knowledge of Indian History and Chronology. Two circumstances, as gratefully acknowledged by the Doctor himself, aided in the determination of the Gupta epoch. The first was the discovery of the Mandasir Inscription by Dr. Fleet, which

'supplied what had always been felt to be a most urgent desideratum, *viz.*, a date for anyone of the Early Gupta Kings, recorded in a standard era, capable of identification, other than the era that was habitually used by the Early Guptas themselves.'

"It furnished the date of the Malawa year *i.e*, the Vikrama year, 493 expired, corresponding to A.D. 436-437 current for Kumara Gupta I; and thus, with also a revised translation given to me by Professor Wright, of a well-known passage in Alberuni's writings, I was enabled to prove, for the first time. what had often been asserted, but had never been proved before,—*viz.*, that the Early Gupta Kings rose to power in the 4th century A. D. and that the dates of their records run, not from A.D. 77-78, A.D. 166-167 or A.D. 190-191 but from A.D. 319-320 or very close thereabouts."

It is but fair to add that Dr. Fleet's entire dependence on the conflicting statements of eras by Alberuni is not completely absolved from doubts and this defect has been remedied by Mr. K. P. Pathak's demonstration of the accuracy of Dr. Fleet's results by furnishing independent proofs from Jaina sources.

The other happy circumstance that helped Dr. Fleet to discover the initial date of the Gupta Era is thus narrated by the departed Doctor in a note he left behind and which his lifelong friend and colleague, Sir. R. C. Temple, published in the *Indian Antiquary*.

> I was in charge of the Sholapore District and was in camp at Barsi towards the end of 1886. "Mr. Dikshit who was then an Assistant Master in the English School at that town came to my tents and made himself known to me. * * * *. He was well versed in Astronomy, both Hindu and European, and was in fact, a joint worker with other people in the making of almanacs. And he made the calculations "some of them very laborious, which enabled me to prove that the first Gupta King began to reign in A.D. 320. The matter, however, did not end there. At my request, Mr. Dikshit published an explanation of the process by which we could calculate the exact Christian date of any given Hindu lunar date by means of Tables which had been published by Professor Kero Lakshman Chhatre, a well-known Mathematician and Astronomer."

The next important publication of Dr. Fleet was 'the Dynasties of the Kanarese Districts' incorporated in the *Bombay Gazetteer* Vol. I., Part ii. Like Sir R. G. Bhandarkar's *Early History of the Deccan* it is a source-book by itself. Not only does it contain the summary of the results achieved by various investigators in the same field but the Doctor himself has furnished fresh information on almost every topic dealt with by him. More original than revisional both in its conception and subject matter, the Dynasties of the Kanerese Districts throws a flood of light on the hitherto little known history of the races that inhabited the Western part of India and there is no student of the History of India that does not reverentially take up the *Bombay Gazetteer* for information and right guidance which he may lock for in vain from other sources.

Dr. Fleet's fame as an Indologist rests, however, not on the publication of works we have mentioned above and which alone the busy work-a-day world sees but on the endless series of epigraphic notes and historical notices in the pages of the *Indian Antiquary*. Referring to this Sir Richard Temple says:

"One of the interesting things that command our attention from a survey of Fleet's contributions to this Journal is that it discloses the history of Indian Epigraphical research almost from its commencement as a systematic study. The very first note he contributed relates to the clearing of inscriptions covered with paint and oil after the Indian fashion, so that they may be properly read and reproduced."

Though Indian Epigraphy and Chronology occupied his main attention, he had contributed original matter on almost every topic connected with Indian studies. Between 1875 and 1891 he had given to the world of

Oriental scholarship 196 critically edited Sanskrit and Old Kanarese Inscriptions, together with disquisitions on the dates, pedigrees and facts disclosed by them. Of perennial interest and importance are some of his longer articles which are in the nature of a regular treatise on Epigraphy. Who is there that does not to-day agree with most of what Dr. Fleet said in his famous article printed in the *Indian Antiquary* (1901)—"The Present Position of Indian Historical Research"? The object of this paper was to arouse a more general and practical interest in the Epigraphic records among the specialists in literature, philosophy, history of the religions and other lines. After pointing out that for our knowledge of ancient political history of India we were indebted only to inscriptions and not to any historical work bequeathed to us by the Hindus, Dr. Fleet says:—

"There is, in short, a vast amount of work still to be done, in all the various lines of research connected with the part of India. We hope, in particular, that the present sketch of the position at which we have arrived, may do something towards attracting more attention to the principal materials, the Epigraphic records and towards inducing more scholars to join us in exploiting them. But we hope, also, that others may be induced to co-operate, by examining more methodically and critically the subsidiary sources of information, and by bringing forward their results in such a way as to make them available for being easily worked in with the more special results derivable from the Epigraphic records. *The principal materials are the Epigraphic records.* And a brief study of some of them will suffice to show the specific importance of them, and to excite a desire to join in exploring them. But the subsidiary materials also are numerous and interesting. And anyone who will take any of them in hand systematically, with just enough knowledge of the results derived from the epigraphic records to shew the objects that require to be kept in view and the general lines of work that should be followed, can render assistance, the value of which will be made clear enough when his results are put forward in an accessible form, even if it may not be fully realisable by him while he is actually at work."

Though Dr. Fleet's enthusiasm for Epigraphic records knew no bounds, yet he is careful to warn workers against the acceptance as genuine of all sorts of records. Under the title of 'Spurious Indian Records' he read a paper, before the Indian Section of the 12th International Congress of Orientalists held at Rome on the 10th October, 1899, the substance of which was subsequently printed in the *Indian Antiquary* (1901). Just as there are numismatic and even literary forgeries, so also there are spurious, counterfeit or forged records. Dr. Fleet in this all-absorbing article shews how these forged documents betray themselves in a variety of ways.

In 1884 Dr. Fleet published at much expense and labour, faithful facsimiles of the Pillar Edicts of Asoka at Delhi and Allahabad. From 1885-1891 he continued to edit the

Indian Antiquary. During this period "he filled the Journal with article after article and note after note * * * * * by way of direct contributions or of criticism of the work of contemporary writers. Any kind of information which could throw light on the story of Ancient India at once claimed his earnest attention." Between 1892 and 1910 he wrote largely on ancient place-names and the identification of their sites. Of his work and its value, thus writes Doctor Fleet himself:—

"I have not much more to say. If life were long enough, I should like to re-edit up to date almost everything that I have published. In all the lines of research in which I have worked, our progress was for a long time very tentative indeed, in some respects it is still so. In such circumstances, it is impossible to avoid making mistakes and I have written much that I should like to correct and something which I should like to cancel altogether. However, I doubt if I shall ever see my way to doing much in that direction: new points of urgent interest arise so constantly that it is dificult to go back on past ground, except in the way of incidental and sometimes quite tacit correction. I can only express the hope that writers who may wish to quote me will look to my later writings in preference to earlier ones."

Sir Edwin Arnold.

INTRODUCTORY.

SIR Edwin Arnold was one of the greatest of the interpreters of the East to the West. He revealed to the West the wonderful inner world of thought and emotion created by the great poets and seers of the East. It was his deep love of the ideals of the East and his special love for India that enabled him to do this work marvellously well. We may say of him what he said of the Englishman (obviously describing himself in that character) in the book *With Sa'di in the Garden.*

Some that he dreamed the West and East would meet
On some far day, by some fresh opened path,
In sisterly new truths, and strove for that;
I think he did but find Wisdom's wide stream
Nearest the fountain clearest, India's air
Softer and warmer than his native skies;
And liked the gentle speech, the grave reserve,
The piety and quiet of the land,
Its old-world manners and its reverent ways,
And kind simplicity of Indian homes,
And classic comeliness of Indian girls,
More than his proper people and his tasks,
He was to blame, but he loved India.

His many-sided work in fulfilling his great task of interpretation of the East to the West may well be described in his own words in the *Proeme* to his volume of verse entitled *With Sa'di in the Garden*:—

Sweet friends who love the Music of the Sun,
And listened—glad and gracious—many an one,
While on a light strung lyre, I sought to tell
Indian Sidhartha's wisdom; and the spell
Of Jayadev's deep verse; and proud deeds wrought
By Pandu princes; and how gems are fraught
With meanings; and to count his golden bead
Of Allah's names of Beauty; and to read
High tender lessons Upanishads teach—
"Secret of Death," and subtle soul of speech
In holy Om; and to con—line by line—
The lofty glory of the "Lay Divine"—
Arjuna's speech with Krishna;—once more come
And listen to the Vina and the Drum!
Come once more with me from our sombre skies
To hear great Sa'di's tuneful mysteries.

LIFE.

Sir Edwin Arnold was born on 10th June 1832 at Gravesend. He was the second son of Robert Coles Arnold of Whartons Fram field and elder brother of Sir Arthur Arnold. He was educated at King's School, Rochester, at King's College, London, and at University College, Oxford. He graduated in 1854 and became a Master of Arts in 1856. Although he got only a third class in the final classical school, he read classical poetry with a great deal of love and enthusiasm. In 1852 he obtained the Newdigate prize with a poem

Belshazzar's Feast. He published it in 1852 and afterwards included it in his volume entitled "Poems Narrative and Lyrical" published in 1853. He was second master at Birmingham in the King Edward's School for a short period. In 1856 he was nominated Principal of the Deccan College, Poona. He describes in a beautiful way his stay at Poona in the chapter on "the Garden of Repose" in his book *East and West.* It shows what sincere love he had for his students and how sincerely they esteemed and loved him. It was this stay in India that enabled him to steep his soul in the outer and inner glories and enchantments of India.

He became a Fellow of the Bombay University and studied Eastern languages including Turkish and Persian. He translated *Hitopadesa* and his translation was published with fine illustrations by Harrison Weir. He wrote a pamphlet on Education in India in 1860 pleading for a more scientific grafting of Western knowledge on the learning of the East. He wrote also a history of Lord Dalhousie's administration. His kind and sympathetic attitude during the troubled times of the great Indian Mutiny won for him the love of the people and the appreciation of the Government of India. He returned to

England in 1861, and got the post of leader writer on the *Daily Telegraph*. George Augustus Sala describes how early in 1862 a sweet and attractive Eastern note began to be felt in the leading articles of the *Daily Telegraph*. He was since then connected with the paper as editor also. He became the chief editor in 1873. As editor for 28 years, he had a staff that included Edward Dicey, James MacDonnell, and H. D. Traill. On 1st January 1877, he was made a C. S. I. He was all this time busy with the great life-work of interpreting the life and thought of the East. In 1879, he published his epic poem, "The Light of Asia," to which he owed most of his fame. By the end of the century it went through sixty English and eighty American editions. His poem on "The Light of the World" was published in 1891.

It dealt with Christ as the previous poem dealt with Buddha. Other books by him are: *Pearls of the Faith, With Sa'di in the Garden, the Secret of Death and other Poems, The Song Celestial or Bhagawad Gita, Poets of Greece, Indian Idyls, Lotus and Jewel, Tenth Muse and other Poems, Adzuma or the Japanese Wife, Potephar's Wife and other Poems, In My Lady's Praise, Indian Poetry, The Voyage of Ithobal, Wandering Words, Japonica, Seas and Lands,*

East and West, India Revisited, In Tent and Bangalow, The Queen's Justice, etc. In 1888, he was made a K C.I.E. In 1889, he started with his daughter upon a travel, chiefly to the Pacific Coasts and Japan. He repeated his visit to Japan later on as he was fascinated by the artistic and social sides of Japanese life. His books on Japanese life spread optimistic views of Japanese progress in England. While he was editor, he arranged on behalf of the proprietors of the *Daily Tele graph* in conjunction with the *New York Herald* for the journey of "H. M. Stanley" to Africa to discover the course of the Congo. He must also be credited with the first idea of a great trunk line traversing the entire African continent. In 1891, he undertook a reading tour in America and also received foreign decorations from the rulers of Turkey, Persia, Siam, and Japan. He expected the reversion of the laureateship after Tennyson died, but did not get it. During the last nine or ten years of his life, he lost his sight but still maintained his keen interest in contemporary affairs. His third wife was a Japanese lady. He died at his house in Bolton Gardens, London, on 24th March 1904. He was cremated at Brookwood, and his ashes were bestowed in the chapel of his old College at Oxford.

His Personality.

Arnold's nature was gentle and loving, and his poems and books of travel contain numerous personal touches bearing ample testimony to the sweetness of his soul. At the same time he had great strength of nature and courage of convictions. His "Light of Asia" was anathematised on many pulpits and offended the taste of many devout Christians. But he never wavered for a moment in his worship of the light that illumined his soul. Again, he was a great traveller and had a special love for the bright tropical regions of Asia. His travels gave him breadth of vision and depth of love and lifted him above that insularity which is admittedly one of the defects of the British character. His brief career as a Principal in an Indian college gives us glimpses of other rare traits of his character—his insight, his sympathy and his love. Above all his insight into Indian life and character and art and his love of India are among the highest elements of his nature. He says in regard to Indian architecture and sculpture:

It is the Hindu only who revels in imitations of Nature and loves to reproduce in marble climbing plants or the leaves and blossoms of the lotus. The Moslem shunning all likeness of living things, has yet, woven out of lines, circles, and triangles, and above all, from the plastic characters of the Arabic alphabet, designs of exhaustless fancy through the fairy-like tracery of which the bright light winnows as if golden wine were poured through lace . . . . It is characteristic of the Hindu art, which the Moslem also in this respect adopted, to leave no naked places in the stone.

His revelling in Indian poetry and his passionate love for it are well known. For Indian philosophy and religion he had true love and genuine reverence. He says:

The Hindu is quite assured that he has lived many previous lives and has many more to experience, and whether Vaishnav or Saivite, is troubled with none of the dismal doubts of modern materialism.

It is in his insight into the true glory of Indian manhood and womanhood and his sense of the immemorial greatness, serenity, and refinement of the Indian race that we find the most perfect manifestations of his rare gifts of vision and love. He says: "Wherever you encounter Parsees in India, you will find intelligence, enlightenment, and energy." He says of Indian refinement: "There is nowhere greater grace or cordiality of greeting than among the educated families of India; but in truth, this is the land of fine and noble manners." He says of Rajputana: "Rajputana is measurelessly old. The bluest blood of Europe is but of yesterday compared with that of the haughty families of this reigion." Of the wonderful architectural monuments of Moghul rule, he says that "the Moghuls designed like giants and finished like jewellers." He says of Indian women: "The Indian wives and mothers, among whom are to be counted humble saints and angels by the lakh—gentle, patient, laborious, faithful, pure, contented, cheerful, and affectionate souls."

What true love and insight throb beneath his fine words of farewell to India!—

> I leave my heart behind me on leaving these Indian peoples, who have taught me, as I have wandered among them, that manners more noble and gentle, learning more modest and profound, loyalty more sincere, refinement more natural, and sweeter simplicities of life and love and duty exist in the length and breadth of British Asia than even I had gathered from my old experiences, before India was revisited.

NATURE AND TRAITS OF ARNOLD'S ART.

The greatest and most admirable trait of Arnold's art is his deep and vivid insight into the artistic and religious ideals of the great cultures of the world that still live and mould the lives of millions of men and women. The debt that the whole English-speaking world owes to him in this respect is immense. Islam, Buddhism, Christianity, and Hinduism have all been interpreted by him with a sincerity, an insight, and a passion of love that carry conviction to our hearts. Great and loving souls like Arnold's do more to soften the animosities of ages born of imperfect sympathies and partial comprehension than all the Diplomats, the Governors, and the

Evangelists put together. Wherever they bear their uplifted torches of love and learning the darkness of the heart flies afar routed by the forces of light.

Another aspect of his art that deserves prominent mention is his passionate love of beauty. It is so deep and dominating in him that he has been criticised for over-sensuousness. In this respect he carries forward the great literary tradition of Keats and Tennyson.

A further characteristic of Arnold's art is his catholicity of taste. He was equally at home in the literatures and arts of Islam, India and Japan.

He has an ornate style and felicitous versification. His blank verse is on the Tennysonian model; but, though fluent and sometimes grandiose, it is lacking in distinction and melody.

Some Fruitful Ideas from His Works.

One great idea that he was never tired of repeating is that the East should not give up its peculiar graces and glories but preserve them while assimilating the most modern culture from the West. He says in respect of Japan:—

> You cannot, gentlemen, import our civilisation; you must make science Japanese by time and patience. . . . But I cherish the hope that your path of

progress will never lead you entirely out of sight of your own peculiar refinements. and that the primary duty of national self-assertion will never finally efface that which is so special and so precious in our own charming civilisation.—*Seas and Lands.*

He gave the same advice often to Indians also.

One of the ideas that he owed to his sympathy with Eastern ideals and his study of the East is his reverence for life and his sense of the sacredness of life. He speaks with contempt of modern methods of butchery. He refers to them as

those sanguinary establishments where a minute and a quarter of merciless machinery converts hog after hog, to the number of thousands in the day, from such earthly pleasures as a pig can know to the posthumous honours of bacon.—*Ibid.*

He was a firm believer in democracy and its ability to draw out the finer element of manhood and womanhood. He quotes with approval President Eliot's remarks:—

It is unnecessary, however, to claim any superiority for democracy in this respect; enough that the highest types of manners in men and women are produced abundantly on a democratic soil. It would appear, then, from American experience that neither generations of privileged ancestors nor large inherited possessions are necessary to the making of a lady or a gentleman.

Ideals of self-restraint, self-sacrifice, and self-respect have to be made a living part of life if the highest manhood and womanhood are to be attained. All national education and national endeavour should be so moulded as to bring about this glorious consummation. Arnold points out how despite the caste system there is true democratic spirit in India. He says: "For all that strong survival of caste, the Hindus are a democratic and easy-going people."—*India Revisited.*

Arnold realised and said that the highest womanhood is the greatest glory of each civilisation. He quotes with approval President Eliot's remark: "The lady is the consummate fruit of human society at its best." It has been well said: "Men are very much the same all the world over: they are like the coarse grass which grows everywhere. But the flowers, you know, are different in every country." It is the duty of Indians to preserve the highest elements of true womanhood, the realisation of which was and is one of the great dreams of our race.

Above all he pleaded for more beauty, grace, and repose in individual and national life and for religious toleration and the attainment of a truly self-sacrificing and spiritual life. He was himself an example, a living embodiment, of the great ideal that he gave to the world, and his ideas have a special value and appeal to us Indians as those of a man who had the deepest love and reverence for India while possessing perfect clarity of vision and insight into the great dreams and ideals of the East and the West.

Four Great Religious Poems.

The volume of poems entitled the ***Pearls of the Faith*** is of great beauty in parts though it does not maintain a uniformly high level of poetic achievement. The most beautiful and inspiring elements of the great religion of Islam are well depicted therein.

As Sir Edwin Arnold well says in his preface to the book: "The soul of Islam is its declaration of the unity of God: its heart is the inculcation of an absolute resignation to His will." The fifteenth poem about Abraham's offence shows a lofty spirit of toleration alien to the spirit of historical Mahomedanism but not really alien to the true essence of the faith of Islam. The description of Mahomed that:

> If one
> Be burdened with a thousand woes, his work
> Dismisses them and makes the sorrow joy,

is very fine. Equally beautiful is the sentiment that our real gain is what we lose for God.

> Bestower! grant us grace to see
> Our gain is what we lose for Thee.

The following description of the evil heart in the fifty-seventh poem is as true as it is beautiful:—

> The likeness of the evil heart, bestowing
> That men may praise, is as the thin-clad peak,
> Wherefrom the rain washes all soil for growing,
> Leaving the hard rock naked, fruitless, bleak.

Sir Edwin Arnold's poem "The Light of the World" describes the holy life of Christ and all that he accomplished for man to make him realise his essential divinity. It was evidently written as a companion poem to "The Light of Asia,' but somehow lacks the serene beauty, the uplifting power, and the harmony of numbers that make the poem on the Buddha a work of great beauty and power. The treatment of the subject is inadequate, and there are frequent infelicities due to his not rising to the height of the subject. The life of Christ is narrated in smoothly flowing lines by means of a long dialogue between Mary Magdalene and one of the three wise men of the East who were led by the star of Bethlehem to the place where Jesus was born.

Sir Edwin Arnold's *The Light of Asia* is perhaps the most widely known and most beautiful of his works. It tells the story of the life of one of the greatest spiritual leaders of the world; it maintains a lofty ethical tone while delineating a great variety of incidents and thoughts; and it is written in a style fluent, impassioned, musical. It is wonderful that he has been able to attain such vivid local colouring and to assimilate so thoroughly the faith of the Enlightened (the Buddha) as is evident from the poem. The scholar and the philosopher in him are not less remarkable than the singer. The supreme ethical fragrance of the flower of Buddha's doctrine is felt in every page of the book. He says of it in his preface: "It has been composed in the brief intervals of days without leisure, but is inspired by an abiding desire to aid in the better mutual knowledge of East and West. The time may come, I hope, when this book and my 'Indian Song of Songs' and 'Indian Idylls' will preserve the memory of one who loved India and the Indian peoples."

Various translations of the poem by Sir Edwin Arnold have appeared in almost every European and numerous Oriental languages. It has been well said:

> It may probably be claimed for it that many people otherwise well-read and educated would never have had more than the faintest notion of the exquisite beauties of the Buddhistic faith, had they not been presented to them in so delightful and at the same time so accurate a form as by the "Light of Asia."

The world has always felt drawn to the sublime ethical teachings of Buddha, and even more to the sweet personality of the great teacher. It has yearned, to quote the beautiful stanza of Annie Herber Barker:

> To hear in old words breathing balm,
> The secret of the Wordless balm,
> The equipoise of chastened will,
> The Master's comfort, "Peace, be still."

Sir Edwin Arnold says in *Seas and Lands*: "I have often said, and I shall say again and again, that between Buddhism and modern science there exists a close intellectual bond." He then proceeds to prove this statement in a long passage full of beauty, and concludes:

> That the destiny of men has been and must be and will be worked out by himself under eternal and benign laws which never vary and never mislead; and that for every living creature the path thus lies open, by compliance, by effort, by insight, by aspiration, by goodwill, by right action, by loving service, to that which Buddhists term Nirvana, and we Christians 'the peace of God that passeth all understanding.'

Various Oriental scholars have found fault with the presentation of Buddhism as contained in the *Light of Asia.* But whatever its imperfections, the essential elements of Buddha's gracious message to the world are well brought out in it, while the poem contains permanent elements of beauty in its presentation of the picturesque and pathetic elements in the story of Buddha's life.

One of the finest passages in the poem is that where the old sage Asita sees the babe Buddha and tells Buddha's father, King Suddhodana:

> Know, O King!
> This is the Blossom on our human tree
> Which opens once in many myriad years—
> But opened, fills the world with wisdom's scent
> And Love's dropped honey; from thy royal root
> A heavenly Lotus springs.

The episode of the wounded swan which first made Buddha meditate upon the ills of life is beautifully narrated.

He saw
The thorns which grow upon this rose of life.

King Suddhodana's attempts to fetter Buddha's soul in silken bonds of love and luxury and Buddha's shaking them off and going forth in a passion of love for all to seek a sovereign remedy for the diverse ills of life are very vividly and imaginatively described. Buddha tells his queen Yasodhara:

Nay, though we locked up love and life with lips
So close that night and day our breaths grew one,
Time would thrust in between to filch away
My passion and thy grace, as black night steals
The rose-gleams from yon peak, which fade to grey
And are not seen to fade. This have I found,
And all my heart is darkened with its dread,
And all my heart is fixed to think how Love
Might save its sweetness from the slayer, Time,
Who makes men old.

His going away from his sleeping queen in search of Light is thus beautifully described:

So, with his brow he touched her feet, and bent
The farewell of fond eyes, unutterable,
Upon her sleeping face, still wet with tears,
And thrice around the bed in reverence,
As though it were an altar, softly stepped
With clasped hands laid upon his beating heart.

Buddha's meditation and penances in search of truth are next described.

Buddha's attainment of illumination under the *Bodhi* tree and his giving of his gracious message to the world are delineated in verses throbbing with feeling and full of splendour of style and sound. I shall quote here only a few stanzas describing Buddha's doctrine.

Ye are not bound! the Soul of Things is Sweet,
The Heart of Being is Celestial rest.
Stronger than woe is will; that which was Good
Doth pass to Better—Best.

* * *

Ye suffer from yourselves. None else compels,
None other holds you that ye live and die,
And whirl upon the wheel, and hug and kiss
Its spokes of agony,
Its tire of tears, its nave of nothingness,

* * *

Such is the Law which moves to righteousness,
Which none at last can turn aside or stay;
The heart of it is Love, the end of it
Is Peace and Consummation sweet. Obey!

One of the poet's masterpieces is *The Song Celestial*, which is a translation of the *Bhagawad Gita*. It has great elevation of tone and majesty and dignity of style. The blank verse is strong, yet pliable and musical and sweet to the ear. There are many translations of the *Gita* but Arnold's translation has a place apart among them by its accuracy and the grave harmony of the verse.

The translation is dedicated by the poet to India. The dedicatory verses are in Arnold's own translation:—

So have I read this wonderful and spirit-thrilling speech,
By Krishna and Prince Arjun held, discoursing each with each;
So have I writ its wisdom here, its hidden mystery,
For England; O our India! as dear to me as she!

Sir Edwin Arnold says in his preface:

This famous and marvellous Sanskrit poem occurs as an episode of the *Mahabharata*, in the sixth—or "Bhishma"—Parva of the great Hindu epic. It enjoys immense popularity and authority in India, where it is reckoned as one of the "Five Jewels"—*pancharatnani*—of Devanagari literature. In plain but noble language it unfolds a philosophical system which remains to this day the prevailing Brahmanic belief, blending as it does the doctrines of Kapila, Patanjali, and the Vedas.

It is not my purpose to set out here the teachings of the *Gita*. I shall however make a reference to them in the course of quoting a few excellent passages from Arnold's translation. Sri Krishna at the very outset dispels the main cause of Arjuna's illusion and sorrow by teaching the immortality of the soul.

Never the spirit was born; the spirit shall cease to be never;
Never was time it was not; End and Beginning are dreams!
Birthless and deathless and changeless remaineth the spirit for ever;
Death hath not touched it at all, dead though the house of it seems!

Sri Krishna then teaches the blessed doctrine of *Karma Yoga*.

Find full reward
Of doing right in right! let right deeds be
Thy motive, not the fruit that comes from them.

He further teaches in the second chapter:

But, if one deals with the objects of sense
Not loving and not hating, making them
Serve his free soul, which rests serenely lord,

Lo! such a man comes to tranquillity:
And out of that tranquillity shall rise
The end and healing of his earthly pains,
Since the will governed sets the soul at peace.

The following is a fine translation of a famous and beautiful verse in Chapter II.

Such is the saint!
And like the ocean, day by day receiving
Floods from all lands, which never overflows;
Its boundary line not leaping, and not leaving,
Fed by the rivers, but unswelled by those:—
So is the perfect one! to his soul's ocean
The world of sense pours streams of witchery;
They leave him, as they find, without commotion,
Taking their tribute, but remaining sea.

In Chapter II the Lord continues his discourse on *Karma Yoga*.

He that abstains
To help the rolling wheels of this great world,
Glutting his idle sense, lives a lost life,
Shameful and vain.

The Lord teaches that work should be done without attachment to its fruits and as an act of worship to God.

In Chapter IV He reveals the gracious doctrine of incarnation and says that He comes often to the earth out of a spirit of compassion to put down evil and exalt righteousness.

When Righteousness
Declines, O Bharata! When wickedness
Is strong, I rise, from age to age, and take
Visible shape, and move a man with men,
Succouring the good, thrusting the evil back,
And setting virtue on her seat again.

In Chapter V the Lord pursues Karma Sanyasa Yoga or renouncing the fruit of works.

In Chapter VI He teaches the methods and the goal of Yoga or self-discipline,

> See!
> Steadfast a lamp burns sheltered from the wind;
> Such is the likeness of the Yogi's mind
> Shut from sense-storms and burning bright to Heaven.

In Chapter VII the Lord reveals the nature of Himself and the Universe and the methods of discerning the truth. In Chapter VIII He describes the life faithful unto Him till death, His love for His devotees, and the future of liberated and unliberated souls. In Chapter IX He reveals His glories by detailed description. In Chapter X He reveals them by mentioning special manifestations. In Chapter XI He shows Arjuna the blessed vision of His Universal Form. In Chapter XII He teaches the gracious doctrine of Love of God.

> Fix heart and thought on Me! Adore Me! Bring
> Offerings to Me! Make Me prostrations; Make
> Me your supremest joy! and, undivided
> Unto My rest your spirits shall be guided.

In Chapter XIII He shows the separateness of body and soul, describes the elements of wisdom, and teaches the nature of Godhead. In Chapter XIV He describes the nature of the three Gunas (attributes). In Chapter XV He shows how He is the not of all. In Chapter XVI He differentiates the *Daivi Sampath* (the pure condition) and the *Asuri Sampath* (the impure condition), and says that the former alone leads to God. In Chapter XVII the same discussion and the discussion of the three *Gunas* are continued. In Chapter XVIII the whole teaching is summed up; the functions of the four castes are described; and the soul is led through the golden gate of renunciation to the Throne of Grace.

> Give Me thy heart; Adore Me! Serve Me! cling
> In faith and love and reverence to Me!
> So shalt thou come to Me! I promise true,
> For thou art sweet to Me;

ARNOLD'S INDIAN POEMS.

Sir Edwin Arnold's volume of poetry entitled 'Indian Poetry' contains many exquisite translations and adaptations from Sanskrit Literature. The first poem is a rendering of Jayadeva's *Gita Govinda.* As has been well said: "Nothing could be more graceful and delicate than the shades by which Krishna is portrayed in the gradual process of being weaned by the love of Beautiful Radha, Jasmine-bosomed Radha, from the allurements of the forest nymphs in whom the five senses are typified." A breeze laden with the odours of Eastern flowers and spices seems to blow through its pages. The supreme literary grace and musical flow of diction which make the original poem unique even in Sanskrit literature are well brought out in Sir Edwin Arnold's translation. The very commencement strikes the key which is the very soul of the poem:

> O, Radha, Radha! take this soul, that trembles,
> In life's deep midnight, to Thy golden house.

The rapturous attainment of divine communion after life-long yearning and search for God is well brought out by the poet who has thus been able to enter into the innermost shrine of the temple of Love and Beauty built to music by Jayadeva's artistic and spiritual genius. The following song in praise of Love is worth remembering:—

> Love—the mighty Master,
> Lord of all the stars that cluster
> In the sky, swiftest and slowest,
> Lord of highest, lord of lowest—
> Manifests himself to mortals,
> Winning them towards the portals
> Of his secret house, the gates
> Of that bright Paradise which waits
> The wise in love...........
> Mighty love sways all alike
> From self to selflessness.

The passage where Radha sends her maid to bring Krishna who was dallying with the *Gopis* by whom the senses are typified is equally full of beauty:

> To yield him up my bosom's maiden splendour,
> And fold him in my fragrance, and braid
> My shining hair for him, and clasp him close
> To the gold heart of his Rose.

The repentant Krishna yearns for Radha,

having risen above the entrancements of the senses. He says:

> Yet all day long in my deep heart I woo thee,
> And all night long with thee my dreams are sweet.

The following beautiful lines conclude the poem:—

> Then she, no more dallying, entered straight;
> Her step a little faltered, but her face
> Shone with unutterable quick love; and—while
> The music of her bangles passed the porch—
> Shame, which had lingered in her downcast face,
> Departed shamed......and like the mighty deep
> Which sees the moon and rises, all his life
> Uprose to drink her beams.

The poem entitled *The Rajput Wife* does not strike a high note, though the subject lends itself to moving and impassioned narration. It describes how a brave and devoted and true Rajput wife avenged the murder of her loving husband and then followed her husband's soul through the shining gate of fire by performing *Sati*. The *spirit* of *Sati* is one of the greatest graces of womanhood in India though the *form* of *Sati* which was often associated with much cruelty is happily gone. The "Adi Granth" of the Sikhs says: "They are not Satis who perish in the flames, O Nanak! Satis are those who live on with a broken heart." The old *Sati* ritual was solemn and sublime. The *Sati* bathed, put on new and bright garments, and holding *Kusa* grass in her left hand, sipped water from her right palm, scattered *tila* grains, and looking eastward said with cheerful looks and happy heart:

> I die by fire that I may enjoy with my husband the felicities of Heaven . . . . that pardon may be given to my lord's sins . . . . I call upon you, guardians of the eight regions of the world, of sun, moon, air, of the fire, the ether, the earth, and the water, and my own soul, Yama, king of death, and you, day, night, and twilight! Witness that I die for my beloved by his side upon his funeral pile.

Other poems in the book describe details of Indian life. One poem deals with the ascension of the Pandava Princes to Heaven, and the other describes the night of slaughter in the *Sauptika Parva* of the *Mahabharata*. The volume concludes with translations from that mine of wordly and moral wisdom—the *Hitopadesa*. The translations have great merit and combine true poetic beauty with fidelity to the original. We shall quote here a few of them:

> Twofold is the life we live in—Fate and Will together run:
> Two wheels bear life's chariot onward—will it move on only one?
> True religion!—'tis not blindly prating what the *gurus* prate,
> But to love, as God hath loved them, all things, be they small or great.
> And true bliss is when a sane mind doth a healthy body fill;
> And true knowledge is the knowing what is good and what is ill.
> Would'st thou know whose happy dwelling Fortune entereth unknown?

His, who careless of her favour, standeth fearless in his own;
His, who for the vague to-morrow barters not the sure to-day—
Master of himself, and sternly steadfast to the rightful way:
Very mindful of past service, valiant, faithful, true of heart—
Unto such comes Lakshmi smiling—comes, and will not lightly part.

The volume of verse called *Indian Idylls* consists of eight graphic episodes from the *Mahabharata.* They reveal the poet's chief traits—his grace of style and his tenderness of tone—in a remarkable manner. It has been said: "Nobody who reads the heart-stirring epics put into magnificent rhythm which are contained in this book can ever again affect to despise the people whose genius established such an imperishable monument." Another writer says:

From these mighty poems the author well describes these Indian epics, compared with which Homer is a modern; he has translated some beautiful and touching episodic legends, and readers of "Savitri, or Love and Death," for example, will feel grateful to him for having revealed to the somewhat jaded sensibilities of our poets of to-day such a mine of inexhaustible spiritual fertility, and such treasures of emotional tenderness and imaginative freshness and simplicity.

The poem 'Savithri' describes the heavenly life and the love stronger than death that make the story of Savitri unique in the whole range of literature in point of beauty and uplifting power. But Sir Edwin Arnold's treatment of the story is unsatisfactory as it misses in some undefinable way the high note of deep passion and watchful selfless love which must be movingly and powerfully brought out if the real beauty of the story is to be realised by the poet and communicated to the soul of the reader. The following description of Sávitri in her self-chosen woodland home is very beautiful :—

> From her neck and arms she stripped
> Jewels and gold, and o'er her radiant form
> Folded the robe of bark and yellow cloth
> Which hermits use, and all hearts did she gain
> By gentle actions, self-government,
> Patience and peace.

The story of 'Nala and Damayanthi' is the next in the volume and is very long. It also lacks distinction and fire, though it, like all other poems of Arnold's, has a sweet flow of diction and a uniform elevation of sentiment. The following description of Damayanthi in the forest is very good :—

> Those breasts
> Beauteously swelling, form of faultless mould,
> Sweet youthful face, fair as the moon at full,
> And dark eyes by long curving lashes swept.

The poem contains also various passages full of true beauty of thought and style.

> Having the eyes of Lakshmi, long-lidded, black and white.
> So that unmet, unknowing, unseen—in each for each
> A tender thought and longing grew up, from seed of speech.

Splendidly invisible
In weakness, loftily defying force,
A living flame of lighted chastity.
Bright-browed, long-tressed, large-hipped, full-bosomed, fair.

With pearly teeth and honeyed mouth,
The large deep lotus-eyes,
That like to Rati's own, the queen of love
Beam, each a love-lit star, filling the worlds
With longing.

The poem in 'The Enchanted Lake' describes the episode known as *Yaksha Frasna* in the *Mahabharata*, and contains the quintessence of Indian thought on life here and hereafter. "The Saint's Temptation" narrates how the pure-hearted child Rishya Sringa. whose holy presence in a country ensures the coming of rain, was beguiled by the sweet ways of women to go into a land thirsting for rain :

Once more she clasped her soft brown arms
About him, and with eyes fixed on his eyes
Withdrew ; having enkindled passion's flame
Where only fires of sacrifice had burned.

The poem on "The Birth of Death" describes how when Mritya (Death) was created, she out of exceeding compassion prayed to the Creator not to be given the task of killing, and how God then willed that death should be caused directly by men's evil acts and sins and by diseases. "The Night of Slaughter" describes the murder of Pandu chiefs in the night by Aswathama, and "The Great Journey" describes the journey to Heaven by the Pandava heroes.

The volume entitled "The Secret of Death and Other Poems" contains smooth and polished verse but does not rise to the height of some of the other volumes of his poetry.

The volume of poems called 'Lotus and Jewel' does not contain the poet's best work, but it has the great merit of containing some of his original poems.

The following lines about chastity have a peculiarly sweet beauty of their own:—

> For lovely is the flower of chastity,
> Lasting its fragrance, and its fruit more fair
> Than chance fruits borne on boughs whence all may pluck.

The poet's insight into the social life of India which is revealed only to the sympathetic vision of a true friend and which is quite unknown to casual observers and unsympathetic eyes is clear from the following lines:—

> Oh and full well I know what happy hearths
> Are here in India, and what stainless wives
> Live their sweet lives and die their gentle deaths
> Under your suns.

There is a sweet and pathetic beauty in the concluding lines:

> Life is not life, if we must live thinking of love's last day;
> Oh, never come, my Love and Life! or never go away.

The miscellaneous minor poems in the volume are not particularly noteworthy. We may however quote here an excellent sonnet bidding adieu to India:

India! farewell! I shall not see again
  Thy shining shores, thy peoples of the Sun,
  Gentle, soft-mannered, by a kind word won
To such quick kindness! Oe'r the Arab main
Our flying flag streams back; and backwards
      stream
  My thoughts to those fair open fields I love,
  City and village, maidan, jungle, grove,
The temples and the rivers! Must it seem
Too great for one man's heart to say it holds
  So many Indian sisters dear,
So many Indian brothers? that it folds
  Lakhs of true friends in parting? Nay! but there
Lingers my heart leave taking; and it roves
From hut to hut whispering 'he knows and loves'!

The poems from the Sanskrit at the end of the volume are an adaptation from Kalidasa's poem about summer in his famous Nature-poem of Ritu-Samhara, and an adaptation of the story of the killing of Kichaka from the *Makabharata*. They have no special poetic beauty but contain a few fine passages. Some of these are given here below:

          Dear Draupadi! whose life
Was glad with garlands, fragrant with fine airs,
Dainty with gems and flowers, and golden cloths!
Ah! eyes so large and lustrous! him they woo
Must helplessly take fire!
Thou art a child, standing on the sea's brink
Who thinks to cross, and dips one foolish foot.

We shall finally refer to Arnold's poem, *The Story of the Snake* describing the doctrine of

Kārma: it is a translation from the *Anushasana Parva* of the *Mahabharata.* We shall quote here the following fine passage containing Bhishma's words of wisdom:

"For will makes deeds,
And deeds make Karma, and the Karma makes
The outcoming. As when ye press the clay
This way and that, and see it harden, so
Men for themselves shape Fate. Shadow and light
Are not more surely tied each unto each
Than man to Karma and to Karma man.
Forget all grief and reach to peace of mind
For Heaven and Hell and all things come to all
By Karma."

The above are the most important of Arnold's Indian poems. They are of great beauty in themselves and also show how India is yet the true home of romance and idealism despite the stress of materialism and competition. The revelation of the treasures lying unknown in the books, folklore, and customs of India is a great work which can be best done by Indians themselves, and the world is waiting for the great Indian genius who shall reveal the supreme ideals of India in poems:

Grateful to hallowed minds, lofty in sound,
And couched in dulcet numbers,

("Indian Idylls").

ARNOLD'S MISCELLANEOUS POEMS.

In Arnold's *The Secret of Death and Other Poems* we have various fine miscellaneous poems, some of them dealing in a beautiful way with Greek subjects and ideals.

In the volume *Lotus and Jewel*, the series of poems called "A Casket of Gems" describes various precious stones and legends about them and interweaves the descriptions with exquisite love poetry.

The volume called '*With Sa'di in the Garden*' consists of a long poem excellently conceived and executed. It opens with a description of the Taj Mahal and introduces us a learned Mirza, two songstresses, and an Englishman who pass the night in the Mosque attached to the Taj, reading the chapter of Sa'di and 'Love' and conversing thereon. The book consists not only of translations from Sa'di but contains various exquisite lyrics and verse-tales full of Oriental passion and picturesqueness. The following opening description of the Taj is full of beauty :—

Not architecture! as all others are
But the proud passion of an Emperor's love
Wrought into living stone, which gleams and soars
With body of beauty shining soul and thought
In so much that it haps as when some face
Divinely fair unveils before our eyes
Some woman beautiful unspeakably—
And the blood quickens, and the spirit leaps,
And will to worship bends the half-yielded knees,
While breath forgets to breathe; so is the Taj.

Or again :—

He has not eyes to see whose eyes have seen
The glory of the beauty of the Taj
Nor knew and felt—at seeing—how man's hand

Comes nearest God's herein, touching His charm
Of rounded silvery clouds in that poised dome
Which hangs between the sky's blue and the stream's—
Fixing the fleeting structures of His snow
In those piled alabasters and stainless flats
Which mount and mount—delicate, drifted, still;—
Simple, yet subtle, as the curves and shades
Of the white breasts of her it celebrates,
Arjamand Banu, Queen of Love and Death;
A passion, and a worship, and a faith
Writ fast in alabaster, so that earth
Hath nothing anywhere of mortal toil
So fine-wrought, so consummate, so supreme—
So, beyond praise, Love's loveliest monument
As what Agra, upon Jumna's bank,
Shah Jahan builded for his Lady's grave.

The volume entitled *Potiphar's Wife and Other Poems* is not of much merit, though here and there we come across pieces of fine poetry.

The Japanese poems in the volume are more interesting than the Egyptian poems but are not of greater poetic value. The miscellaneous poems in the volume are of greater beauty and interest. The following lines to the British Empire are very fine:—

She alone knew, of victors first and best,
To fold the vanquished to her pardoning breast;
To gather 'neath her wings, in one great brood,
The tribes of Man, by might, then love, subdued,
Mother, not queen, calling those sons by birth
Whom she had conquered—linking ends of earth.

The volume entitled *In my Lady's Praise* contains the poems called 'A Casket of Gems' which have been collected in the volume

'Lotus and Jewel' and which have been reviewed above, and a few other poems. The other poems are mostly elegiac poems in sorrowful praise of his dead wife.

In his *Indian Poetry* already referred to, there are various fine miscellaneous poems. The poem called *King Saladin* narrates an adventure during the times of the Crusades. The other poems therein do not call for any special mention.

Arnold's miscellaneous poems do not as a whole touch a high level of lyric achievement or dramatic vividness of story-telling interest or philosophic depth. They show that he possessed a soul alive to beauty and a command of melodious verse but they are not the work of a great poet dealing with physical and ethical beauty in a profound and fascinating manner and do not contain his best work.

ARNOLD'S DRAMA.

His drama entitled 'Adzuma' is of value as throwing light on some Japanese ideals, though it is not a high work of art.

ARNOLD'S PROSE WORKS.

Sir Edwin Arnold's *Wandering Words* is a book of travels which deals more with the interpretation of the soul of the lands he visited than with the recording of mere outer incidents. It is especially valuable as an interpretation of Japanese and Indian life. He says:

> To see popular gatherings alive and brilliant with happy colours, and to find the lost repose and delightfulness of daily life extant, and visible, and placidly prized, one must wander to-day among Indian cities and enter the precincts of the temples of their gods and the courts of the Hindu princes.

He describes Japanese womanhood with true insight and sympathy, and says: "She is, in point of fact, the most unselfish, the most self-denying, the most dutiful and patient woman in the world, as well as the most considerate and pleasing." His description shows how there are intimate points of resemblance between Japanese and Indian womanhood. The stories of love and devotion in the book show what an admirable story-teller the poet is. The book is full of beautiful reflections and is quite worthy of the poet.

Sir Edwin Arnold's *East and West* is a book of traveller's impressions. It contains a few exquisitely narrated stories and some sketches of Indian and Japanese life.

"*India Revisited*," from which we have already quoted, is an excellent book of travels, full of picturesque description and sympathetic interpretation of the East. The chapter on "New Bombay" gives a full and glowing description of the queen of the Indian Ocean. The description of the

Elephanta caves is very fine. He says of the statue of *Ardhanareeswara*:

This statue, of colossal size, is nevertheless very delicately cut, and the limbs and features possess an almost tender beauty. But the right half of the deity from head to foot is male, and the left moiety female. On one side of the figure are the knotted hair, the breast, the limbs of a god-like man; on the other the smooth and braided tresses, the swelling bosom, the rounded contour of a goddess.

The description of his going to see his old college to which he often recurs with longing affection is pathetic and beautiful:

An old gate-keeper of the College—not so much older than he used to look, notwithstanding these many years—makes many salaams, and 'Sadhoo' presently brings up other people of the quarter who recognise the former 'Principal.' A good many well-remembered faces have however, quitted this world of illusions for 'Swarga.' Krishna Sastri is dead, Kero Punt is dead, Baba Gokhley is dead!

In regard to Indian sculpture he says:

Everywhere—on plinth and abacus, frieze and entablature—appears the same lavish wealth of work and fancy; for it is characteristic of the Hindu art, which the Moslem also in this respect adopted, to leave no naked plans in the stone"

He notes the still surviving skill of our artists despite the infamous neglect of them by the so-called 'patriotic educated' India. He says:

"While all exhibited great dexterity and artistic gifts, it was positively wonderful to watch one boy of fourteen summers from Shekrawati, whose nimble chisel and unerring mallet seemed to make the pattern leap, as it were, alive from the hard wood."

He speaks "of these indigenous crafts and of the manner in which the son acquires them from the father, perpetuating from generation to generation that admirable precision and feeling of pure native art which will be acknowledged by all good judges." Arnold describes later on the Kutub Minar and says that it "lifts its lofty beauty to the sky, a pillar of fluted masonry two hundred and forty feet high." What shall we say of his description of the Taj, when his description of the lesser architectural beauties is so great! He says:

> When the full glory of this snow-white wonder comes into sight, one can no more stay to criticise its details than to analyse a beautiful face suddenly seen. Admiration, delight, astonishment blend in the absorbed thought with a feeling that human affection never struggled more ardently, passionately, and triumphantly against the oblivion of Death.

He speaks of it as "that tender elegy in marbles which by its beauty has made immortal the loveliness that it commemorates." The description of Benares—the soul of India—is full of truth and charm; and so is the description of Buddha Gaya, the Mecca of Buddhism. Then follow the descriptions of Calcutta, Madras, Ceylon and Ootacamund. He speaks of the Minakshi temple at Madura thus:

> Each *gopuram* looks like a mountain of bright and shifting hues, in the endless detail of which the

astonished vision becomes lost . . . Imagine four of these carved and decorated pyramidal pagodas, each equally colossal and multi-coloured with fine minor ones clustering near, any one of which would singly make a town remarkable!

The following wise words of Arnold to England and India are worthy of serious attention:—

The time is gone when we could hold India by mere force. She must be 'ours' in the days to come because England is 'hers,' because the basis and purpose of our sovereignty there are her advancement and her benefit; because the best thing for the two populations is that they should dwell sisterly, the stronger protecting the weaker. What is good for India, in the sense of wisely and naturally developing her social and political emancipation, must henceforth be gladly done . . . . . : There are no longer two policies—one which suits the Empire, and one which satisfies India; there is but one henceforward, to find and to follow—the policy, that is to say, which is best for India.

Sir Edwin Arnold's *Seas and Lands* is a brilliant book of travels containing the picturesque descriptions of landscape, men, and manners.

The volume entitled "In Tent and Bungalow" is a book of short stories describing Anglo-Indian life.

The Queen's Justice is a work relating the facts of a murder case in India and the final vindication of justice in it by the courts established in India. It is dedicated to his third wife Jama Kurokawa, Lady Arnold.

Sir Edwin Arnold's "The Marquess of Dalhousie's Administration of British India" is in two volumes and was published in 1862. He finely says at the commencement of the work:

"He confesses to approach this labour with a conviction that India should be ruled for the Indians and that no imperial necessity can be stronger than imperial obligations."

These are wise and weighty words that deserve to be treasured up in all true hearts. Lord Wellington when he was in India said once: "I would sacrifice every political consideration ten times over rather than sanction the slightest infraction of British good faith." There is a serene jubilation dignified by a high sense of duty in the following passage in Arnold's book:—

Strength, indeed, is sure to be respected in practice; but it demands the regard of the philosopher also, being of its nature divine; and, at least a presumptive title to authority. Strength, inspired by benevolence, needs only wisdom to be the earthly analogue of the Divine Government. The two first are present together on all the pages of the history of the English in India. Sordid those pages sometimes are with the contact of money, blotted sometimes with innocent blood, but they always recite a progress to other gain than gold, and to other conquest besides territory. . . . . But, when all is conceded that envy or candour can ask, there remains that wherein England may challenge the comity of nations to match her work. The mantle of the Roman is descended upon us; bringing a larger gift, and a better spirit. We have overspread the earth; for our own gain, truly, but not for that alone—nor always for that at first. Where we we have come, justice, the best we know, is done; benefits, the best

we possessed, have been imparted. . . . . .
If we have not yet gained the affections of of India, at least we have never yet despaired of deserving them; and the temptation of a military mutiny has failed to enlist against us the accusation and hostility of her working people. . . . . We have deserved to keep what we have dared to acquire, and they read history ill, and fail beside in duty to their country, who speak of our Indian annals as fair to apologize for them. Let them be written, extenuating nothing and enlarging nothing, and a record will stand which the future will value and the present may be proud of.

Let all Englishmen remember the following precious words of Arnold:—

We are introducing in India an idea unknown to the East, as it was unknown to Europe before commerce and the Italian cities taught it—the idea of popular rights and equality before an impartial and written law. If in that mission we violate justice, and let our ambition get before our duty, we shall spoil our own work; which will else bring the circumference of civilization back to its starting point, and completing the round of human intercourse, repay to the East the heavy debt due to it from the West, in religion, art, philosophy, language—in almost everything but the science of government.

Ralph T. H. Griffith.

"GRIFFITH was not only the most voluminous but also the best translator of ancient poetry that Great Britain has produced," writes Prof. Macdonell and it is sufficient distinction for the inclusion of his name in this series of eminent Orientalists. As a translator of the *Vedas* and the *Ramayana* he has rendered services for the diffusion of a knowledge of Sanskrit literature in the West which cannot be easily forgotten by posterity. As an educationist who presided with great distinction over the Queen's College, Benares, for nearly two decades, he has left an honoured reputation behind him in the United Provinces of Agra and Oudh. To people in Southern India, the life and work of Griffith must be of special interest as he spent the last years of his life at Kotagiri on the Nilgiris and much of his literary work was accomplished in retirement at that quiet and beautiful South Indian hill-station. This writer must confess to a peculiar sense of personal satisfaction at being furnished with this opportunity of paying this tribute of praise to the memory of the great scholar, engaged as he is in educational work in the same ancient city of the Hindus where he himself laboured with such splendid fruit and has often passed along the very sights which he must have witnessed in the course of his active life in India.

The life of a scholar and educationist does not bristle sufficiently with interesting incidents to make his biography a matter of great attraction to those who are not specially interested in the history of intellectual achievement. Griffith's was no exception to this rule. Ralph Thomas Hotchkin Griffith was born at Corsley in Wiltshire on the 25th May, 1826. His father was the Rector of Corsley and that ensured his receiving a very good education at home after which he proceeded to Westminster School and then to the Queen's College in Oxford, where he took his B. A. degree in 1846 and his M. A. degree in 1847. While yet a student at Oxford, he had the privilege of coming under the influence of the well-known Sanskrit Scholar, Horace Hayman Wilson, who had laboured for Oriental scholarship in an earlier generation with all the enthusiasm with which he himself was to labour in later life. Winning the Boden Scholarship he pursued Sanskrit learning with great zeal and it is interesting to know that, even before coming to India as Professor of English Literature at the Queen's College, Benares, in the year 1853, he had distinguished himself by literary work relating to Oriental Scholarship. *Specimens of Indian Poetry* containing translations of selected passages from the *Ramayana* and the *Mahabharata* and a translation of the *Kumara Sambhava*, or the *Birth of the War-God* of Kalidasa, were the credentials he had even before coming to India at the early age of 27. He had also the valuable experience of four years' service as Assistant Master at the Marlborough College. He was Professor of English first and later Principal of the College and he ultimately rose to be Director of Public Instruction of the Provinces from which high office he retired in 1885 with a "Companionship of the Indian Empire", to spend the rest of his days in peaceful pursuit of the muses in Southern India, "in the sweet, half-English Nilgheri air," to whose attractions many other devoted Europeans have borne equally eloquent testimony.

As an educationist, Griffith enjoyed the esteem of all with whom he came into contact and had the reputation of being not only a very able exponent of the subject, English Literature, which he actually taught at College, but also a sympathetic friend and guide, to whom the students could always look up for help. His interest in the work of his students was real and abiding and always extended to their careers in life after leaving the portals of his institution. This writer has had the privilege of listening many an evening to enthusiastic accounts of his work at College from one of his most distinguished students—the late Mahamahopadya Adityaram Bhattacharya, at one time Professor of Sanskrit at the Muir Central College, Allahabad and later Pro-Vice-Chancellor of the Benares Hindu University. It was an inspiration to watch his face brighten up whenever he had occasion to speak of his old master. There was a new fire in his voice in spite of his advancing years and he spoke of him with an affection and joy which left an indelible impression on his listener. As a compliment to Griffith's splendid services, the College which was originally the Government College, Benares, was renamed the Queen's College, after his own *alma mater* at Oxford. During the period of his educational work in the Provinces, Griffith was not content with the mere acquisition of Sanskrit scholarship. His fondness for literary expression was almost a passion with him and it found vent during the period in the *Idylls from the Sanskrit*, *Scenes from the Ramayan* and the mellifluous translation of the love romance of Yusuf and Zulaika from the Persian of Jami.

He was destined to produce his *Magnum Opus*, the translation of the *Vedas*, only in his retirement at Kotagiri. The *Hymns of the Rigveda*, the *Hymns of the Sama Veda*, the

Hymns of the Yajur Veda and the *Hymns of the Atharwa Veda* followed in quick succession between 1889 and 1897, all of them appearing appropriately from Benares, the centre of Hinduism and Sanskrit culture. Years of strenuous work left their impression on his energies and the last few years of his life were spent in absolute peace without any attempts at further literary responsibilities. He died at the age of eighty in 1906 and lies buried at Kotagiri where he found a haven of rest towards the close of his long life of active work. He sleeps amidst surroundings which he loved so much, far away from the din and turmoil of crowded cities in seclusion so dear to his scholarly temperament.

This writer does not feel himself particularly competent to express an opinion on one aspect of his work, its value to accurate and profound Sanskrit Scholarship. He is content to quote the testimony of Prof. Macdonell in the matter: "Griffith's command of poetical diction enabled him to reproduce the form and spirit of the ancient hymns better than by means of prose or of rhyming verse. His method of interpretation is eclectic; it follows partly the mediæval commentators, partly the researches of Western scholars, supplemented by investigations of his own. His rendering cannot be considered authoritative, but they are the only versions that present the general spirit of the ancient hymns to the English reader in an attractive garb."

It is easy enough to indulge in cheap common places in condemnation of the art of translation in general; to join the Italian proverb which condemns all translators, as traitors *traduttori traditori*, and to repeat Dante Rossetti's advice, "never translate, never translate." But the translator has a very, valuable part to play in the diffusion of the world's knowledge and it is difficult to over-estimate the usefulness of the work done by writers of Griffith's type. Scrupulously accurate Oriental scholarship satisfying modern standards of investigation and research may not be the special distinction of Griffith, but his memory will be cherished with gratitude by a wide circle of readers all over the English-speaking world, to whom his translations have unlocked, probably for the first time, some of the imperishable treasures of Sanskrit literature. Introduced to a new world of romance and literature under his auspices, the English-speaking reader may exclaim with Keats:

> Then felt I like some watcher of the skies
> When a new planet swims into his ken.

As a translator, Griffith was free and rapid in his method and with his real command of versification he could always write in a manner which would interest the popular reader. Here is his tribute to the glory of the sun, based on a passage in the Rig Veda :

> Such the majesty and power,
> Such the glory of the Sun,
> When he sets at evening hour
> The worker leaves his task undone ;
> His steeds are loosed and over all
> Spreadeth Night her gloomy pall
> When he rides in noontide glow,
> Blazing in the nations' sight,
> The skies his boundless glory show,
> And his majesty of light,
> And when he sets, his absent might
> Is felt in thickening shades of night.

Every reader of Sanskrit will feel thankful for his translations of stray passages from such masterpieces as *Sakuntala*, the *Cloud Messenger*, and the *Ritusamhara* of Kalidasa and the *Gita Govind* of Jayadeva, which are not less valuable than his translation of such a complete work as the *Ramayan*, though very much smaller in compass. His rendering of the great epic into English is the best and the most popular which has yet been achieved in the medium of the English language. He has endeavoured to interpret his master with great faithfulness, whether he describes a scene of nature in the forests of Dandaka

> The very fowl that haunt the mere
> Stand doubtful on the bank, and fear
> To dip them in the wintry wave

As cowards dread to meet the brave.
The frost of night, the rime of dawn
Bind flowerless trees and glades of lawn;
Bennmbed in apathetic chill
Of icy chains they slumber still.

or writes with impressiveness of the marching armies, "like autumn clouds in long array," or narrates the triumphant entry of Rama into Ayodhya:

Then o'er the earth let thousands throw
Fresh showers of water cool as snow;
And others strew with garlands gay
With loveliest blooms our monarch's way.
On tower and temple, porch and gate
Let banners wave in Royal state
And be each roof and terrace lived
With blossoms loose and chaplets twined.

Much water has sped down the Ganges since the days when Griffith sought thus to bring the literature of India, sacred and profame, to the notice of the West. Sanskrit scholarship has advanced in many directions; Papyrus and Stone have made new revelations to a wondering world and musty manuscripts have been dragged into the day light of scholarship and knowledge has grown into the poet's phrase, from 'more to more', but it will be long before we will see another writer with a similar record of devotion to the great classics of India and with achievement of similar magnitude in the course of its diffusion over the civilised world.

Sister Nivedita

AMONG the small band of European scholars who have attempted to interpret the culture of the Orient, Sister Nivedita holds a unique place by virtue of her transcendent genius in identifying herself completely with the life and spirit of Hindu civilisation. Where other savants tried to approach the portals of Oriental thought through laborious learning in the technics of language and grammar, Sister Nivedita chose the better and the truer path of practical life in the very heart of Hindu society and drew her inspiration from the life of the people around her—people steeped in the age-long traditions of Ancient India. She thus reflects the very Soul of India *from within.*

Sister Nivedita (Miss Margaret Noble) was born on October 28, 1867, and was of Irish parentage on both sides, her father, the Rev. S. R Noble, being a Congregational Minister. She received a thorough modern education, and was widely known in London before she came to India as a prominent educationist who strove to realise the principles of Peztallozzi and Froebel. She was chiefly instrumental in founding the famous Sesame Club, and was the head of a school of her own at Wimbledon, London, when she came under the influence of Swami Vivekananda.

Of her early life Mrs. J. C. Bose has given a beautiful account:

"It was no accident that had shaped her life. Her father, an eloquent English clergyman of great promise, had ungrudgingly sacrificed his young life in the service of the poor in Manchester. A great love existed between the father and the child. A friend of his, a preacher in India, had come on a visit. Being struck with the spiritual earnestness of the child's face, he had given her his blessings and said that one day the claim of India would touch her. This seemed prophetic of what was to come. Her father, too, before his death had told her young mother that he knew that one day a great call would come for the child and that the mother should then stand by her. Thus it was that she was consecrated, so that when the call did come, though the mother's heart was full of anguish at the thought of parting, the memory of her dead husband strengthened her. Henceforth India, the object of her daughter's devotion, became hers too; and Indians always found a touch of home in her house at Wimbledon"

The child gradually developed rare intellectual powers. Even Huxley had been struck by her intellect. In time, she became the centre of a great educational movement, an outcome of which was the famous Sesame Club. At the very time when there was opened before her great possibilities in London for her splendid intellectual gifts, the call of India reached her."

She had lost faith in dogma and creed, but the motive of *service* still remained. As she herself writes: "For to me the mystery and tragedy of London, had long been the microcosm of the human problem, standing as the symbol of the whole world's call." And she was busy with educational schemes when the call of India reached her through Vivekananda.

THE CALL OF INDIA.

In September of the year 1895 Swami Vivekananda went to London in response to invitations. Miss Noble (as she then was) was one of the select circle who were brought into intimate contact with the Swami. She heard the lectures of the season, but was not conquered. She says:—

"His system as a whole, I for one, viewed with suspicion, as forming only another of those theologies which, if a man should begin by accepting, he would surely end by transcending and rejecting. And one shrinks from the pain and humiliation of spirit that such experiences involve,.................The time came, before the Swami left England, when I addressed him as "Master." I had recognised the heroic fibre of the man and desired to make myself the servant of his love for his own people. But it was his *character* to which I had thus done obeisance. Nor did I, at that time, though deeply attracted by his personality, dream of the immense distance which I was afterwards to see as between his development and that of any other thinker or man of genius I could name."

But what were the things that marked out to her the Swami's personality at the time?

"These, then, were the things I remembered and pondered over concerning the Swami, when he had left England, that winter, for America,—first, the breadth of his religious culture; second, the great intellectual newness and interest of the thought he had brought to us; and thirdly, the fact that his call was in the name of that which was strongest and finest, and not in any way dependent on the meaner elements in man."—*The Master As I Saw Him.*

The Swami returned to England in the year 1896, but Miss Noble's attitude towards the Swami still remained unchanged. But with his magical insight the Swami had marked her out as his faithful disciple.

"It was in the course of a conversation much more casual than this," she writes, "that he turned to me and said, 'I have plans for the women of my country in which you, I think, could be of great help to me and I knew I had heard a call which was to change my life..................The friend who afterwards called me to her side in India, chose a certain evening in London, when both the Swami and myself were her guests for an hour, to tell him of my willingness to help his work."

Having thus proffered her help Miss Noble sailed for India in the early part of 1898.

THE MASTER AND THE DISCIPLE.

Even after arriving in India she rebelled long against her Master. It was only gradually that the greatness of the Swami dawned on her in all its full glory and her own doubts were stilled. She accompanied the Swami in his wanderings in the year 1898, and at the end of the year we find her writing in her diary;—

"Beautiful have been the days of the year. In them the ideal has become the real.........................

Everywhere have come hours never to be forgotten, words that will echo through our lives for ever, and once at least a glimpse of the Beatific Vision."

She finally cast in her lot with Vivekananda only when she had had personal experiences warranting the truth of what he taught. But let us describe in her own words the story of her attitude towards Vivekananda till it culminated in loyal acceptance and passionate worship. She writes:—

Under the influence of the Swami Swarupananda, I began seriously the attempt at meditation. And if it had not been for this help of his, one of the greatest hours of my life would have passed me by. My relation to our Master at this time can only be described as one of clash and conflict. I can see now how much there was to learn and how short was the time for learning to be, and the first of lessons doubtless is the destroying of self-sufficiency in the mind of the taught. But I had been little prepared for that constant rebuke and attack upon all my most cherished prepossessions which was now my lot. Suffering is often illogical, and I cannot attempt to justify by reason the degree of unhappiness which I experienced at this time, as I saw the dream of a friendly and beloved leader falling away from me, and the picture of one who would at least be indifferent and possibly, silently hostile, substituting itself instead.

Fortunately it never occurred to me to retract my own proffered service, but I was made to realise, as the days went by, that in this there would be no personal sweetness. And then a time came when one of the older ladies of our party, thinking perhaps that such intensity of the pain inflicted might easily go too far, interceded kindly and gravely with the Swami. He listened silently and went away. At evening, however, he returned, and finding us together in the verandah, he turned to her and said with the simplicity of a child, "You were right. There must be a change. I am going away into the forests to be alone, and when I come back I shall bring back peace." Then he turned and saw that above us the moon was new, and a sudden exaltation came into his voice as he said, "See! the Mohammedans think much of the new moon. Let us also with the new moon begin a new life!" As the words ended, he lifted his hands and blessed, with silent depths of blessing, his most rebellious disciple, by this time kneeling before him.........It was assuredly a moment of wonderful sweetness of reconciliation. But such a moment may heal a wound. It cannot restore an illusion that has been broken into fragments. And I have told this story only that I may touch upon its sequel. Long, long ago, Sri Ramakrishna had told his disciples that the day would come when his beloved "Noren" would manifest his own great gift of bestowing knowledge with a touch. That evening at Almora, I proved the truth of this prophecy. For alone, in meditation, I found myself gazing deep into an Infinite Good to the recognition of which no egoistic reasoning had led me. I learnt, too, on the physical plane, the simple every-day reality of the experience related in the Hindu books on religious psychology. And I understood, for the first time, that the greatest teachers may destroy in us a personal relation, only in order to bestow the Impersonal Vision in its place.

Having thus convinced herself Miss Noble was formally admitted into the Order of Ramakrishna and became Sister Nivedita (dedicated), dedicated in very truth to the service of India. Henceforth she became a servant of servants to the Indian people. And here it is worth noting, that though she had accepted Hinduism, yet never did she pose as a religious leader. She never appeared to be *teaching* but only *serving.*

It was the spirit of the work, more even than its form, its freedom from parade and vainglory, its *silent strenuousness*, that is of infinite value to us. Those who want to realise the true greatness of Vivekananda and Nivedita's interpretation of his teaching, should read her beautiful book, *The Master as I Saw Him*, from which we shall give one other quotation touching the significance of Vivekananda's life:

"But in good sooth it is not of these things that I am attempting, in the course of the present pages, to speak. Mine is the broken and faltering witness of one who is fain to tell—not of geography nor of politics, nor yet of the ways and customs of interesting peoples and unknown races, but rather of the glimpses vouchsafed to her of a great religious life of the ancient order living itself out amidst the full and torturing consciousness of all the anomalies and perplexities of Modern Transition. Sree Ramakrishna had been, as the Swami himself said once of him, "like a flower, living apart in the garden of a temple, simple, half-naked, orthodox, the ideal of the old time in India, suddenly burst into bloom in a world that had thought to dismiss its very memory." It was at once the greatness and the tragedy of my own Master's life, that he was not of this type. His was the modern mind in its completeness. In his consciousness, the ancient light of mood in which man comes face to face with God, might shine, but it shone on all these questions and all those puzzles which are present to the thinkers and workers of the modern world. His hope could not pass by unheeded, it might include or it might reject—the hope of men of the nineteenth century. That sudden revelation of the misery and struggle of humanity as a whole which has been the first result of the limelight irradiation of facts by the organization of knowlege had been made to him also, as to the European mind. We know the verdict that Europe has passed on it all. Our art, our science, our poetry, for the last sixty years or more, are filled with the voices of our despair. A world summed up in the growing satisfaction and vulgarity of privilege, and the growing sadness and pain of the dispossessed; and a will of man too noble and high to condone the evil, yet too feeble to avert, or arrest, this is the spectacle of which our greatest minds are aware. Reluctant, wringing her hands, it is true, yet seeing no other way, the culture of the West can but stand and cry, "To him that hath shall be given, and from him that hath not shall be taken away even that which he hath." *Væ Victis*! Woe to the vanquished!

Is this also the verdict of the Eastern wisdom? If so what hope is there for humanity? I find in my Master's life an answer to this question. I see in him the heir to the spiritual discoveries and religious struggles of innumerable teachers and saints in the past of India and the world, and at the same time the pioneer and prophet of a new and future order of development. In the place which a problem took in his mind I find evidence regarding its final solution which—short of my own definite arrival at an opposite conclusion, as he himself would have been the first to point out—is of the highest value to myself. And thinking thus, I believe that each trace of those higher and uncommon modes of thought and consciousness to which he held the key, has its significance for the modern age. I believe much which has passed myself by, uncomprehending, will fall on its proper soil in other lives. And I pray only to give always true witness without added interpolation or falsifying colour."

Nivedita was among the greatest of the great legacies of Vivekananda to his country.

LIFE AT CALCUTTA.

In order to do the work to which her Master had called her, she had to win for herself a place in orthodox Hindu society, a Herculean task, surely! Of the life she led at Calcutta and of how she entered the very heart of Hindu society, such that even the most conservative of Hindu women thought it a privilege to partake of the bread broken by her, we shall quote the testimony of an eye-witness, Mrs. J. C. Bose. She writes:—

"A few months after the interview in which I could hold out very little hopes for her success in her educational efforts among our orthodox sisters, I was invited to her little house in Bosepara Lane. I was astonished. She had accomplished the impossible. Having secured a house in the midst of orthodox surroundings, at first no Hindu servant would serve her; but she went without any help rather than wound the feelings of her neighbours. Many a day passed when there could be no cooking, and she lived on fruits and on what some kindly neighbour would send her. After a time, however, the people about came to regard her as their own in so far that even the most orthodox and saintly women felt happy to live in the house as her guest.

It is a wonderful story—how little by little she completely won the heart of the people by her patient love."

Her First Literary Achievement.

Her first literary achievement was *Kali the Mother* issued in 1900 from an English publishing firm. In this little book she expounds the conception of Kali. There are many 'educated' Indians—of Christian missionaries we need not speak—who think that Kali is some blood-thirsty deity worshipped by barbarous people. To such people this book ought to be a revelation. The conception of God as Love is but half the truth, and ought to be supplemented by the conception of God as Terror. Even those who are repelled by the conception will be fascinated by the beauty and golden glow of the style of this book.

TRAVELS IN INDIA.

After the passing of her Master in July 1902, she travelled over the greater part of India and delivered lectures in all the chief cities. All the chief places of pilgrimage she visited, often travelling long distances on foot in the manner of the pilgrims of old.

HER *Magnum Opus*.

It was in the year 1904 that she published her greatest work, by which she is chiefly known in England and America—"*The Web of Indian Life*." Of this book, it may at once be said that it is the greatest in the English language upon India. It is not a book of travel or description, it is the revelation of the soul of a people. To those who have read it praise would be superfluous and halting; to those who have not read it praise would be meaningless. One cannot conceive of this book growing old or stale. Its literary power and its insight ensure its immortality. Whoever cares to understand India, whether alien or child of the soil, must take up this book. The style is strong, grave, concentrated, piercing. Passages of sustained eloquence abound. In almost every sentence there is some phrase or artistic touch which abides with us. In splendour of language and marvel of insight the book is undoubtedly great; in its humanity, catholicity and sweetness, it is simply sublime.

Nothing that has yet been written of Indian women is more beautiful or truer than Sister Nivedita's sketches of the home life of Bengal. Indeed with the vision of a poet and the sympathetic imagination of an artist she probed into the heart of Indian womanhood and reflected in her rythmic and eloquent prose the natural simplicity and spiritual fervour of the women of India. Women, she contended, are the embodiment and repository of the ancient wisdom of the East. They are the inheritors of a radiant orthodoxy, unspoilt by age and undimmed by the passing fashions of the day to which men so easily succumb.

But Sister Nivedita was quite alive to the fact that the Hindu woman must be modernised, and a new education is necessary. On that point she writes :—

It is clear that, as the objective of the old education of Indian woman lay in *character*, the new cannot aim lower. The distinctive element, therefore, in their future training cannot be reading and writing—

though these will undoubtedly grow more common—but the power to grasp clearly and with enthusiasm the ideas of nationality, national interests, and the responsibility of the individual to race and country.

WANTED A DYNAMIC ORTHODOXY.

Orthodoxy must become aggressive, and boldly face the new order of things. She writes :—

The weakness is easy enough to probe. The West conquers the East, as long as the East on the one hand shuns it as contamination, or, on the other, accepts it as a bribe. The idea of assimilating just so much of Western science as shall enable India to compete in the same market by the same processes as the West is as delusive as it is mean. The idea of refusing to participate in Western methods, and dying of starvation if need be, martyrs to national purity, is manifestly impracticable for the people at large, even if it had not long ago been carried out of reach of all on the high tides of economic disaster. What then? *Western Science must be recognised as holy. The idea of that Science must be grasped and pursued for its own sake.* Modern Astronomy must claim its "star intoxicated" prophets in the East as in the West. Geology, Physics, Biology, and the sublime and growing sciences of man, history and morals, must be left in India as new modes of the apprehension of truth, studied passionately without ulterior object, as the religious experience is now followed at the cost of all.

THE MESSAGE OF THE GITA.

In the chapter on the *Gita*, she writes :—

The book is nowhere a call to leave the world, but everywhere an interpretation of common life as the path to that which lies beyond. "Better for a man is his own duty, however badly done than the duty of another, though that be easy." "Holding gain and loss as one, *prepare for battle.*" That the man who throws away his weapons, and permits himself to be slain, unresisting in the battle, is *not* the hero of religion, but a sluggard and a coward; that the true seer is he who carries his vision into action, regardless of the consequences to himself; this is the doctrine of the "Gita" repeated again and again. The book is really a battle-cry. Spirituality is with it, no retreat from men and things, but a burning fire of knowledge that destroys bondage, consumes sluggishness and egoism and penetrates everywhere. Not the withdrawn, but the transfigured life, radiant with power and energy, triumphant in its selflessness, is religion.

That indifference to results is the condition of efficient action is the first point in its philosophy. But there is no doubt that the action should be strenuous. Let every muscle be hard, every limb well-knit, let the mind sweep the whole horizon of fact; with the reins in hand, the fiery steeds under control, with the whole battlefield in view, and the will of the hero lifted high to strike for justice, "Arise!" thunders the voice of Sri Krishna, "and be thou an apparent cause!"

It is the supreme imperative. Play thy whole part in the drama of time, devoting every energy, concentrating the whole force. "As the ignorant act from selfish motives, so should the wise man act unselfishly."

THE UNIQUE CONTRIBUTION OF INDIA TO THE WORLD.

It is from India that we shall gather that intellectualisation of belief which is to re-establish, in the name of a new and greater synthesis, our confidence in our own past. In this new synthesis every element of your own thought must find a place—the conception of humanity and the worship of truth of course, because without these it would have no *raison d'etre*. But even the emotionalism of the Negro must not go unplaced, uninterpreted, any more than that wondrous mood in which the explorer of knowledge finds himself launched on a vision of Unity that he dare not name. Neither the Catholic organisation of Monasticism nor the Protestant (taken from the Mohammedan) inspiration of common prayer can be left out. There must be a religious consciousness strong enough to recognise the anguish of denial as its own most heroic experience, and large enough to be tender and helpful to the ignorance of a child.

In the new up-growth of our own days, many preparatory influences now at work are to find fulfilment. All who have felt the love of the disinherited and oppressed, all who have followed truth for its own sake, all who have longed to lose themselves in a paradise of devotion and been refused by the armed reason standing at the gate, all who have felt out for a larger generalisation as they saw the faith of their babyhood falling away from them,—all these have helped and are helping to build up the new consciousness, to make the faculty that is to recognise and assimilate the doctrine of the future. But the evangel itself will be mainly drawn from India.

The book closes with the following note of joy and hope:—

Jackals prowl about the buried cities and deserted temples of the Asokan era. Only a memory dwells within the marble palaces of the Moguls. Is the mighty Mother not now exhausted? Having given to the world, is it not enough? Is she again to rouse and bestir herself for the good of her own household? Who can tell? Yet in all impotence and desolation of the present, amidst the ruin of his country and the decay of his pride, an indomitable hope wakes still in the heart of the Indian peasant. "That which is shall pass: and that which has been shall again be," he mutters "to the end of time." And we seem to catch in his words the sound of a greater prophesy, of which this is but the echo—

"Whenever the Dharma decays, and Adharma prevails, then I manifest myself. For the protection of the good, for the destruction of the evil, for the firm establishment of the national righteousness I am born again and again."

The Task Before Us.

"But to-day," she says "in the deliberate adoption of an agressive policy, we have put all this behind us. Realising that life is a struggle we are now determined that our wrestling, with the powers that are against us, shall enable us to contribute to the World's sum of culture, not merely to make adaptations from it."

Our part henceforth is active, and not passive. The Indianising of India, the organising of our national thought, the laying out of our line of march,—all this is to be done by us, not by others on our behalf. We accept no more programmes. Henceforth are we become the makers of programmes. We obey no more policies. Henceforth do we create policies. We refuse longer to call by the name of education the apprenticeship necessary for a ten-rupee clerkship. We put such things in their true place. We ordain ourselves intellectually free. What, then, is the task before us?

Our task is to translate ancient knowledge into modern equivalents. We have to clothe the old strength in a new form. The new form *without* that old strength is nothing but a mockery; almost equally foolish is the savage anachronism of an old-time power without fit expression, Spiritually, intellectually, there is no undertaking, but we must attempt it.

Great realms of the ideal open for our exploration, new conceptions of life and duty, and freedom, new ideals of citizenship, untried expressions of love and friendship, into all these we must throw ourselves with burning energy, and make them our own.

We must create a history of India in living terms. Up to the present that history, as written in English, practically begins with Warren Hastings, and crams in certain unavoidable preliminaries, which cover a few thousands of years, and troublesome as they are cannot be altogether omitted! All this is merely childish and has to be brought to the block. The history of India has yet to be written for the first time. It has to be humanised, emotionalised, made the trumpet-voice and evangel of the race that inhabit India. And to do this, it must be reconnected with *place.* Calcutta, Madras and Bombay are the present view-points! Surely the heroes that sleep on ancient battle-fields, the forefathers that made for themselves the wide-walled cities, the scholars that left behind them precious thought and script, have laughed sometimes, when they have not wept to see from high heaven the grotesque docility of their descendants! The history of India consists in truth, of the strata, of at least three thousand years. Ocean-bed and river-sands, forest marsh, and ocean-floor again lie piled one upon the other—and in each period some new point is centre. Ayodhya and Hastinapura, Indraprastha and Pataliputra, Ujjain and Delhi, Conjeeveram and Amaravati, what of the vanished worlds of which all these were born? There is no evangel without worship. Throw yourselves, children of India, into the worship of these and your whole part. Strive passionately for *knowledge.* You are the spades and mattocks of this excavation. For with you and not with the foreigner, are the thought and language that will make it easy to unearth the old significance. India's whole hope lies in a deeper research, a more rigid investigation of facts. With her, encouragement and not despair, is on the side of truth.

Great literatures have to be created in each of the vernaculars. These literatures must voice the past, translate the present, forecast the future. The science and the imagination of Europe have to be brought, through the vernacular, to every door. India cannot afford to imitate foreign institutions. Neither can she afford to remain ignorant of foreign ideals. The history of the past has to be re-written, in simple terms. True hope for the time to come must fill all hearts, like a nation's Common Prayer. On the creation of such vernacular literatures, depends the effective education of women.

Art must be re-born. Not the miserable travesty of would-be Europeanism that we at present know. There is no voice like that of art, to reach the people. A song, a picture, these are the fiery cross * that reaches all the tribes, and makes them one. And art *will* be re-born, for she has found a new subject,—India herself. Ah! to be a thinker in bronze and give to the world the beauty of the Southern *Pariah*, as he swings scarce clad, along the Beach-Road at Madras! Ah! to be a Millais, and paint the woman worshipping at dawn beside the sea! Oh! for a pencil that would interpret the beauty of the Indian *Sari*; the gentle life of village and temple; the coming and going at the Ganges side; the play of the children; the faces, and the labours of the cows!

But far more, on behalf of India herself, do we need artists, half poets and half draughtsmen, who can wake in us the great new senses. We want men of the Indian blood who can portray for us the men of old—Bhishma and Yudhisthira, Akbar and Sher Shah, Pratap Singh and Chand Bibi—in such fashion as to stir the blood. We want through these to feel out, as a people, towards the new duties of the time to be. Not only to utter India to the world, but also to voice India to herself—this is the mission of art, Divine Mother of the ideal when it descends to clothe itself in forms of realism.

At each step then, the conquest must be twofold. On this side something is to be added to the world's knowledge, and on that, an utterance to be given for the first time for India to herself. This is the battle that opens before the present generation. On our

* A rough cross of charred wood used to be passed from clan to clan in the Scottish Highlands, as the call to war. We all know the folded chapathy of the Indian villages.

fighting—a good fight, the very existence, it may be of the next, depends. Our national life is become, perforce, a national assault. As yet the very outwork of the besieged city is almost unstormed. Herewith then let us sound the charge. Sons of the Indian past! do ye fear to sleep at nightfall on your shields? On, on, in the name of a new spirituality, to command the treasures of the modern world, sack! On, on soldiers of the Indian Motherland, seize ye the battlements and penetrate to the citadel! Place garrison and watch within the hard-won towers, or fall, that others may climb on your dead bodies to the height ye strove to win.

OTHER WORKS.

In 1907, she published her "*Cradle-Tales of Hinduism.*" In it she has thrown Hindu stories into enchanting literary form. The stories gain inexpressibly when Nivedita is the narrator. In 1909 she published another short work, "*An Indian Study of Love and Death.*" We cannot think of a better offering to people in sorrow over bereavement than this little book. In 1910 was published "*The Master as I saw Him,*" her beautiful account of Vivekananda. She had been engaged for some time before her death in completing two great works on India. We do not know if they have been completed. All this does not, however, exhaust her literary productivity. She was contributing to many magazines, and whatever she wrote the reader was sure to find peculiarly original and brilliant, even though the theme should be trifling.

THE SISTER'S SERVICES TO INDIAN ART.

Not the least of the Sister's services to India was her interpretation of Indian art to India and the West. Her exquisite art criticisms contributed to the "*Modern Review*" will never be forgotten by those who read them. They were sometimes, as has been said, as great efforts of the pen, as the pictures dealt with were as efforts of the brush.

THE SISTER AND THE NATIONAL MOVEMENT IN INDIA.

Her influence upon the National movement in India, and especially in Bengal, it would be impossible to exaggerate. Two such competent judges, as Messrs. Blair and S. K. Ratcliffe, estimate that she, more than anybody else, created a passion for nationality in Bengal in recent times. Mr. Blair is of opinion that "she probably did more to create an atmosphere of unrest than all the newspapers in the world." Mr. S. K. Ratcliffe, speaking from intimacy of knowledge, wrote in the *Daily News*:—

"It was through her spoken and written word that the idea of nationality became a living and absorbing force."

THE END.

We are now bringing this fragmentary sketch of the life of this great soul to a close. Her life had been lived at a very high level, and the strain of overwork had manifested itself in frequent illness. She had gone to Darjeeling for a change. She was attacked with hill dysentery and on the 13th October, 1911, passed away. Her last mortal remains were borne to the burning-ghat on the shoulders of Hindu gentlemen and cremated. Some of the most distinguished sons of Bengal formed part of the funeral procession which was the largest that Darjeeling had ever witnessed. Her last words were "The boat is sinking but I shall see the Sun rise."

So lived and passed away this great soul. "I have seen the greatest thinkers in England, France, America, religious leaders, social workers, politicians and scholars filled with admiration and reverence for her clear vision and keen intellect and noble personality," says Mrs. J. C. Bose. And no wonder. Such a life would shed a glory over any country. Her life and achievements will live and abide with us as a cherished possession, a sweet and radiant presence, to be bequeathed as a treasure and an inspiration to coming generations.

William D. Whitney

TO European savants of Oriental literature, India owes much indeed. Professor Max Muller, in particular, did a great deal to popularise Sanskrit and open the rich fields of Indian civilisation and culture for systematic research on scientific lines. At about the same period, the Western Hemisphere too saw the birth of Oriental studies. Pre-eminent among the American Orientalists, Prof. William Dwight Whitney distinguished himself in the field of Sanskrit studies carried on over more than half a century.

William Dwight Whitney was born on the 9th Feb. 1827 at Northampton in Massachusetts. After graduating in 1845 he began his career as a bank clerk studying Sanskrit off and on. After being at the Yale College during 1849-50 he came to Berlin on a three years' trip to attend the lectures of Profs. Francis Bopp and Albrecht Weber. At Tubingen he attended the lectures of Prof. Roth. Thus completing his Sanskrit studies under the supervision of the best scholars of the day, Whitney returned to America in 1854 as Professor of Sanskrit at Yale College.

His well-earned leisure began to bear early fruits. In 1856 Whitney achieved, as joint editor with Prof. Roth, a most distinguished service for science by the issue of the *editio princeps* of the Atharva Veda. The same year he married Miss Elizabeth Wooster Baldwin. From 1855 onwards he began his connection with the American Oriental Society—whose Literary Journal was kept up at such a high level by his special endeavours. Whitney was the Librarian of the Society from 1855-1873, the Corresponding Secretary from 1857-1884 and since then President of the Society till his death.

Prof. Whitney wrote and published many works; the more important of his works are mentioned below. In 1860 appeared the translation of the "Surya Siddhanta" in the *Journal of the American Oriental Society.* He published the "Atharva Veda Pratisakhya" with text, translation and notes in 1862. In 1867 appeared the " Language and the Study of Language" being lectures delivered on various occasions. In 1871 he published "Taittiriya Pratisakhya" of the Yajur Veda which earned for him the Bopp Prize from the Berlin Academy. Between 1873 and 1875 appeared the "Oriental and Linguistic Studies" in two volumes. In the latter year, "Life and Growth of Language" was published in the International Scientific Series.

In 1879 Prof. Whitney published his *magnum opus* "A Sanskrit Grammar including both the Classical Language and the Older Dialects of the Veda and Brahmana." The book was written in response to an invitation from Messrs. Breitkopf and Hartel for inclusion in the *Indo-European Series* projected by them. The chief objects specially held in view in this Grammar are: (1) the presentation of the facts of the language primarily as they show themselves in use in the literature, and only secondarily as they are laid down by the Indian Grammarians, (2) the inclusion of the forms and constructions of the older language as exhibited in the Veda and the Brahmana, (3) the treatment of the language throughout as an accented one, (4) and the casting of all statements, classifications and so on into a form consistent with the teachings of linguistic science. The treatment of the facts of the Sanskrit language has thus been a historical one within the limits of the language itself. This work has proved to be of such indispensable use to scholars and beginners alike, that it has already run into a second and extended edition in 1888 and a third edition in 1896.

In 1881 appeared his "*Index Verborum* to the Atharva Veda" and in 1885 his "Roots," verb-forms and primary derivations of the Sanskrit language.

In 1875 Prof. Whitney became combined Professor of Comparative Philology and Sanskrit at Yale College.

During his lifetime Prof. Whitney enjoyed the confidence and esteem of almost all the leading Orientalists of his day. His theory of the origin of language attracted a good deal of criticism from very able compeers like Prof. Max Muller and others. In this particular case one would seem to think that both these scholars lost themselves a bit. By way of diversion it may be observed in passing that Prof. Whitney wrote of Max Muller: "To me he is simply with all his ability one of the great humbugs of the century. He has always been rated at full ten times his value as a scholar." Prof. Max Muller says of Whitney: "No plagiarism, I am sure, is more delightful than that which we all commit on truth. If we succeed in stealing the same good morsel from the larder of truth we should feel delighted, as I always feel, if others in their own independent way, arrived at the same results at which I have arrived. I thought at first he (Whitney) was honest and sincere, and took the trouble to answer him in a long paper in self-defence. In order to put an end to mere squabbling I proposed to him to choose three judges among his own friends to sumbit the points in question to them and to have done. He showed the better part of valour and declined the trial on purely whimsical grounds. After that he went on sending me articles, anonymous or signed; in fact, he placed himself outside the pale of literary criticism."

Beyond this unseemly affair, Prof. Whitney commanded general esteem. All honours were showered upon him, even as on on his contemporary Prof. Max Muller. Prof. Whitney received honorary degrees from Breslau (1861), William's College, Yale (1868), St Andrews (1875), Harvard (1876) and Columbia (1886). He became the first President of the American Philological Association (1869), and was Knight of the Royal Russian Order, Corresponding Member of the Imperial Russian Academy of Sciences, of the Institute of France and of the Royal Prussian Academy of Sciences, Foreign Member of the Royal Academy *Die Lincei* of Rome, Honorary Member of the Asiatic Society of Bengal, of the Royal Asiatic Society of Great Britain and Ireland, and of the German Oriental Society.

He breathed his last, full of years and honours, on June 7th, 1894, leaving behind him as intellectual legacy to America his own pupil, Charles Rockwell Lanman, who is Professor of Sanskrit at Harvard University.

Professor Lanman is carrying on the great work of his revered master. He brought forth in 1891 the famous "Harvard Oriental Series", the primary object of the series being the elucidation of the history of religions, more especially of those of India. In this series Professor Lanman published in 1905 in two volumes Whitney's translation of the Atharva-Veda Samhita with notes etc. This edition of the Atharva Veda stands unequalled in every respect till to-day. Besides, Professor Lanman has also published many works and contributed valuable articles to the leading Oriental journals of the day. His "Sanskrit Reader" with vocabulary and notes was published by him in 1893 and has run into many editions. He will be chiefly remembered for this work which is an indispensable guide for the study of Sanskrit on modern comparative and scientific lines.

Anundoram Borooah

INTRODUCTORY.

THE latter half of the nineteenth century witnessed a glorious band of workers in the field of Sanskrit research in India. This gifted brotherhood included among its members the late Mr. R. C. Dutt, Raja Rajendralal Mitra, Mr. Dayananda Saraswati, Pandit Indraji Bhagavanlal, Sir Ramkrishna Gopal Bhandarkar and Mr. Anundoram Borooah. The last, by dint of his earnestness of purpose and his lifelong devotion to the cause of Sanskrit scholarship, has won an imperishable name in the annals of Indian Sanskrit research. Thirty-five or forty years ago no Indian *savant's* name had excited greater admiration and applause than Mr. Borooah's, and this feeling was rightly echoed in the Lahore *Tribune* of those days—

"Mr. Borooah's Sanskrit scholarship is as profound and accurate as it is extensive. We are proud of him as a nation and we earnestly hope that our brightest youths may follow his noble, though very arduous, path."

Mr. Borooah was a member of the Indian Civil Service, and was for some years in charge of a heavy district in Bengal. The scope of his work and the range of his scholastic investigations which he strenuously carried on in the midst of his busy official duties show him—to quote Prof. Cecil Bendall's words in *the Tribune's Record*, 1889—"to have been a kindred spirit with administrators like Colebrooke and Burnell among the illustrious dead, and the small band of living workers like Grierson, Fleet and R. C. Temple."

Mr. Borooah is a fine flower of Western culture. The profound erudition of the Oriental scholar, combined with the critical spirit of the West, imparted to Mr. Borooah's works a peculiar value and lustre. As the greatest intellectual representative of the "benighted Province of Assam," Mr. Borooah is the glory of the Assamese; and Assam has not produced a greater man during the space of ninety years that she has come under British rule. His name has been an example and an inspiration to thousands of the youth of Assam.

LIFE.

Mr. Anundoram Borooah, B.A., I.C.S., Barrister-at-Law, was born in May, 1850, at North Gauhati in the district of Kamrup, Assam. Anundoram belonged to the well-known Majindar Borooah family of Assam.

His father—an Assamese gentleman of the older type, was for some years a *Sadar Amin*, a post equivalent to a modern Deputy Magistrateship. Through the efforts of his learned father Anundoram was initiated into the vast potentialities of the *Deva Bhash* even during his childhood. With the help of an erudite Sanskrit Pandit who was appointed to teach him Sanskrit, Anundoram mastered and got by heart the whole of the immortal lexicon *Amarkosha* before he was fourteen, at which age he also passed the Entrance Examination of the Calcutta University. He read for the First Arts Examination in the Presidency College of Calcutta, and there he had as his teachers the great educationalists, Mahamohopadhya Moheshchandra Nyayaratṇa C.I.E., in Sanskrit, and Sir Gurudas Banerjee (then Mr.) in Mathematics. Sir Gurudas Banerjee has once fittingly remarked,—

> "The First Year Class of the Presidency College of 1865 was a splendid one containing many very brilliant students......and Mr. Borooah was unqestionably the brightest of this bright band of young students."

Anundoram stood sixth in the First Class in the F. A. Examination held in December, 1866, securing the Duff Scholarship in Mathematics, and in January, 1869, he stood second in the First Class in the B. A.

Examination of the Calcutta University. Emulated by the noble example of the glorious *trio*, Mr. Surendranath Bannerji, Mr. Beharilal Gupta and Mr. Romesh Chandra Dutt who had left for England a few months ago, Mr. Borooah made up his mind to proceed to England and sit in the competitive examination for the State scholarship tenable in England. The Syndicate of the Calcutta University in their sitting of the 29th January, 1869, elected Mr. Borooah to the scholarship. Besides the State scholarship Mr Borooah won by open competition the Gilchrist Scholarship as well, and the total value of these stipends amounted to £ 300 a year.

Mr. Borooah proceeded to England in the spring of 1869 with Mr H. Woodrow, M.A., sometime D.P.I. of Bengal, who had taken a kindly interest in this young prodigy from Assam, and introduced him to Lord Mayo, the then Viceroy and Governor-General of India. Mr. Borooah joined one of the Civil Service coaching institutions in London, studied Science in the London University and Law in the Middle Temple. His aptitude for scientific studies was so great that Dr. Carpenter, Professor of Zoology in the London University and Principal of the University College, London, once remarked,—

"Mr. Borooah was the most inquisitive student that I have ever come across." Mr. Borooah passed the I.C.S. Examination in 1871, was called to the Bar in the subsequent year, and is said to have passed also the B.Sc. examination of the London University. He stood first in Mathematics in the Civil Service Examination. During his stay in England Mr. Borooah contracted intimacy with the late Sir Taraknath, Palit, D. L., and it ceased only with the death of Mr. Borooah. It may be noted here that Mr. Borooah was the first Assamese graduate, the first Assamese Barrister and the first Assamese Civilian.

Mr. Borooah returned to India in the autumn of 1872, and was appointed Assistant Commissioner of the Sibsagar district in his Province of Assam. After a year of service in Assam Mr. Borooah secured transfer to Bengal where he passed the remaining years of his life. His short stay in Sibsagar was marked by his scholastic habits and his independence of attitude for which he had occasional misunderstandings with his superiors. His usual dress was the old-fashioned aristocratic *Chouga* and *Chapkan* and he used to have a book by his side, even, in the court, which he read in the intervals of his magisterial functions.

Mr. Borooah served as an Assistant Magistrate in several places in Bengal ; and when after a prolonged agitation, which had as its great patron and supporter Sir William Hunter, Indian Civilians were first entrusted with the charge of districts, Mr. Borooah and Mr. R. C. Dutt were eventually appointed District Magistrates and Collectors. And as is always the case when Indians are given fair opportunities to prove their mettle they always respond magnificently. Mr. Borooah and Mr. Dutt discharged their duties without any hitch or trouble, and thereby paved the path for the Indians to secure the highest responsible posts under the Government.

Mr. Borooah did not allow his literary zeal to be damped by the heavy responsibilities of a magistrate's duties,—there issued forth from his pen every year book after book, lexicons, grammars, new editions of old Sanskrit texts and compilations from old Sanskrit authors. In 1881 Mr. Borooah projected the compilation of a "Comprehensive Grammar of the Sanskrit Language" in twelve volumes of one thousand pages each, and in order to be able to consult the Oriental books and manuscripts of the British Museum, London, he took two year's furlough from November 1881 and sailed for England. He carried on his investigations in England, and in this undertaking his great helpers were Prof. Cecil Bendall, the Keeper of Oriental Books in the British Museum, Mr. Nicholson, the Bodleian Librarian at Oxford, and Dr. Reinhold Rost, the learned Librarian of the India Office. After collecting sufficient materials Mr. Borooah returned to India in October 1883.

In 1885 Mr. Borooah was appointed a Fellow of the Calcutta University and was attached to the Faculty of Arts. Two years after he was placed for the second time in charge of the Noakhali district in Bengal, and there by his learning, benevolence and sympathetic temperament and various acts of public utility Mr. Borooah won the hearts of the people. He helped many poor students with books and money, and educated a meritorious Bengali student even in England. He had a staff of erudite Sanskrit Pandits whom he paid handsomely. This learned *congerie* of orthodox Pandits helped Mr. Borooah in the mechanical portions of his literary labours. As an official too he won the trust and confidence of the Government.

In the winter of 1888 Mr. Borooah became ill. A sudden attack of paralysis disabled him, and he took leave for three months. He went to Calcutta, lived at the Ballygunge residence of his old friend, Sir Tarak Nath Palit, and placed himself under the treatment of the best Allopathic, Homœpathic and Ayurvedic physicians of the day. But even their united efforts failed to cure that fell disease. Mr. Borooah passed away in the afternoon of the 19th January, 1889.

LITERARY WORKS.

Mr. Borooah's literary career spread over a period of twelve years only, and considering the shortness of the period, the character of his productions, both in their qualitative and quantitative aspects was simply marvellous. His *English-Sanskrit Dictionary* appeared in three volumes between 1877—1880, and for many years it was the only work of its kind written by an Indian. On the completion of this *magnum opus,* Mr. Borooah was congratulated from all quarters, including among them the illustrious names of Lord Northbrooke, Governor-General of India, and Prof. F. Max Muller. To the second and third volumes of his Dictionary Mr. Borooah added two other original and useful works, viz., his *Higher Sanskrit Grammar* and *Ancient Geography of India* respectively. This was followed by an edition of Bhavabhuti's *Mahaviracharitam* with Mr. Borooah's own lucid commentary in Sanskrit called *Janakiram Bhasua* after his beloved brother

Janakiram Borooah. Mr. Borooah's next literary ventures were, first, a critical dissertation named *Bhavabhuti and His Place in Sanskrit Literature*, which contained an exhaustive treatment and examination of the *Ramaic* drama, besides Bhavabhuti and his age; and secondly, *A Companion to the Sanskrit-Reading Under-Graduates of the Calcutta University*, being a few notes on the Sanskrit Texts selected for the F. A. and B. A. Examinations. Small though in bulk the latter book is an important contribution to the Sanskrit scholarship. Mr. Borooah's comments were suggestive rather than detailed.

The next literary enterprise of Mr. Borooah was, to quote Mr. R. C. Dutt's words—" A Sanskrit Grammar of formidable size and erudition." In 1881 Mr. Borooah projected the compilation of *A Comprehensive Grammar of the Sanskrit Language, Critical, Analytical and Historical*, in twelve volumes, of one thousand pages each. Its object—as described by Mr. Borooah in a prospectus which was circulated among his friends and the lovers and promoters of Sanskrit culture —" was to simplify the rules of Grammar as far as possible, to examine their historical growth, and illustrate them fully from the existing literature, both ancient and modern, and to offer a complete commentary on all the Vedas." "The first volume of the series, which was on Sanskrit Prosody, came out in 1882 under the somewhat eccentric title of Volume X. The next Volume was on Letters and their changes—*Nanarth-Samgraha,* and came out in 1884 as Volume III of the series. Learned world was startled at the encyclopædic character of Mr. Borooah's great undertaking. Professor Max Muller wrote to Mr. Borooah from Oxford,—"I confess I felt almost overhhelmed by the grandeur of it, but if only you carry out some portion of it, you will have done a very useful work...... It is a great undertaking and will require for its completion a lone life, a long purse and long patience."

Mr. Borooah did not live to complete this great literary project. The remaining years of his life were spent in publishing scholarly editions of *Saraswati-Kanthabharanam*, Amara's *Namalinganusasanam* with the commentary of Kiraswami, Dhatukosh and *Dhatuvrittisara*.

Besides these Sanskrit works Mr. Borooah had arranged to compile a Dialectical Dictionary of the Bengali Language and had for this purpose negotiated with the Government of Bengal for its help and co-operation.

Mr. Borooah was a Sanskrit poet of no mean order. In his edition of *Mahaviracharitam* he has added towards the end of each act a few autobiographical verses in Sanskrit. These scattered lines and his address to the Sanskrit Muse prefixed to the second volume of his Dictionary show how this eminent Indian Sanskritist had assimilated the rhythm and melody of the language of his forefathers.

CONCLUSION.

Mr. Borooah's useful career was cut short by his untimely death ; but his indefatigable exertions on behalf of Sanskrit learning will always be an example to the rising generations of India. His earnestness of purpose is best manifested in his confirmed bachelorhood. As a member of the Indian Civil Service, enjoying the highest emoluments and honour open to an Indian, Mr. Borooah could have led a life of ease.

But Mr. Borooah, whose love of Sanskrit did not allow him to share his heart with any earthly object, preferred to remain a bachelor; and when he was pressed by any friend to marry he would simply point to the vast array of books in his magnificent library and say,—"This is the darling of my life demanding from me my best energy and attention."

Macdonell

THE increasing scope for higher research in Sanskrit and Sanskritic studies has been appreciated by the Government of India to some extent at least. The Government of India now awards two scholarships, tenable abroad, for Advanced Post-Graduate work in languages. Scholars naturally turn to Great Britain to see whether there is any scope for their work there. The Archives of the British Museum, the India Office Library in London and the Bodleian Library at Oxford do indeed contain much valuable material awaiting further elucidation. But more than the material, it is the Professors—the living agencies—that appeal to the novice; for he is eager to be shaped and moulded into the best form of the day.

There are only five Sanskritists to-day in Great Britain. Prof. A. A. Macdonell specialises in Vedic subjects at Oxford. Dr. Barnett is in charge of the Oriental Department of the British Museum and specialises in Archæology and Dravidian subjects. Dr. Thomas is the Librarian of the India Office and an expert with regard to Classical Sanskrit. Prof. Rapson specialises is numismatics etc., at Cambridge. There is Dr. A. B. Keith who is a storehouse of information on all conceivable subjects, at Edinburgh.

Arthur Anthony Macdonell was born on 11th May 1854. He was very fortunate in having a Continental training even from his early days. He was educated at the Gymnasium and University at Gottingen, at the Universities of Leipzig and Tubingen, and at Oxford University also. Even from his boyhood he gave great promise and won many academical honours. At Oxford he was *Exhibitioner* of Corpus Christie College (1876-1880); won the Taylorian Scholarship for German in 1876, the Davis Chinese Scholarship in 1877 and the Boden Sanskrit Scholarship in 1878. He took his B. A. degree in 1880, and M. A. in 1883 at Oxford and obtained the Ph. D. of Liepzig in 1884, submitting for his thesis 'a critical edition of the *Sarvanukramani* with commentary," which was published later on at Oxford in in 1886 in the *Anecdota Oxoniensia* series.

At Oxford, Prof. Macdonell decided to begin his career. From 1880-1899 he was Taylorian teacher of German; was Deputy Professor of Sanskrit from 1888-1899 and has been Boden Professor of Sanskrit and Keeper of the Indian Institute since 1899.

From the very beginning of his career, Professor Macdonell has always been engaged in doing some work or other with regard to Sanskrit. A man of very unassuming habits, he impresses his pupils and friends very well indeed. He is a keen and regular worker, so studious indeed, that he rarely exhibits any symptoms of that Oxford polish—of *sociability*. One wonders whether any one of his more brilliant pupils have ever known Dr. Macdonell, the man.

The literary output of Professor Macdonell may not perhaps favourably compare with other Orientalists in point of volume. But surely from the point of solid work achieved, the Professor will always hold a high place. To his first noteworthy publication—the *Sarvanukramani*—we have already referred. In 1886, he published a "Sanskrit Grammar for Students"—a valuable companion for students of Sanskrit, executed on modern European lines. This book has been so useful that it has already run into the third edition. In 1892 appeared the "Sanskrit Dictionary" the chief value of it being the large inclusion of Vedic words also. *Vedic Mythology* was published in 1897; in that famous Series "Grundriss der Indo Arischen Philologie and

Altertumskunde" projected by Buhler, Keilhorn and others. This work is of immense use to scholars. It deals in a systematic and critical manner with the conceptions of the Vedic peoples. The author traces these conceptions in respect of every individual deity from their earliest references in the Vedas. To the students of Comparative Religions as well as to those of Indian Religious Systems and Metaphysics, the book is a veritable treasure-house. In 1900 appeared " A History of Sanskrit Literature" in the " Short Histories of the Literature of the World" Series edited by Edmund (Jones) Gosse. Till today, this book holds its place and is the only trustworthy history that is yet available. In the preface, Professor Macdonell says :—

"The student is in want of a guide setting forth in a clear and trustworthy manner, the results of research down to the present time.........................

....

In writing this history of Sanskrit literature, I have dwelt more on the life and thought of Ancient India, which the literature embodies, than would perhaps have appeared necessary in the case of a European literature. This I have done partly because Sanskrit literature, as representing an independent civilisation entirely different from that of the West, requires more explanation than most others, and partly because, owing to the remarkable continuity of Indian culture, the religious and social institutions of modern India are constantly illustrated by those of the East."

The book, besides a number of appendices, contains also very valuable " Biographical

Notes." The work has run into many impressions, but unfortunately it has not yet been revised and republished as recent researches have necessitated important additions and corrections in many places. In the "Harvard Oriental" Series was published in 1904 the "*Brihaddevata*" in two volumes, the first volume containing the original Sanskrit text critically edited with an introduction and seven appendices, and the second volume containing the English translation with critical and illustrative notes. 1910 saw the publication of the "Vedic Grammar" in the "Indo-Aryan" Series of Buhler. This will remain the greatest work of Professor Macdonell, a work by which he will take his place among the greatest of Orientalists. In the introduction we read—

> "Vedic Grammar has never till now been treated separately and as a whole. Both in India and in the West, the subject has hitherto been handled only in connection with Classical Sanskrit.........In view of the prominent position occupied by the Indo-Aryan branch in Comparative Philology and of the fact that the language of the Vedas represents the foundation of the subsequent strata, it seems important for the sake of clearness and definiteness that the earliest phase should be treated as a whole independently of later developments. As the linguistic material of the Rig Veda is more ancient, extensive and authentic than that of the other Samhitas, all of which borrow largely from that text, it is taken as the basis of the present work."

Almost all the researches from 1850 onwards down to about 1905 are incorporated in the work. Each chapter has at the beginning a list of the more important works on the subject and the book is full of notes and references at each and every page. Surely, a monument of industry, perseverence and patience. This book can, by its very nature, be used only as a reference book. The author recognising the need for a handy volume for use by students, issued in 1916 " A Vedic Grammar for Students". In the preface, the author says—

> "The present book is to a great extent based on my large 'Vedic Grammar'". It is, however, by no means simply an abridgment of that work. For being besides differently arranged, so as to agree with the scheme of the "Sanskrit Grammar," it contains much matter excluded from the 'Vedic Grammar' by the limitations imposed on the latter work as one of the volumes of Buhler's "Encyclopædia of Indo-Aryan Research." Thus it adds a full treatment of Vedic Syntax and an account of the Vedic metres...............The present work therefore constitutes a supplement to, as well as an abridgment of, the Vedic Grammar, thus in reality setting forth the subject with more completeness as a whole, though in a comparatively brief form, than the larger work."

Even with these valuable helps, the study of the Vedic language is not an easy task. The applications of the methods of critical interpretation by those who are acquainted with Classical Sanskrit, but are only beginners in Vedic, necessitates the help of a teacher. To remedy this in some measure at least, Professor Macdonell published in 1917

"A Vedic Reader for Students" containing thirty hymns of the Rig-veda in the original Sanskrit and Pada texts, with transliteration, translation, explanatory notes, introduction and vocabulary. The scope of the work is amply explained by the author in the preface where he says—

"In conjunction with my 'Vedic Grammar for Students,' the "Reader" aims at supplying all that is required for the complete understanding of the selection without reference to any other book. Each hymn is preceded by a special introduction describing briefly the deity or the subject with which it deals. The text of every stanza is printed in three different forms.........Next follows the transliterated Samhita text, in which by the removal of vowel contractions, the resolution of semi-vowels, and the replacement of *A*, the original metre of the Rig Veda is restored and, by the use of punctuation, the sense is made clearer. The translation which follows, is close, accounting for every word of the original and is based on the critical method of interpretation. The notes furnish minute explanations of all matters concerned with grammar, metre, accent, syntax and exegesis. The general introduction gives a concise account of the form and the matter of the Rig Veda, describing in outline its arrangement, its language and metre, its religion and mythology, besides the critical method here applied to the interpretation of its hymns. The vocabulary supplements the translation and notes by giving the derivation of every word...... Anyone who has worked his way carefully through the page of the "Reader" ought thus to have laid a solid foundation in Vedic scholarship, and to be prepared for further studies on independent lines."

Besides these, in 1912, the "Vedic Index of Names and Subjects" was published in two volumes in collaboration with his illustrious pupil—Dr. A. B. Keith. Professor Macdonell has also contributed very useful articles on varied subjects to the *Encyclopædia Britannica*, the *Journal of the Royal Asiatic Society* and others. Among his articles, mention may here be made to his contribution to the "Bhandarkar Memorial Volume" published in 1917, where the place of honour was given to him. Indian scholars may not often agree with his unjust and unmerited tirades on Pandit scholarship in India. It needs indeed a far higher mental vision to appreciate approximately the Pandit and discern his gifts from his shortcomings. Professor Macdonell made a tour of study and research in 1907-08 throughout India. That perhaps has entitled him to dogmatise on Pandits. We, for our part, know that a good deal of the Vedic Research of the last half a century lie embedded in the Pandit-produced Vedic literature of India; only, her modern descendents have been criminally slow to resuscitate them to life.

The Oriental and literary world has not been slow to appreciate and honour Professor Macdonell. He was elected Fellow of the most distinguished College at Oxford—Balliol, as early as 1900, which he continues to hold, Representative of Sanskrit Language and Literature at the Congress of Arts and Sciences,

St. Louis, U. S. A. in 1904 and Fellow of the Royal Danish Academy. He has been Fellow of the British Academy from 1906 onwards, and on the Council of the Royal Asiatic Society of Great Britain and Ireland, besides being one of its Vice-Presidents. He continues to take keen interest in Oriental problems in spite of advancing years. He was one of the prominent figures at the recent *entente* Oriental Congress held in London in 1919, when he read a paper, "*On the establishment of a British School of Oriental Studies in India*," which evoked a good and profitable discussion. The Calcutta University has resolved to confer on him the honorary degree of Doctor of Oriental Learning, in recognition of his scholarship, at the Convocation which is to be held to welcome the Prince of Wales.

Vincent Smith

INTRODUCTORY.

DR. Vincent Arthur Smith, C.I.E., I.C.S., was one of the last of the eminent band of Orientalists, scholars and researchers, who, from the time of Sir William Jones and Charles Wilkins have done so much for the advance in Indology that has been effected.

"His knowledge of Indian history and art and all their connections was comprehensive and unrivalled; his experience in India enabled him to use his materials with judicious discrimination, and he coordinated and wrought them up into complete treatises that were acknowledged as authoritative. He accomplished a great work that lay beyond the scope of the researches of other individual scholars and conferred notable boons of permanent value not only on them, but also on all persons interested in India."

The above verdict on the output of Dr. Smith's scholarship, genius for collation and laborious industry is an eminently just and impartial one. For nearly half a century, since his entry into the Indian Civil Service in 1871, did he patiently study the history, archæology and arts of the people of the country which he served for about three decades. He early formed the resolution of writing the ancient history of Northern India from the monuments, collected materials and the results of all researches available. In the midst of heavy official duties, Dr. Smith persisted on in his resolution of devoting all his spare hours to his favourite studies. And from 1875 down to a few months before his death in February 1920, he put forth books, pamphlets and brochures in abundant profusion, first making detailed preparatory studies of the materials and publishing them from time to time—in anticipation of the complete History which was to come out in 1904—in various learned journals. Subsequent to the publication of his *Early History of India*, his energy seemed as if it had doubled in quantity and intensity; and his literary output became larger and more varied than ever. His contributions to Oriental scholarship were immense and valuable; he was an erudite and thorough student of the materials that he collected; and the strength of his conclusions impressed his readers no less than the stores of buried learning which he brought to light.

His Life and Achievements.

The late Dr. Smith was born in Dublin on June; 3, 1848, the son of Aquilla Smith,

M.D., who was a well-known numismatist and archæologist of his days and whose valuable collection of coins was acquired by the British Museum. This fact probably accounts for the great interest that Vincent Smith took in the study of coins from a very early age. He graduated from the Trinity College, Dublin, where he got the highest distinctions. His own University honoured him in the year previous to his death with a Doctorate in appreciation of his high learning and valuable publications. He next passed the open competitive examination for the Indian Civil Service in 1869 and the final examination in 1871, standing at the top of the list of successful candidates. He was posted to the United Provinces where he served in the regular junior magisterial and executive offices for some years. In 1874 he was taken into the Land Settlement Department of the Province which had been organised most thoroughly by Merttins Bird; he wrote the *Settlement Officers' Manual for the North-Western Provinces* in 1881. He continued in that Department until he was appointed Magistrate-Collector in 1889. He became District Judge in 1895 and three years later was promoted to the position of Chief Secretary to the Provincial Government. Shortly afterwards he was further raised to the post of Divisional Commissioner. But he did not care to enjoy the high official position that had become his for long. "The call that history made on him led him to retire from India comparatively early, in July 1900, in order that he might devote undivided attention to it." Soon after his retirement he was appointed Reader in Indian History and Hindustani in the University of Dublin. He settled at Cheltenham for some years for the sake of his health, but finally removed to Oxford where he joined the staff of St. John's College. He was subsequently nominated to the post of Curator of the Indian Institution at that place, and was the Literary Adviser to the Syndicate of the Clarendon Press in the matter of their Oriental publications. Dr. Smith was elected a member of the Council of the Royal Asiatic Society in 1915 and promoted to be one of its Vice-Presidents four years later. The Society awarded him in 1918 its Triennial Gold Medal which was founded in 1897 and the recipients of which included such honoured names as Prof. E. B. Cowell who did much for Sanskrit studies at the English Universities, Sir William Muir, the great authority on Islam and Islamic history, Dr. G. U. Pope, the well-known Tamil scholar, Sir George Grierson, Director of the Linguistic Survey of India, and Dr. J. F. Fleet, the founder of Scientific

Sanskrit Epigraphy. Dr. Smith continued to work with his usual industry down to the last days of his life; he, however, began to fail in health seriously in December, 1919, and died on the 6th February following.

CONTRIBUTIONS TO LEARNED JOURNALS.

Dr. Smith's literary activities covered a period of nearly forty-five years. To *The Indian Antiquary* alone he was a valued contributor of more than forty years' standing. His connection with that Journal dates from 1878 beginning with a query on Saka and Samvat Dates. Especially since 1885 when *The Indian Antiquary* passed into the hands of Dr. J. F. Fleet and Sir Richard Temple, Dr. Smith became a constant contributor to its columns. The coins of the Gupta Dynasty, the Inscription of Mahanaman at Bodh-Gaya, the Tibetan affinities of the Lichchhavis, the History and Coinage of the Chandel Dynasty, the Palas of Bengal, Discovery of the Plays of Bhasa, a predecessor of Kalidasa;—these were among the important subjects on which he wrote to the *Antiquary*.

The *Journal of the Bengal Asiatic Society* was vastly enriched by his contributions on the coins of the Gupta Dynasty and on the probable estimate of Græco-Roman influence on the civilisation of Ancient India. The *Journal of the German Oriental Society* and the *Ostasiatischen Zeitschrift* contained a number of articles from his pen on the Andhras and their coinage, the Indo-Parthian Dynasties, the Sakas in Northern India, the Indian Travels of Apollonius of Tyana and others. But it was to the *Journal of the Royal Asiatic Society* that he contributed most frequently. His first article to the Journal was on the coinage of the Guptas written in 1889, and the last ones, contributed only a short time before his death, were on the invasion of the Punjab by the Sassanian Ardeshir of Persia, and the identification of the Ka-pi-li country of the Chinese authors.

First Literary Productions.

His first literary productions bore on the history and architecture of the province of Bundlekhand. It was from these first fruits that his grand scheme of compiling the ancient history of Northern India developed. He soon came to be considered as an expert authority in the study of coins; and his monographs on the Gupta coinage were specially valuable and formed the basis of a paper which he read before the International Congress of Orientalists in 1892. It was he who wrote extensively on the Gupta Dynasty and brought home to Indians the greatness and glory of India under their rule. In 1896 he published a memorandum on the Buddhist Remains in Kasia (Gorakhpur District). This memorandum, written at the express request of Sir Antony Macdonnell, the then Lieutenant-Governor of the United Provinces, adduced various arguments to disprove the theory of Sir Alexander Cunningham that Kasia was identical with Kusinagara where the Buddha attained *Nirvana.* In a paper which he subsequently contributed to the *Journal of the Royal Asiatic Society* in 1902, he further asserted that the scene of the Buddha's death was to besought in the Nepal country. Dr. Vogel who was entrusted with the work of excavations at Kasia has come across a number of inscribed clay seals which were found bearing dates from *cir* 400 to *cir* 900 A. D. belonging to the Congregation of the Reverend Friars of the Temple of the Great Decease. If they should belong to the spot where they were found—the variety of their dates and the similarity of their legends would suggest this conclusion—they would then vindicate Cunningham's identification and refute Dr. Smith's conclusions.

Another Government work was undertaken by him, *viz.*, *The Jain Stupas and other Antiquities of Mathura* (1901). The book was based on the previous labours of Dr. Fuhrer of the Lahore Museum; but it contains a few suggestive notes from the pen of Dr. Smith. In the same year was published *Asoka, the Buddhist Emperor of India*, one in the series of the *Rulers of India*, a popular yet scholarly account of the great Buddhist emperor "who sought to combine the piety of the monk with the wisdom of the king and to make India the kingdom of righteousness as he conceived it, a theocracy without a God; in which the Government should act the part of Providence and guide the people in the right way." This book was intended to be the first of the *Rulers of India* series and by Professor Rhys Davids. But circumstances led to Dr. Smith taking up the task; and he accomplished it as thoroughly and efficiently as the great scholar of Pali Buddhism would have done. He relied mainly on Buhler's translations of Asoka's inscriptions, but checked them by comparison with the versions of other scholars. He was the first writer to arrive at a true estimate of the historical value of the legends enveloping Asoka and keep them separate from authentic history. A second edition of *Asoka* came out in 1909; and yet a third was in preparation at the time of the author's death.

THE EARLY HISTORY OF INDIA.

In 1904 appeared the first part of his long-contemplated history as *The Early His-*

tory of India—the result of antiquarian studies in the shape of a connected relation of the lost history of India, made possible by the researches of a multitude of scholars spread over a century. This was a very ambitious and arduous task where "the materials are so imperfect, the lacunae so great and so much is in dispute." The epigraphic evidence had been digested and finally settled for two periods only, the age of Asoka and that of the Guptas; with regard to the period of the Sakas, Parthians and Kushans matters have long been in dispute. The evidence of coins is very scanty altogether east of Allahabad, while the testimony of Greek writers and Chinese travellers is limited to certain brief periods. The Puranas are not very useful in the work of construction; and the chance references to historical events in native literature are still less valuable. It is only from the time of the Guptas that matters improve somewhat; and before the close of the mediæval period we begin to have some real local histories like Kalhana's *Rajatarangini*. As Dr. Vogel has remarked "generally speaking, we have darkness illuminated by gleams of light, and although the outlines are perceptible the details are unknown."

Dr. Smith's preliminary studies on Alexander's campaigns, on Asoka, the Indo-Scythians, the Kushans, the Gandhara sculptures, the coinage and chronology of the Guptas have acquainted scholars with the views that he systematised in his *Early History*. This work the learned author humbly regarded but as "the taking stock of the accumulated stores of knowledge." The work was so highly appreciated and the edition was so rapidly sold out, that a second improved edition appeared in 1908. The full acknowledgment of the Parthian influence is the chief feature of the second edition, as well as a fuller treatment of the mediæval history of Northern India which was "meagre, lifeless and inadequate" in the first edition. The history of South India was also largely rewritten; and Kanouj had its history elaborated since, in the words of the writer, "Kanouj was to the uprising Rajput tribes what ancient Rome was to the Northern Barbarians, and Byzantium to mediæval Europe."

A third and improved edition was brought out in 1914 which, according to the author, is "a view of the early history of India as it appears to me after nearly forty years of study." He continues;

"It is as accurate and up-to-date as I can make it, but does not pretend to be final, because finality in a work dealing with a subject so progressive is unattainable. The mass of new matter and fresh

discussion accumulated since the publication of the last edition little more than five years ago, is so great that difficulty has been experienced in maintaining the decision to confine the book within the limits of a single volume of reasonable size and moderate price.

In this edition much new matter was inserted regarding the age of the Puranas, Kautilya's *Artha-Sastra*, the Kushans and the Andhras and the mediæval history of Kanouj and Bengal.

Dr. Smith, in the *Early History*, designedly confined himself to the plain narration of of political events. His dictum was that a sound frame-work of dynastic annals must be provided before the story of Indian religion, literature and art can be told aright. The book was designed to be primarily a political history and a presentation of dynastic facts, and not "an encyclopædia of Indian antiquities as some critics seem to think that it ought to be." The hope that sustained the author in this apparently dull task of collaborating the results of researchers was expressed in his own words thus:—

"Although the names of even the greatest monarchs of Ancient India are at present unfamiliar to the general reader and awaken few echoes in the minds of any, save specialists, it is not unreasonable to hope that an orderly presentation of the ascertained facts of ancient Indian history may be of interest to a larger circle than that of professed Orientalists, and that, as the subject becomes more familiar to the

reading public, it will be found no less worthy of attention than better known departments of historical study."

Dr. Smith remarks, with a generous enthusiasm for Ancient India, rare among English civilians, and echoing the words of an Indian writer, that

"India suffers to-day, in the estimation of the world, more through the world's ignorance of the achievements of the heroes of Indian history than through the absence or insignificance of such achievements."

In his work he has proved conclusively that the deeds of our great ancestors like Asoka, Chandra Gupta, Vikramaditya and Harsha, not to speak of a host of lesser figures, are fully worthy of remembrance and deserving of rescue from the oblivion in which they have been buried for so many centuries.

THE CATALOGUE OF COINS.

In 1906 Dr. Smith issued the first volume of *The Catalogue of Coins in the Indian Museum, Calcutta.* Dr. Smith has given us within the covers of a single volume a succinct account of all the ancient and mediæval non-Mussalman coinage of India which would serve as a hand-book to the student by enabling him to easily find out the class to which belongs any specimen that he might have.

HISTORY OF FINE ART IN INDIA & CEYLON.

The next great work of Dr. Smith is his *History of Fine Art in India and Ceylon* (1911). In this fine volume was presented for the first time a comprehensive survey of the whole field of Indian fine art in all its branches, from its beginnings to the present day.

Dr. Smith's treatment of the development of Indian fine art is practical though not always consistent. He first deals with the indigenous styles of architecture, but includes early importations of foreign methods as in the case of the Gandhara sculptures. Later, foreign influences are dealt with, connected with the Central Asian and Persian art introduced by successive Mussalman invasions. He deals with the art of Ceylon, the sculptures of Java and the architecture of Tibet. Tibetan and Javanese art can however be considered Indian only so far as their original inspiration is concerned; and each shows signs of varying ethnical elements. The chapters on architecture may be compared with great advantage with the latest edition of Fergusson, as revised by Burgess, especially in the part relating to Muhammadan buildings.

For the benefit of Indian schoolboys he compiled in 1912 a small manual, *The Ox ford History of England*, and also wrote *The Oxford Students' History of India*, a short work which has gone through several editions.

AKBAR, THE GREAT MOGUL.

In 1917 was published his *Akbar, The Great Mogul, 1542-1605*. In the preface to this book he wrote :

> "Twenty-four years ago when I was editing the *Rambles and Recollections* of Sir William Sleeman, and was under the influence of that author's enthusiastic comment that 'Akbar has always appeared to me among sovereigns what Shakespeare was among poets,' I recorded the opinion that the competent scholar who will undertake the exhaustive treatment of the life and reign of Akbar will be in possession of perhaps the finest great historical subject as yet unappropriated."

The hope that he would be that competent scholar had at last become a reality : and as a result of two years' strenuous labour he produced this biography which he thought "although not on the scale once planned, may be at least better than anything now in existence on the subject." Elphinstone's estimate of Akbar, written in 1839, though accurate so far as it goes, was based on a limited number of authorities which alone were then available. He had not access to the abundant Jesuit testimony written in the Latin and Romance tongues which has subsequently been made accessible to scholars by the efforts of Father Hosten and others. The *Commentaries* of Monserrate, du Jarric, Peruschi, and various other contemporary Jesuit missionaries who were invited to the Mogul court, as well as the writings of early European travellers have been made full use of by Dr. Smith. One outstanding feature of Dr. Smith's book is that it brings out prominently the greatness and the genius of Tulsi Das—"the tallest tree in the magic garden of mediæval Hindu poesy."

Akbar's greatness does not come out scathless from Dr. Smith's pen; but the picture that he draws is not an unfair one on the whole. He says:

"Although I have ventured to indicate that it is a mistake to regard Akbar as perfect, I do not wish to leave the impression of being insensible to his real greatness.........He founded or at least re-founded the Mogul Empire which received from him life and vigour enough to endure as a great power for a century after his death, He had the broad views of a true far-seeing statesman and knew how to choose, use and keep loyal servants. His policy of impartial toleration was all his own. Personally he was one of the most kingly of kings and his superlative qualities

enabled him to keep a firm hand upon the sceptre even to the end. His aberrations must be viewed in proper perspective and should be regarded as only spots on the Sun."

This is indeed far removed from the picture that an Indian writer would draw of the great Emperor who sought to unite the Hindus and the Mussalmans and who appeared to the learned Abul Fazl as "the Orient where the light of form and ideal dawns"; and "a guide to the world of action, and a comforter in lovely retirement."

THE OXFORD HISTORY OF INDIA.

Dr. Smith's *Oxford History of India*, published in 1919, was his last great work. Its purpose is to provide a compendious up-to-date history of India as a whole, based on the results of modern research and marked by "scrupulous accuracy of statement and impartiality of judgment." The period treated covers nearly 3,000 years and the information given is encyclopædic in its variety and value. Even hostile critics have to acknowledge its distinctive merits of comprehensiveness, painstaking thoroughness and an intimate study of all available material. Yet we are tempted to ask, after a perusal of the book, whether the author's reputation for impartial judgment would not have been greater had he died before he brought out the work. Its demerits from the Indian national and patriotic points of view greatly outweigh its good features.

As Mr. Benoy Kumar Sarkar has remarked :

> Dr. Smith has been led in spite of himself to interpret the entire story with an eye to the event of 1757, as if the three or four thousand years of Hindu political life and Indo-Saracenic evolution were merely preliminary to Plassey."

Occasionally he throws light on the economic conditions of various epochs, but always shows a tendency to contrast British plenty and security with the misery and poverty of the people in pre-British times.

Dr. Smith has presumably intended this volume to be a hand-book on loyalty and to create the impression that the British Empire in India is "the only empire in the world's history which is not stained with the blood of innocents." "The author has neither the enthusiasm of a Guizot, nor the scholarly eloquence of a John Richard Green, for the theme of his investigations and his style seldom rise above that of a gazetteer writer."

HIS LAST WORK.

The last work of his that we have got to notice is *Indian Constitutional Reform Viewed in the Light of History* (1919). This only confirms us in the belief that Dr. Smith was intensely sceptical about the ability of Indians to govern themselves or show any true democratic progress. Perhaps it was an irony of fate that the rescuer of ancient Indian history and greatness from oblivion should become the deprecator of the modern Indian's capacity for political progress!

We have noticed all his works except his editions of Bernier's *Travels in the Mogul Empire* and of Sleeman's *Rambles and Recollections of an Indian Official* and his contributions to *The Oxford Survey of the British Empire*. His death has cut off a prominent worker in the field of Indian History and in him India has lost a valuable pioneer in collation and many lines of research.

Arthur Berriedale Keith

AMONG the younger generation of Sanskrit scholars, from whom the Oriental world may well expect a substantial contribution to the further exploration and elucidation of the knotty problems in the domain of Sanskritic research, we have no hesitation in assuring our readers that Dr. A. B. Keith will hold the premier place among them. A man of good physique, with a massive and commanding head, Dr. Keith is always genial and pleasant to all who may have occasion to approach him. There is that atmosphere of scholarly brilliance about him, that attracts towards him many an ardent young inquirer, with confidence.

Arthur Berriedale Keith was born on April 5th, 1879. After completing his early education at Edinburgh, he entered the University of Oxford in 1897 as an under-graduate of Balliol College, which was then the most coveted of colleges, Dr. Benjamin Jowett's (master) fame being still quite green. During the five years of his academical career at Balliol, Keith did full justice to the high intellectual traditions of his *Alma Mater*. He won the Boden Sanskrit Scholarship in 1898 and qualified himself for the B. A. degree, passing with first-class in two successive years in two different branches of knowledge —first-class in 'Oriental Studies' in 1900 and first-class in Literaris Humanioris in 1901. His successes did not stop here. He took the degree of Bachelor of Civil Law in 1905 and became a Doctor of Civil Law in 1911. He was also admitted to the Degree of Master of Arts at Edinburgh University, in 1897. Besides these he also won seven class medals, three scholarships and the Guthrie Fellowship in Classics at Edinburgh, and the Fergusson Scholarship in Classics at Glasgow. By dint of his indomitable energy and acute brain, he easily won the first places in the Home Civil Service and the Indian Civil Service Examinations.

In 1901 he entered Government Service at the Colonial Office in London. Very often he was called upon to undertake work of far-reaching national importance requiring the greatest tact. These he fulfilled not only to his own satisfaction, but also to the admiration and gratitude of the parties concerned. In 1903, he received thanks from the British Agent for services in connection with Alaska Boundary Arbitration. From 1903-05, he was Secretary to the Crown Agents for the Colonies, and later on served the Colonial Office in various capacities. Meanwhile he entered the Inner Temple as Barrister in 1904 with Honours Certificate, having been first in the Final Examination. In 1907, he represented His Majesty's Government at the Colonial Navigation Conference. In 1910 he was Secretary to the Imperial Copyright Conference and also Junior Assistant Secretary to the Imperial Conference. He received the Coronation Medal in 1911. From 1912 he was Private Secretary to the Permanent Under-Secretary of State for the Colonies for some years.

During 1907-08 when Professor Macdonell was out on tour in India, Dr. Keith was appointed Deputy to the Boden Professor of Sanskrit. About 1915 when Professor Eggeling of the Edinburgh University left for Europe, Dr. Keith was appointed to the vacant Regius Professorship of Sanskrit at that University. Dr. Keith resigned his Colonial Office appointment and took up the Professorship. Since then he has had comparative leisure which has enabled him to devote himself more assiduously to Sanskrit.

In 1904 Dr. Keith published a Catalogue of Sanskrit and Prakrit MSS. in the Indian Institute, Oxford, and in 1906 was published in colloboration with Professors Aufrecht and Winternitz '*the Catalogue of Sanskrit MSS.*' in the Bodleian Library, Oxford. These two catalogues must have taxed him not a little; and they already exhibited unmistakable signs of his devotion to duty and masterly accuracy of minute details—elements so essential to an efficient scholar.

1907 saw the publication of his '*State Succession in International Law.* In 1909 he published his translation of the *Sankhayana Aranyaka.*

In 1909 he published his book on "*Responsible Government in the Dominions.*" which, in its enlarged edition of three volumes, won for him the Doctorate in Civil Law at the Oxford University in 1911. Even to-day, this book commands a wide popularity and is quoted frequently as an authority on the subject.

In 1910 he published the *Aitareya Aranyaka* with critical text, notes, translation and introduction and also issued a 'Supplement to Aufrecht's Catalogue of Sanskrit MSS. in the Bodleian Library.' In 1911 he published his "Catalogue of Prakrit MSS." in the Bodleian Library, and in 1911 he collaborated with Professor Macdonell in his edition of "Vedic Index of Names and Subjects" published in two volumes.

In 1914, he published the greatest of his extant works. *The Veda of the Black Yajus School* entitled the *Taittiriya Samhita,* being a translation from the original Sanskrit prose and verse, in two volumes, in the famous "Harvard Oriental Series." This is an invaluable work to scholars.

In 1916, Dr. Keith published his "Imperial Unity and Dominions". Part I of this book deals with limitations of the autonomy of the Dominions and their possible relaxation while Part II deals with the possibities of union. In 1918 he published in the "World's Classics" "Selected Speeches and Documents on British Colonial Policy, 1763-1917" in two volumes and in 1919 appeared his book on "The Belgian Congo and the Berlin Act."

Professor Keith has been of recent years engaged in writing short, lucid and instructive manuals on Indian Philosophy. In 1918 he published in the "Heritage of India Series", his work on "*Samkhya System.*" This work deals with the development of the fundamental doctrines of the Samkhya school historically and is the best readable book on the subject and can well serve as a very good introductory book to students. He published in 1921 a companion volume to the above on *Karma Mimamsa*. Mimamsa has always been a 'White Elephant' to students, European and Indian alike. Professor Keith deals with the subject exhaustively, though in a short compass, under the headings—the Development and Literary History of the Karma Mimamsa, the Problem of Knowledge, the World of Reality,

God, the Soul and Matter, the Rules of Ritual Interpretation, and the Mimamsa and Hindu Law.

Besides having been on many committees, Professor Keith has been a member of many learned societies. He is member of the International Colonial Institute, the Royal Asiatic Society of Great Britain and Ireland, the Hellenic, African and Hardwicke Societies, and the American and German Oriental Societies. His articles and reviews have often appeared in the Journals of the Royal Asiatic Society and the Society of Comparative Legislation, as well as in the *Zeitschrift der Deutschen Morgenlandischen Gesselschaft.*

We are just in receipt of two of his latest works, representative of the two departments of knowledge that claim him as an authority. The Oxford University Press which have published most of his others works, announce his "Dominion Home Rule in Practice" as well as his "Indian Logic and Atomism". The latter work must be of great value to Sanskritists as our Nyaya and Vaiseshika systems have always been, to the Western scholars, very hard nuts to crack.

Professor Keith is still in the prime of his manhood and much may be expected of him.

Bal Gangadhar Tilak*

TILAK is well known as a politician of great power and personality, who did his best to promote the political freedom of his country. Yet, the field of politics to which he devoted the best years of his life was not the one for which he was made. Tilak was by nature a scholar and only by necessity a politician. Not for nothing did he come from the Mahratta country. Latterly it has not been possible for the thinking minds of India to be indifferent to the political situation. The subjection of the country worked persistently on the mind of Tilak and triumphed over his natural bent. Politics in India, when taken up seriously, is not only exacting but also exhausting. If one has to succeed in it, one must give up all other pursuits. The jealous mistress cannot brook the rivalry of other intellectual exercises involving patient labour and continued thought. Tilak who fell a victim to the political struggle was unable for a long time to give his best to

---

* For biographical details see "Tilak" in *Biographies of Eminent Indians Series.* G. A. Natesan & Co., Madras.

Oriental studies. The Government however came to his rescue and enabled him to practise a little more economy of interest, by forcibly retiring him from public life. The prison cell was the place where his brave soul could pursue its congenial vocation. In the ten years of enforced leisure spent in Mandalay and elsewhere, Tilak did his best literary work, by which he will be remembered even after his fame, as a politician, grows dim.

Tilak's literary work is not the traditional distraction of an unemployed statesman. As a rule, the transformation of a professional politician into a man of letters is not successful. But Tilak's natural aptitude had been in the direction of Oriental studies and so we find in his work, instead of the discursiveness of the amateur, the solid learning and the keen insight of a trained scholar.

While his chief investigations in Oriental scholarship are in the domain of the Vedas and the Bhagavad Gita, he also wrote several miscellaneous essays on kindred topics, the chief of them being an article on "A Missing Verse in the Sankhya-Karikas." His discussions, as we shall see, are marked by a very liberal spirit. He does not accept everything established; nor does he slavishly adhere to authorities, Eastern or Western, in the interpretation of ancient texts.

The *Orion* is an essay on the antiquity of the Vedas. Pressing into service his great knowledge of astronomy, Tilak argues that the hymns of the Rig Veda, those at any rate which have a reference to the word *Agrayana* or *Agrahayana*, must have been composed at a time when the year began with the Sun in the constellation of *Orion* or ***Mrigasirsha*** *i.e.*, before 4000 B.C. From the Greek tradition of *Orion*, he infers that it was also the period before the Greeks separated from the Hindus. Tilak's presentation of his case elicited warm praise from eminent scholars like Max Muller and Jacobi, Weber and Whitney. According to Bloomfield, "the book is unquestionably the literary sensation of the year—history, the chronic re-adjuster, shall have her hands uncommonly full to assimilate the results of Tilak's discovery and arrange her paraphernalia in the new perspective."

In his next work, *The Arctic Home of the Aryans*, Tilak makes out that the neighbourhood of the North Pole was the original home of the Aryans. He bases his conclusions on the results of research in Geology and Archælogy. The Arctic regions, though they are now desolate and unfit for human habitation, enjoyed, before the glacial epoch, a mild and temperate climate fit for habitation. There are indirect references in the Vedas to some astronomical phenomena peculiar to the North Pole such as those of day for six months and night for six months. On the hypothesis of a long night of six months, the rapturous utterances about the dawn and the anxiety relating to it are easily explained. Corroborative evidence from the Zend-Avesta is cited. Of course a theory so startling in its nature is not easily accepted. It is however acknowledged that Tilak made out a good case for his position. According to Dr. Warren, "the array of evidences set forth is far more conclusive than any ever attempted by an Indo-Iranian scholar in the interest of any earlier hypothesis. Absolute candour and respect for the strictest methods of historical and scientific investigation characterise the discussion throughout."

In the second number of *Sanskrit Research*, (Oct. 1915) is found the article on "*A Missing Verse in the Sankhya-Karikas.*" Tilak points out that there is a consensus of authority for the view that the Sankhya Karikas are seventy in number. If we exclude last three verses which do not belong to the doctrinal part of the text,—they give us only the Guruparampara or the line of succession of teacher and pupil—we have only 69 verses in the Indian (Gaudapada's) and the Chinese (Paramartha's) editions. One verse is missing.

Tilak tries to trace the lost verse with his acute powers of deduction.

The commentaries in the two editions contain a passage developing a refutation of the four possible causes of the world : Iswara, (God), Purusha (Soul), Kala (Time) and Swabhava (Nature). The commentator argues that the first two being nirguna, cannot be the cause of the saguna world and the last two being vyakta cannot be subtler than the avyakta, Prakriti. Obviously this discussion should be based on some text. The 61st Karika contends that Prakriti is the cause of the world and there is nothing more subtle than that (Sukumarathara). The comparative degree suggests that the author of the Karikas had in view other alternative hypotheses. Besides, the commentator introduces the discussion of the four possible causes by the statement, "Tatra sukumaratharam Varnayati." [He describes (the meaning of) subtler]. From the contents of the commentary Tilak works up the verse which reads as follows:

Karanameeswarameke purusham kalam pare swabhavam va
Prajah katham nirgunatho vyaktah kalah swabhavascha

Tilak, a born fighter of evil and injustice, did not feel inclined to support the quietistic interpretation of the teaching of the Bhagavad Gita. It is not right to think that one on whom the light of God's peace has settled, need not worry about the work of the world. Wisdom or Jnana is not an end in itself. Moral heroism is the fruit of the heavenly vision. The scholastic commentators have used the Bhagavad Gita in the interests of their own metaphysical and religious views and twisted out of its shape the true message of the Gita. Tilak attempts to restore the natural sense of the Bhagavad Gita by making Karma Yoga its central secret.

It is needless to say that it is Tilak's robust patriotism that predisposed his mind to this activistic view. It is often said, not without justification, that the spirit of contemplation and repose is responsible for the present state of the country. The Indian accepts the principle "my mind to me a kingdom is" and bows to the inevitable in a spirit of resignation. Tilak makes out that the Gita, which has a supreme place in Indian spiritual life, stands for the do-and-dare spirit. The whole setting of the Gita supports Tilak's view. Arjuna comes to the battlefield to fight the enemy but at the psychological moment shrinks from his duty. Looking at friends and comrades arrayed on both sides, his heart is torn with anguish, his mind is divided by doubt and he lays down his bow under the impression that it is not proper for him to trample on the ties of kindred and slay those who deserve worship. The message of the Gita enables him to take up his bow and fight. It is not action that is forbidden but interested action. So long as the heart of man vibrates in perfect harmony with the Supreme Self, action does not result in entangling him in the world of Samsara. It is silly to shrink from our appointed task, afraid of the consequences. The Gita asks us to work in imitation of the Lord, for the purpose of Lokasangraha or unification of the entire humanity in the bonds of a deep and common sympathy. The Bhagavad Gita is designed as a solution of the universal problem of life. It reconciles spiritual freedom with work in the world. Mere sense of repose or mere devouring energy are extremes to be avoided. Work wedded to wisdom, Arjuna the Archer, guided by Krishna the Seer or the Yogeswara, is the ideal.

There are however passages in the Gita which declare that the final end is the calm of an immutable self in whose equality and oneness, we cast off all desire and passion. If it be so, then no action is possible in the ultimate condition. Sankara takes his stand on these texts. The Gita gives us also the vision of a divine being from whom all, world and souls, proceed. Freedom is to become one with Him. We do not so much die in Him as recover our lives in Him by an integral self-finding. On this view, action is compatible with freedom. Whether activism or quietism is the truth of the ultimate state is thus not a question of ethics, but one of metaphysics. Tilak seems to adopt Sankara's view in metaphysics though he fights shy of its logical implication of quietism. If the inactive, inpartial, immutable self is the reality, then freedom means a passage from the world of action into one of inaction. If, on the other hand, it is possible for us to be active in the freed state, then Sankara's reality is not the final expression of truth. Perhaps Tilak had in his own mind reconciled Sankara's metaphysics with ethical activism. It is however not brought out in his writings.

Paul Deussen.

THAT the Orientalist in the realm of Sanskrit should possess a profound knowledge of that language is, perhaps, a truism. That the Orientalist in the realm of Sanskrit (or Indian) philosophy should himself be a philosopher seems not to be equally apparent. And yet, nothing can be more evident on a little reflection than that the categories, the *Weltanschauung* of a system of philosophy can best be appreciated only by one whose Spirit has been through the Dialectic mill. In the world of thought, as in that of perception, preparedness accounts for a great deal of the final apprehension; the apperceptive system accounts for much more than is usually laid to its credit. Nowhere else has this been made clear, perhaps, as much as in India, where systems have been appraised, praised and condemned for very various and conflicting reasons by various rival schools. Sankara, the stern opponent of Buddhism, was known in this country as *pracchanna Bauddha*. And the present writer remembers a very able plea set forth by an Indian medical man in London, a plea for logical *materialism*; and the logical materialism he advocated was the *Advaita Vedanta*.

At a time when we in this country had become apathetic towards all that was Indian culture, when we required to be re-assured of its value only by chits from Western savants, it required not merely a Sanskritist, but a philosopher to wake us up to the realisation of our own philosophical heritage. A philosopher, be it noted, not one acquainted with philosophical jargon, nor a student of the history of philosophy. The mischief that a scholar of the latter kind can perpetrate is painfully evident in the *Philosophy of the Upanishads* by A. E. Gough. According to this writer, "the real movement of philosophic thought begins, it is true, not in India, but in Ionia" (p. v); "I think he (the general reader) will pronounce that India had little intellectual wealth for exportation to the Alexandrian Emporium" (p. xii). The very name of Absolutism seems to be anathema to this person. Anyone who cannot get out of such an atmosphere of prejudice cannot deserve to be considered a philosopher. We had, therefore, to wait for a philosopher in very truth to interpret to us and to the Western world the significance of a metaphysics that had so long failed to be understood. And this philosopher was Prof. Paul Deussen of the University of Kiel.

The fact of primary significance in Deussen's work is that he came to the study of Indian philosophy *as* a philosopher. He was not primarily a Sanskritist. His study of Sanskrit under Prof. Lassen was, as in the case of many other great things of the world, a matter of accident. There was no one to advise him to take up the study, none to encourage him therein except his Professor. The study was taken up because it was found to be attractive, and persisted in because the student was Deussen. The result of that study was the production of the two monumental works on *The System of the Vedanta* and *The Philosophy of the Upanishads*, not to mention his translation of the *Sixty Upanishads*, and other works of less note. The *Elemente der Metaphysic*, however, deserves special mention, as a noteworthy attempt to make the Western metaphysical student get familiar with and assimilate Indian metaphysical conceptions.

Deussen was steeped in the philosophies of Plato and Aristotle, Spinoza and Kant. When he came to the study of Indian philosophy, notably the *Advaita Vedanta,* he could not help remarking the extraordinary similarity between this system and that of Kant. The Kantian philosophy, according to Deussen, supplies the scientific back-ground for *Vedantist* metaphysics. The similarity between Spinozism and the *Vedanta* is not less clear but this is not a fruitful analogy, as both can be (and are) dismissed as merely mystical. Kant was interested in the sciences, mathematical and physical, and in establishing their validity; and it was in pursuing this inquiry that he evolved his own metaphysics. If this metaphysics can be shown to be very similar to, perhaps substantially identical with, the *Vedanta*, surely it will be a triumph for the latter; for it can no longer be dismissed as a misty and mystical dream. Such was the line of thought and the procedure adopted by Deussen.

Kant, by examination of the validity of the sciences, had found that the forms of perception—Space and Time—and the categories of the understanding—Causality etc.—are subjective and are super-imposed by us upon the external manifold. The manifold comes to us first through our own forms of perception, and is then distinguished and related by our understanding under its categories. The empirical world which is manifest to us is, in this sense, our own creation. But it is none the less real, being the only world that can be known by our senses and the understanding. The sciences cannot dispute this subjectivity, which is their only true objectivity, for in seeking objectivity elsewhere, they inevitably land in scepticism and commit suicide, as David Hume had shown. This world, then, is empirically real. But there is still the Thing-in-itself, outside of and beyond our categories, that which is presented as the manifold of sense and is systematised by the understanding. To this our mental faculties do not apply. And this, considered as the real, makes our world but ideal. The world we know is empirically real, but transcendentally ideal. This transcendent reality may not be known by Pure Reason; but Practical Reason which holds its sway in the domain of action, demands its postulation.

The *Vedanta* considers time, space, and causality as essentially subjective modes of apprehension. *Brahman* is above these modes and cannot be known through them. But the world, as apprehended through these modes, is not unreal, though it is not real *as such.* For the practical man, the man who is still at the *Vyavaharika* stage (what Deussen calls the exoteric stage) of apprehension, this world of particulars is real. Such knowledge, however, is not *Paramarthika.* (esoteric). From that point of view, the empirical world becomes ideal, a creation of *Maya*. *Brahman,* which for the *paramarthika jnani* is the sole real, cannot be known by reasoning. It is, rather, to be understood from the *Sruti,* the words of the Rishis—great seers and noble men—and then realised in *anubhava.*

All this indicates a striking resemblance to the Kantian system. And the credit for perceiving the resemblance and bringing it out must go to Prof. Deussen. It cannot be doubted that one result at least of this work was a stimulus to a closer and a more scientific study of the *Vedanta* than had been attempted earlier. And the study that has been the result of such a stimulus has been all to the good of India.

One peculiarity of Deussen's exposition may be noted. Systematic German that he is, he always divides his subject under the four heads—Theology, Psychology, Cosmology, and Eschatology. This classification is present in all his expositions of the Vedanta, whether in a short lecture or in a lengthy treatise. His method, like the subject of his exposition—the Vedantic Brahman—seems to be *anoraniyan mathormahiyan*. That such a method is of considerable value to the student goes without saying.

It will be doing a disservice to Prof. Deussen and the magnitude of his work, if we fail to draw attention to the defects of his analogy. The resemblance he has brought out is important, but the difference is at least as important. And it is in noting this difference that the comparative study of the *Vedanta* and Western metaphysics should receive a fresh stimulus. The Kantian

Thing-in-itself has been well characterised as an irrelevant ghost. If our forms and categories are complete in themselves, if they can and do constitute a workable world, where is the necessity for invoking this abstraction? If, on the contrary, these forms which constitute our mental furniture are essentially defective and call for completion from without, their defective nature must be exhibited as also their mode of completion in this Thing-in-itself. The transcendent reality must be exhibited as an immanent necessity of our empirical world itself. This Kant does not show. And then, the dualism of the Pure and the Practical Reason. Does Pure Reason know that it cannot know the Real? Then, does it not transcend its limits in possessing even this degree of knowledge?

Such are the main defects of the Kantian system. They are not reproduced, but got over in the *Advaita Vedanta*. Time, Space, and Causality are considered defective, not because they are subjective (for all knowledge must be so in some sense or other) but because of their inherent nature. These categories cannot be conceived intelligibly except when so whittled down as necessarily to posit the absolute *Brahman*. The concept of causality, for instance, does not bear analysis. We are finally reduced to saying that the same thing must be cause *as it were*, and effect *as it were*; and this is but the Advaita doctrine. Thus is exhibited the immanent necessity of the postulation of *Brahman*.

Again, *Brahman* is not a Thing-in-itself standing over and above the empirical world. It is that which is immanent in our world, and it is also that in which our world lives and moves and has its being. "Who but for that atmosphere of *ananda* can move or even breathe?" asks the *Taittiriya*. It is the ocean into which all individual streams flow and are merged. This is not the negation of individuality, either, but its perfection, for how else can the river fulfil its individuality but by flowing into the sea?

The distinction between intellect and intuition is not absolute in the *Vedanta*. One has to walk here with careful steps as this is controversial ground. This much at least will be admitted by all, *viz.*, that the faculty wherewith *Brahman* is realised is conceived rather as something which fulfils Reason, making of use of Reason in the earlier stages of the inquiry, than as an entirely independent and distinct faculty. This in itself indicates that the *Advaitic* distinction bears but little resemblance to that between the Pure and the Practical Reason. Further, there are numerous passages in Advaitic works where the demonstration of Brahman by Reason is attempted. One such is a chapter of the *Gaudapada Karikas* on the *Mandukya Upanishad.* The condemnation of Reason, as it occurs in the *Vedanta Sutras,* is again suggestive. ***Brahman*** cannot be known by Reason as it ***(Brahman)*** has no characteristic marks. This would seem to suggest the absence of a middle term, which absence makes syllogistic reasoning impossible. The inference does not seem to be unwarranted, that what the Advaitin condemns is not Reason, but the syllogising faculty. It has been contended that the *Vedantin,* far from condemning Reason, has indeed a much higher conception of it than is to be met with anywhere else in the metaphysics of the East or the West. (See in particular two articles by Mr. V. Subramanya Aiyar, Registrar, Mysore University, one in in the *Sanskrit Research,* July, 1915, and the other in the *Indian Philosophical Review,* Vol. I. Mr. Subramanya Aiyar, it may be mentioned, seemed to find considerable support for his thesis from the late Nrisimha Bharati, the late incumbent of the Sringeri Mutt).

These considerations lead us to imagine that a comparison of the *Vedanta* with later Western metaphyics, as expounded by Hegel or by his English followers, Bradley and Bosanquet, will be more fruitful at the present day. We may now be told that all that was said earlier about the value of apperceptive systems and so on has been falsified by Deussen's own example! The comparison between Kant and Sankara is not very exact; and this inexactitude was not noted by Deussen. Should this not be set down to his prepossession in favour of Kant, to his looking at the *Vedanta* through Kantian spectacles? This may be admitted. And yet it would not follow therefrom that he or another scholar without any prepossessions would have done better. As likely as not, the supposed absence of pre-conceived notions may be a symbol of intellectual inanity. Man, as finite, is limited to angles of vision; the synoptic vision of man, as infinite, must be a development which includes and transcends the finite point of view. To do without points of view at all, because each as such is defective, can only lead to closing the eyes firmly and refusing to see anything. To use a particular view-point—the best attainable—and then rise superior to its limitations, that is the mark of the truly great man.

What we have had to say, by way of criticism of Deussen's work, should not be taken as minimising its value. Deussen must be taken to be the pioneer of this comparative study, the value of which is so apparent, but the pursuit so rare. If we at the present day or in times to come, pursue that path and enrich our philosophical literature, our thanks will in no small measure be due to him. The ignorance of Sanskrit prevalent when he began the study of that language and thè prejudices he had to overcome cannot easily be imagined. The admirers of Sir William Jones have set up a statue for him in St. Paul's, and on the pedestal are inscribed the words *Courma Avatar* underneath the figure of a fish rising out of the waters. And in the second decade of the twentieth century, Mr. William Archer—an eminent art critic and a Liberal politician—wrote a book about *India and the Future*, which bade fair to become notorious. These may illustrate to some degree the ignorance and prejudice mentioned above. It will always be said to the lasting credit of Paul Deussen that with so little encouragement and living in such an atmosphere, he yet kept brightly burning his passion for Truth, and pursued her even through the baffling difficulties of a distant land, a dead language, an alien culture, and a remote age.

Dr. Bhandarkar.

EARLY LIFE AND OFFICIAL CAREER.

OF all the eminent Indians who adorned the past generation some of whom are happily alive, it would be difficult to name any one who represented what was best in Ancient Indian culture more finely than the veteran educationist, the great Sanskrit savant, reformer and revivalist—Sir Ramakrishna Gopal Bhandarkar. Those who are privileged to study, amidst the stormy political controversies of the day, the writings and speeches of the venerable sage, may well realise the need of the present generation, to cultivate those traits of character that won for Dr. Bhandarkar a high place in the republic of letters. Accurate in scholarship and always sound in judgment, of pleasant manners and yet possessed of an indomitable will, Dr. Bhandarkar's early life and career is a source of deep inspiration to young men of India. Thoroughly patriotic in the best sense of the word, Dr. Bhandarkar's life is a living example of what can be achieved by patience, perseverence and singleness of purpose.

Sir Ramakrishna Gopal Bhandarkar was born on 6th July 1837 of poor Maharashtra Brahmin parents. His father was a clerk under the Mamledar of Malwan. Want of facilities prevented young Bhandarkar from receiving a very early education. But when his father was transferred to the District Treasury of Ratnagiri which boasted of an English school, a great career opened itself before him. Young Bhandarkar entered the school at about the same time that some of his illustrious contemporaries such as Mandlik and Barve left it, to prosecute their studies in the Bombay institutions. After completing his education in the Ratnagiri school, Bhandarkar went to Bombay in 1853 and joined the Elphinstone College. There he studied under distinguished professors among whom was our illustrious patriot the late Dr. Dadabhai Nowrojee who was the first to perceive the genius in the boy. He was very assiduous in the college, devoting the day-time to discussions of Western ideas with his fellow-students while "he cheated sleep of a portion of its natural period, by the boyish expedient of tying his hair to the back of his chair as a precaution against an unwary nap." He devoted himself to the study of English literature, History, Natural Science and Mathematics, which last claimed his particular attention.

This partiality for Mathematics besides winning for him the admiration of Dr. Dadabhai Nowrojee, gave him a discipline of mind so essential for scholarly pursuits.

Passing his scholarship examinations, Bhandarkar was in due course appointed a Fellow and subsequently transferred to the Deccan College. It was there that he came in contact with Mr. Howard, the then Director of Public Instruction. Noticing the brilliant academic career of Bhandarkar and full of great hopes in the boy, Howard persuaded him to study Sanskrit. In the midst of his tutorial duties as a college Fellow, Dr. Bhandarkar applied himself diligently to this new task and ere long became very proficient in it. Then came great educational changes. The Bombay University was incorporated and all the Fellows of colleges who underwent the old college course were required to pass the new University tests. He took his B. A. degree in 1862 and his M.A. in 1863, both in English and Sanskrit. A curious mistake is said to have occurred regarding his B. A. results.—

"By a mistake—the University by the way, was even then liable to mistake—the marks assigned to a fellow-candidate were entered against his name and Mr. Bhandarkar was one of those who was found to have failed. He was thereupon ready with his resignation of the Fellowship. Fortunately however, Sir Alexander Grant who was one of the examiners, was struck with the result, being of opinion that the portion of the answer-paper which he himself examined, entitled Dr. Bhandarkar to more marks than were entered against his name for the whole paper. This led to the discovery of the mistake which was soon corrected."

Immediately after passing his M. A. examination, Dr. Bhandarkar thought of joining the law college. The legal profession has attracted some of its best men in the presidency of Madras. But, fortunately in Bombay, some of the most distinguished of our countrymen such as Dadabhai Nowrojee, Gopal Krishna Gokhale, and Dinsha Edulji Wacha, have been able to escape the charms of law. While Bhandarkar was thus hesitating, the tempting offer of the head-mastership of a High School at Hyderabad, (Sindh) was made to him. He at once closed with it and his career was shaped.

In 1865 Dr. Bhandarkar was transferred as the head-master of the Ratnagiri English School, his own "*Alma Mater.*" His management of the school is characterised by vast administrative improvements which practically saved the institution from dissolution. By this time, he had acquired fame by the publication of his first and second books in Sanskrit, text books which have since rendered the study of that language an easy one.

In recognition of his scholarship, the Bombay University first appointed Bhandarkar as one of its examiners in Sanskrit. It was as an examiner that he came to know that talented scholar and antiquarian, Dr. Kashinath Trimbak Telang.

In 1868, Colonel Waddington, the then Acting Director of Public Instruction, on the advice of Dr. Buhler, the great Orientalist, appointed Dr. Bhandarkar temporarily to the Sanskrit chair at Elphinstone College. His method of teaching and his masterly exposition of the subject soon brought crowded classes. The study of Sanskrit and Prakrit languages was by no means easy in those days and the "dry as dust" method of second-rate teachers had done everything to smother all interest in that branch of learning. But the analytical and synthetical methods pursued by the learned Doctor as well as his mastery of the subject soon gave a fresh impetus to the advancement of Sanskrit education on new lines. The lecture hours flew away rapidly, nobody knew how. Unlike the professors of the present day, Dr. Bhandarkar lived with his pupils as they lived with him. This intimate and personal contact with his students soon brought to the field of Oriental research a group of learned scholars.

Thus from November 1867 to 1872, he was acting as Professor of Oriental Languages in the Elphinstone College, Bombay. In 1872 the Sanskrit chair fell permanently vacant.

And contrary to all expectations, Dr. Bhandarkar was superseded and the professorship was given to Dr. Peterson, comparatively a junior. This was a great blow to him and any other in the same position would have felt the ignominy and retired into oblivion. But the revered professor had faith in himself and knew that, by patient waiting, the injustice rendered by the Government would be righted. That, however, he felt and long remembered this incident, this injustice due to colour prejudice, is evident from the following extract of a speech which he delivered in a meeting of the Bombay branch of the Royal Asiatic Society, held in 1899, to place on record its sense of the loss sustained by the death of its President, Dr. P. Peterson.

* * * *

"Dr. Peterson was brought out in January 1873 to supersede me. I had been Acting Professor of Oriental Languages in the Elphinstone College for four years from the beginning of 1867 to the end of 1872. Dr. Peterson was a young man of 25 and was junior to me by ten years. For 15 years before, I had been learning and teaching Sanskrit, while Dr. Peterson could have been studying it only for about 5 years before. Under the ordinary operation of our sinful human nature one would expect that distrust, suspicion and jealousy would have sprung up between us. But such feelings never for a moment took possession of his heart nor mine and a cordial friendship grew between us. * * * * Doctor Peterson was Professor and I his assistant and we worked harmoniously together."

Thus Dr. Bhandarkar continued as assistant to Dr. Peterson. In 1879, Dr. Bhandarkar acted for Professor Keilhorn as Professor of Sanskrit in the Deccan College, Poona, and on his retirement from service towards the close of 1881, Dr. Bhandarkar was made a 'pucca' professor and entered the graded service of the Bombay Education Department. The whole circumstance thus set forth by the Doctor himself will be of great interest.

Dr. Keilhorn of Poona was about to retire on that occasion and the idea had been conceived of getting out a new man from Germany to succeed him there: but since it was considered unfair that I should be passed over another time especially after the literary work I had done, it was arranged that I should be made Professor of Oriental Languages in the Elphinstone College and Dr. Peterson appointed Professor of English Literature. Had this plan succeeded, the world would not have heard of Dr. Peterson as a great scholar. But having deliberately chosen Sanskrit studies as the work of his life, this proposal was not liked by him. He saw the members of Government and personally protested against it in a strong manner and the result was that the orders for a new professor from Germany were countermanded by a special telegram and I was appointed to the Deccan College and Dr. Peterson remained Professor of Sanskrit in the Elphinstone College."

Thus as Professor, Dr. Bhandarkar retired from Government service in 1893. Both as Professor and as University Examiner his services were indispensable to the University and as a member of the Syndicate (1873-1882)' he took a leading part in regulating the affairs of the Bombay University. After his retirement, he was appointed as Vice-Chancellor of the Bombay University, a just and generous recognition by the Government of the great services rendered by the Doctor to the cause of education in general and of Sanskrit learning in particular.

LITERARY ACTIVITY.

The literary activity of Dr. Bhandarkar is almost coeval with the starting of the '*Indian Antiquary*'. That journal, as is well known, was started by James Burgess in 1872 with a view to bring together the results of the researches of Oriental scholars and Dr. Bhandarkar was one of those mainly relied upon to fill the columns of this journal. Nor did he fail to justify the expectations formed of him. Besides the *Antiquary* various research journals and organisations claimed his attention. He was for a long time member of the *Bombay Branch of the Royal Asiatic Society* and identified himself entirely with it. Dr. Bhandarkar and K. T. Telang belong to the third generation of the members of the Society. This Society was started in 1804 by that illustrious scholar and statesman, Sir James Mackintosh, and since then, has been doing yeoman service to the cause of Indian historical research. Membership was confined first exclusively to European scholars; but soon, the time came when European scholarship, unaided by Indian talent and erudition, could not go beyond a limited tether. The first Indian member to be admitted was a Parsi gentleman, Mr. Maneckjee Cursetjee, in 1840. The first Hindu to gain admission, which, in those days, was considered to be very difficult, was a famous Sanskrit scholar, Dr. Bhau Daji, whose collection of MSS. is one of the treasured possessions of the Society. Thus it was scholarship and sound learning that opened the doors of the *Bombay Branch of the Royal Asiatic Society*. And needless to say Dr. Bhandarkar's scholarship was at once recognised by the society and many were the learned papers that he read before the meeting of scholars.

The writings of Dr. Bhandarkar naturally fall into two sections—those that were contributed to research journals and the more permanent portion of his life-work, the books that he had published.

As has already been stated, Professor Bhandarkar contributed many articles to the earliest numbers of the *Indian Antiquary*. Space forbids the review of all of them. During the years 1872, 1873 and 1874, he was engaged in a spirited controversy with Professor Weber of Berlin on the question of the "*Age of Pathanjali*" and "*Pathanjali's Mahabashya*."

In his article on the *Age of Pathanjali*, he successfully contended that the date of the composition of *Pathanjali's Mahabashya* was about the middle of the second century B. C., a result arrived at also by Goldstucker, though for independent reasons. Prof. Weber himself would assign it a date several centuries later. In the same year, 1873, he contributed to the *Journal of the Bombay Branch of the Royal Asiatic Society* another learned paper on the "*Age of Mahabharata.*" This was written with a view to correct Colonel Ellis who suggested that the date of *Mahabharata* should be sought for after 1521 A.D.! In another article, Bhandarkar discusses Pathanjali's and Kathiayana's native places and controverts the views of Goldstucker and Weber. According to Bhandarkar, Pathanjali's native place is to be sought somewhere to the north west by west of Oudh, while Prof. Weber thought that he lived to the east of Pataliputra. As regards Kathiayana, Bhandarkar says he was a native of the south. In 1874, there appeared a very interesting article of his in the '*Indian Antiquary*' entitled "*Allusions to Krishna in Pathanjali's Mahabashya.*" Taking various passages from the *Mahabashya* and discussing elaborately the root-meanings of words, Dr. Bhandarkar established the following propositions, that the stories of the death of Kamsa and the subjection of Vali were popular and current in Pathanjali's time, that Krishna or Vasudeva was mentioned in the story as having killed Kamsa, that such stories formed the subject of dramatic representations in the same way as the Puranic stories are still popularly represented in the Hindu stage and that the event of Kamsa's death at the hands of Krishna was in Pathanjali's time, believed to have occurred at a very remote period. Thus Bhandarkar:

> "I have thus brought together seven passages from a work written in the middle of second century B.C., which show that the stories about Krishna and his worship as a god are not so recent as European scholars would make them. And to these I ask the attention of those who find in Christ a prototype of Krishna and in the Bible the original of Bhagavat Gita and who believe our Puranic literature to be merely a later growth. If the stories of Krishna and Bali and others which I shall notice hereafter were current and popular in the second century before Christ, some such works as the Harivamsa and the Puranas must have existed then."

In about the May of the same year, 1874, he contributed a long article on the "*Veda in India*," where he gave a clear and succinct account of the study of the Veda by the Brahminical families and pointed out the services rendered to the cause of Sanskrit learning by the Vedic reciters.

By this time, the fame of Dr. Bhandarkar as a Sanskritist of great eminence had spread far and wide and he was invited to join the International Congress of Orientalists which met in 1874 in London. For domestic reasons, he could not accept the invitation but wrote a paper for the Congress on "*The Nasik Inscriptions,*" which considerably enhanced his reputation as a scholar. This brilliant paper was published in the "Transactions of Oriental Congress, 1874" and was at once acclaimed as one of the best treatises throwing a flood of light on the Kings of the Satavahana race. In the next year Dr. Bhandarkar was made an honorary member of the *Royal Asiatic Society*. In 1876, was instituted, *Wilson Philology Lectureship* and Dr. Bhandarkar was the first lecturer. His lectures in this connection are of permanent value and interest. They set forth the basis of philological science with its application to Sanskrit and Prakrit lucidly and instructively. It is the opinion of scholars that for fund of information supplied and original ideas set forth they are almost incomparable in their importance. In the same year, he published his edition of *Malathi Madhava*, a Sanskrit play, much admired for critical acumen and scholarship.

It has been previously mentioned that on the retirement of Dr. Kielhorn from Bombay Educational Service, Dr. Bhandarkar was made a permanent Professor in 1881. Two years previously, however, the Government entrusted him with a very important mission. The Government of Bombay had for several years before been conducting a search for Sanskrit MSS. This task required great learning and vast powers of research. Fortunately for Bombay Government when the scheme was launched, the services of Dr. Buhler were available. And he conducted a vigorous hunt for manuscripts. But after the retirement of that gentleman, the work was entrusted to Dr. Kielhorn mainly and partly to Dr. Bhandarkar. After Prof. Kielhorn's departure, Dr. Peterson claimed to be allowed a portion of it and the whole work was divided equally between Dr. Bhandarkar and Dr. Peterson. Dr. Peterson issued interesting *Reports* of his search, while Dr. Bhandarkar issued periodically six volumes of reports regarding his operations. It is not possible to give any fair idea of the magnitude of the task entrusted to and patriotically performed by the revered Professor. In general, one might say, that the *Reports* form vast storehouses of historic information on a variety of topics. Unlike the generality of official documents of ephemeral value these *records* are of permanent interest to the student of Early Indian History. These reports in the words of Dr. Buhler form an important help to every student who has to find his way into the tangled jungle of Sanskrit Literature. They exhibit the most conscientious devotion to the search and are full of instructive and interesting matter. A strong adherent of the critical and historical school of Philology, Dr. Bhandarkar has been able, by supplying correct information, to fill many a lacuna. Old Jaina Bhandars were visited and a large number of Jaina MSS. purchased. The MSS. were carefully edited and Dr. Bhandarkar's own views clearly stated. The editing of these led to re-suscitation of the history of the Jaina sect of whom, till then, very little was known. In the course of his search he was able to gather materials which he subsequently utilized for the publication of his "*Outlines of Vaishnavaism, etc.*" Many philosophical works were also purchased and Dr. Bhandarkar's commentaries and discussions on these are very interesting especially his remarks on Ramanuja's system and Kashmerian Saivism. For an account of Jainism, early Vaishnavaism, Kashmere Saivism and the early Chalukyas, we are mainly indebted to these reports. Dr. Bhandarkar's reports like his "*Early History of the Deccan*" are quoted with profound respect by all scholars, both European and Indian. As these works were appearing in parts and as their contents were being studied by European Scholars, the University of Gottingen thought that such an eminent scholar as Bhandarkar ought to be honoured and that any honour done to him was honour done to itself. It conferred on him, in the year 1885, the degree of PH. D. Next year, the Government of India selected Bhandarkar on behalf of the Kathiawar Chiefs to represent the Presidency of Bombay in the great Congress of Orientalists held at Vienna. This brilliant assembly of some of the most distinguished Orientalists met in the last days of September 1886. The Government and the public of the Austrian capital gave a hearty welcome to the delegates who had come from the various parts of the world. The Aryan section of the Congress was presided over by Professor Von Roth, an eminent Sanskritist. It was here that Professor Bhandarkar read a learned and exhaustive report entitled "*Principal results of my last two years' studies in Sanskrit MSS. and literature with particular refernece to sacrificial, ritual and the Pancharatra system.*" Dr. Buhler warmly praised the merits of the Professor's paper which created such a deep impression that "the whole section proposed and passed by acclamation a vote of thanks to the political Agent and the chiefs of Kathiawar and to the Bombay Government to whom the Congress was mainly indebted for the presence of so distinguished a representative of native learning."

At the end of the proceedings, Prof. Bhandarkar recited his complimentary Sanskrit poem to the section which was, needless to say, much admired. Since this incident in his career, many learned societies in Europe and America vied with each other in honouring him. He was at once elected honorary member of German Oriental Society, American Oriental Society, and the Asiatic Society of Italy. The Government of India were not slow to recognise the special merits of the great Doctor. On his return form Vienna in 1887, he was made a C. I. E. and at the same time nominated a Fellow of the Calcutta University. In 1888 he became a member of the Imperial Academy of Science at St. Petersburg.

It is, therefore, plain that even before his retirement from the Educational service in 1873, Dr. Bhandarkar was acknowledged as the leading Sanskritist in India. Nor did his labours for the cause of Indian historical research cease with his retirement. Before giving an account of his activities after 1893, there is one fact to which prominent reference must be made, *viz.*, the publication of his "*Early History of the Deccan*," in 1884. Dr. Bhandarkar's "*Early History of the Deccan*" is to-day the only reference book on the subject. It is the fruit of his labours in connection with his search for Sanskrit MSS.

It embodies his considered views on the chronology of the various periods in the Deccan History. Since the publication of that book a good deal has been written on the subject, but the Doctor's conclusions in the main remain unshaken. The book was published for the *Bombay Gazetteer* on behalf of the Government of Bombay The political history of the Deccan, before the advent of the Mahomedans was entirely unknown before, and realising the difficulty of ascertaining facts concerning Deccan, Bhandarkar collected all the materials available, most of which he himself furnished in one comprehensive form. He calls the book very modestly "mere congeries of facts." It is not. so. It is an inexhaustible fountain of knowledge that continues to fertilize the vast field of Indian historical research. No decent book has been written on the subject in recent times, which does not contain quotations from Bhandarkar's "*Early History of the Deccan*"

Most Government officials after retirement from service would be thinking of a life of ease and leisure. But Dr. Bhandarkar, every inch a student, has lived only for his studies and, in spite of severe physical strain, continued to evince as much interest and enthusiasm as he did, when comparatively young. He contributed many papers to the

Journal of the Bombay Branch of the Royal Society, the most prominent among which was a very learned paper on "*The work done by the Society towards the elucidation of Indian History on the study of Inscriptions*," which he contributed to its centenary volume. Dr. Bhandarkar took a very prominent part in the centenary celebrations of the *Bombay Branch of the Royal Asiatic Society*, by presiding over the Sanskrit section of it, throughout.

Before we close this section of our sketch, reference should be made to Prof. Bhandarkar's recent contribution to the realm of Indian religious thought. So recently as 1913, in failing health and advanced age, Sir Ramakrishna has been pleased to give us what has been aptly called his "Magnum-Opus," "*Vaishnavaism, Saivism and Minor Religious Sects*." This work constitutes, from the Indian point of view, the most useful of the volumes of the Series "*Encyclopædia of Indo-Aryan Research*." They were planned and carried out in part by the late G. Buhler and F. Keilhorn. Dr. Bhandarkar's book comprises 170 pages and in spite of the technical nature of the subject, he has striven to give as popular an exposition of it as it will admit of.

Both Vaishnavaism and Saivism, according to Bhandarkar, are the offshoots of the Bhakti school and were based on Upanishads. Vaishnavaism is a sort of religious reform on theistic principles and could be traced at least to the fifth century B.C. Its early name was 'Ekantha Dharma' and it had for its background the Bhagavat Gita. Soon acquiring a sectarian form, it was embraced by a tribe of Kshatriyas of the Satwata sect about the end of the 4th century B.C. At the beginning of the Christian era, a foreign tribe, Abhiras or Cowherds, imported into India a new system of religion with which early Vaishavaism got itself mixed up. The result was a new cult, the worship of Krishna. "Thus constituted, Vaishnavaism went on till the end of about the 8th century when the doctrine of spiritual monism and world illusion was promulgated and disseminated by Sankaracharya and his followers." The learned Doctor then traces the history of Vaishnavaism and Vaishnavite systems in various parts of the country. Sankara's teachings, so destructive of Bhakti, were attacked from time to time by Vaishnavite saints who introduced various systems of their own, Ramanuja in the 11th century opened the attack. He was followed by Nimbarka who introduced the worship of Radhâ also. Madhwa or Ananda-Tirtha established in the 13th century the doctrine of pluralism at the same time bringing into prominence the name of Vishnu as the supreme god. Ramananda, in the 14th and Kabir in the 15th centuries gave a new turn to Vaishnavaism. In the 16th century the doctrine of Bhakti was spread by Vallabha and Chaitanya who also introduced the worship of grown-up Krishna. In the Mahratta country Namdev and Tukaram popularised the worship of Vitoba, and their soul-stirring songs were composed in the vernacular of their country. "The two Mahratta saints and Kabir also laid particular stress on the purification of the individual's heart and moral elevation as a means to a single-minded and devoted love of God and as necessary for the attainment of eternal bliss.

Equally interesting are the learned Professor's views as regards the evolution of Saivism and Saivite schools. The various phases of development of Saivism are treated in a popular way and the whole book, without being technical, stimulates interest. It is quite possible to hold a different opinion on one or two points mentioned by the Doctor, *e.g.*, the development of Vaishnavaism in the south but there is absolutely no doubt that the work "is a monument of learning and should be in the hands of all those interested in the study of Hinduism."

THE BHANDARKAR INSTITUTE.

From what has hitherto been stated it is clear that, among the Oriental scholars, no name is held in greater veneration than that of Sir Ramakrishna Gopal Bhandarkar. Towards the middle of 1915, the many loving disciples and admirers of the learned Doctor conceived the idea of founding an Oriental institute offering facilities to research workers and at the same time commemorating the name and work of Dr. Bhandarkar. Receiving the enthusiastic support of the cultured aristocracy of Western India and munificently aided by the merchant princes, Sir Ratan and Sir Dorab Tata, the scheme soon materialised—thanks to the active sympathy shown towards the movement by the Government of Bombay. Thus, named after the old venerable Doctor and conducted by a band of scholars trained up under his influence, this institution has for its object the continuance of the work so dear to Sir Ramakrishna. The Institute was formally inaugurated by His Excellency Lord Willingdon, the then Governor of Bombay, on the 6th of July 1917. Circumstances soon arose which tended considerably to enlarge the scope of its activities. In the year 1919, the organisers of the Institute took the bold step of arranging for an All-India Conference of Oriental Scholars. Congresses of Orientalists have regularly been held in the various capital cities of Europe. Though success attended these meetings and the proceedings had attained a high standard of scholarship, yet, in view of the meagre attendance of Indian members and lack of time and facilities to deal with Indian subjects with such fulness and thoroughness that they required, Prof. Vogel put forward the suggestion at a meeting of distinguished Orientalists held in Simla in 1911 under the presidency of Sir Harcourt Butler, that arrangements must be made to hold a similar congress confined to scholars from India, Burma and Ceylon. The Bhandarkar Institute took up the cue. The first great Conference was held in 1919. It was in the fitness of things that Sir R. G. Bhandarkar was unanimously elected as its President. Unfortunately owing to acute illness, he could not be present and his speech was read out by Professor V. K. Rajwade.

The learned presidential address of Sir Ramakrishna is an important document, containing, as it does, his mature views on a variety of topics concerning Ancient India. More than this, his speech is to be valued for the wholesome advice that the sage gives to young research scholars, who unfortunately rush to conclusions not based upon a thorough knowledge of the things that they talk or write about. It conveys a sound warning to those patriotic historians who find nothing in the methods of study pursued by distinguished scholars of the West. To them Sir Ramakrishna says :—

"Between the Western and Indian scholars a spirit of co-operation should prevail and not a spirit of depreciation of each other. We have but one common object, the discovery of the truth. Both, however. have prepossessions and even prejudices, and the same evidence may lead to their arriving at different conclusions. Often, however, when controversies are carried on, the truth comes out prominently, and there is a general acquiescence when it does so. To express the same idea, in other words the angle of vision, if I may use the expression that has become hackneyed, may be and is different. The Indian's tendency may be towards rejecting foreign influence on the development of his country's civilization and to claim high antiquity for some of the occurrences in its history On the other hand, the European scholar's tendency is to trace Greek, Roman or Christian influence at work in the evolution of new points and to modernize the Indian historical and literary events. It is on this account there has been no consensus of opinion as to the approximate period when the most ancient portion of the hymns of the Rig Veda was composed. Some refuse to assign it a higher antiquity than 15 centuries before Christ, while others carry it far to the beginning of Kali Yuga, *i.e.*, to about 3101 B. C. A scholar may have conceived a prejudice against the Indian race and may look down upon the Vedic Rishis. Thus our critical method is unfortunately too often vitiated by extraneous influences. But this, probably, is due to human weakness. A critical scholar should consider his function to be just like that of a judge in a law-court; but even there human weakness operates, and renders a number of appeals necessary, so that one judge differs from another, so does one critical scholar from another."

Sylvain Levi

Sir Charles Eliot, in his recently published work on Hinduism and Buddhism, makes the following observations in regard to Indian History generally :

"But in Eastern Asia the influence of India has been notable in extent, strength and duration. Scant justice is done to her positon in the world by those histories which recount the exploits of her invaders and leave the impression that her own people were a feeble, dreamy folk, sundered from the rest of mankind by their sea and mountain frontiers. Such a picture takes no account of the intellectual conquests of the Hindus. Even their political conquests were not contemptible and were remarkable for the distance if not the extent of the territory occupied. For, there were Hindu kingdoms in Java and Cambodia and settlements in Sumatra, and even in Borneo, an island about as far from India as is Persia from Rome. But such military or commercial invasions were insignificant compared with the spread of Indian thought. The south-eastern region of Asia both mainland and Archipelago—owed its civilization almost entirely to India. In Ceylon, Burma, Siam, Cambodia, Champa, and Java, religion, art, the alphabet, literature as well as whatever science and political organisation existed, were the direct gift of Hindus, whether Brahmans or Buddhists, and much the same may be said of Tibet, whence the wilder Mongols took as much Indian civilization as they could stomach. In Java and other Malay countries this Indian culture has been superseded by Islam, yet even in Java the alphabet and to a large extent the customs of the people are still Indian.

This wider historical outlook has become possible for the twentieth century historian of Indian culture, thanks to the labours of the nineteenth century savants, chiefly foreign and Continental. The defect of present day Indian history pointed out by Sir Charles is too commonly the characteristic of the work of English historians as yet, though it must be said to the credit of English scholarship that it is an English scholar that draws such pointed attention to this vital drawback. This improved outlook and the attainment of a new perspective in Indian culture-history is due, entirely almost, to the labours of a band of Indologists, the leading places among whom must be given to French savants—the most prominent of these being Burnouf, Julien, Bergaigne, Senart, Chavannes, Chezy and Levi to mention just a few. The new school began with Anquetil Duperron, who joined the French East India Company to come over to India and realize his ambition to acquire some genuine records of Indian culture. Duperron succeeded so far in this laudable ambition of his that his gift to the Biblotheque Nationale of copies of the Vedas and the Avesta gave the start to a new Oriental School in Paris.

A typical product of this school and a *multum in parvo* representative of its ever-widening circle of interest in Indian culture is Sylvain Levi. The labours of this school have not only succeeded in filling many a gap in the study of the history of India herself, but have also carried us a great way to bridge the gulf that yawned between India, the homeland, and those regions where her culture exports flourish in various stages of growth and in varying forms of development. It is to these French savants and to the Dutch that we are indebted for the reclamation of India's forgotten children across the seas, and her equally forgotten nurslings across her borders, seperated now by impassable deserts and mountains, and worse still, impossible human obstacles. The reviving interest in these studies received encouraging support and recognition soon from Governments so that now the achievements in this line have become accessible in some measure even to the English reading public through the munificence of the Government of India, and of learned bodies like the Asiatic Society.

Sylvain Levi, who has borne his own share in this edifying work for close upon 40 years, was born in 1863 and took his degree in 1883 when he was just 20 years old. He was such an extraordinarily good student that both Ernest Renan and James Darmesteter were interested in the talented youth. It was Renan that was responsible for bringing young Levi into touch with Abel Bergaigne, one of the greatest teachers of Sanskrit that Europe produced. A sound student of the Classical languages that he was, he took to Sanskrit studies with great zeal and got initiated at the outset both in the study of the Veda and in the epigraphical and other documents of Cambodian history on both of which Bergaigne was at the time engaged. From the very beginning of his Sanskrit studies, Levi learnt to gain that wider vision and larger outlook which are the dominant characteristics of all his work. Levi's first published work was, in the circumstances, not at all strange, a paper on the Brihatkathamanjari of Kshemendra in the *Journal Asiatique* for 1885-86. He was then appointed "Master of Conference of the School of Higher Studies" in Paris, a professor-prodigy of twenty-three summers. It was in these conferences of his early years that he came into contact with the most brilliant among his pupils, A Meillet, the eminent philologist, and A. Foucher, the illustrious scholar of Buddhist Art and Archæology.

In 1889 Bergaigne died prematurely in the course of an excursion in Switzerland to the great sorrow of young Levi. Levi took the blow so badly to heart that it required a visit from another eminent savant, M. E.

Senart, to revive his drooping spirits. He resolved that the best tribute to the memory of his late master was to continue his good work unimpaired, and set about it in right earnest, when he was nominated to the Council of the French Asiatic Society in the vacancy caused by the death of Bergaigne himself. Levi's first contribution after this was "Bergaigne and Indianism" in the *Journal Asiatique* for 1890. The same year he submitted two theses for his doctorate, one in Latin on "What about Greece Ancient Indian monuments conserved" and the other in French on "The Theatre of the Hindus" which stands still an authority on the subject of Hindu drama. He was made a member of the Faculty of Letters about the same time that he was made Assistant Director of the School of Higher Studies. In 1894 he was appointed to the Chair of Sanskrit in the College de France. Thus at the age of thirty-one he reached the highest educational position and began his life's work as the colleague of such eniment savants as Darmesteter, Maspero and Gaston Paris.

From this time forward he went on lecturing on various subjects relating to his chair, discussing Asoka Inscriptions and organising classes for teaching Chinese and Tibetan, along with Pali and Sanskrit. As his interest widened he set about to found a school of Indology in the East and sent Foucher on this mission. When the scheme was ripe, through the warm interest of the Colonial Secretary, Mr. Guiyesse, he himself came over and laid the foundation (in 1897-98) of the 'Ecole Francaise d'Extreme Orient' with the active assistance of another pupil of Bergaigne, Leon Bourgeoise, then Governor-General of Indo-China.

Levi had already published his studies in the Buddhacharita in 1892 and had collected and edited about 150 verses of Matricheta, and had become acquainted with Edward Chavannes, the great French Sinologist, through the medium of Foucher. The first fruit of this friendship was the publication of the Itenary of Ou-Kong in the *Journal Asiatique* in 1895. Levi took advantage of his visit in 1897-98 referred to above to tour through India, Nepal, Indo-China and Japan. From the date of his return from this tour he settled down to work of an extra-Indian character, though he did off and on make his own contributions to Indian studies as well. In this latter branch he published his monograph on the "Doctrine of Sacrifice in the Brahmanas" in 1898. The same year he became Director of the School of Higher Studies. Soon after the *Journal T'oung-Pao* came under the editorship of his friend,

Ed. Chavannes almost about the same time that the Ecole Francaise d'Extreme Orient began their *bulletine.* These gave new life to the parrallel study of Chinese and Indian culture begun by Remausat and St. Julien. It was in Levi that there was that marvellous knowledge of India that could bear real fruit in comparative study. He brought about this combination in himself by lecturing on these subjects almost together. In 1907 he is found lecturing on Sakuntala on the one side, and on the other, studies the Dhammapada in its Sanskrit and Chinese versions; he discusses on the one hand Kotikarnavadana in its Sanskrit, Chinese and Tibetan versions and on the other, analyses the beauty and sublimity of the Great Epic (the Mahabharata). The year 1908 saw the publication of his monumental work on Nepal in the *Annales Musee Guimet.*

It was in the same year that one of his brilliant pupils, Pelliot, started on a mission of exploration to Central Asia. When Pelliot returned with a collection of Manuscripts in 1910, Levi formed a seminar for the study of these documents, while lecturing on Tibetan and publishing the Sutralankara of Asanga. This resulted in a contribution of the first importance for the decipherment of Tokharian and Koutchean dialects of Central Asia through the combined efforts of Levi, Chavannes and Meillet. The untimely death of Chavannes left a void difficult to fill, but the others continue the good work which is becoming far more important owing to the fresh accessions of records and documents in the line brought in by the " Stein Expeditions".

Levi's activities are not confined to these literary labours alone. His interest in institutions of public benefit is great—It is in connection with one of these that he visited India early in 1922 at the invitation of Rabindranath Tagore at the Santiniketan Visvabharati—His views in regard to the position of India in the history of civilization bring them near enough in idea to *Vishvabharàti*, as he said in concluding his article on Bergaigne and Indianism ; " From Persia to the Chinese sea, from the icy regions of Siberia to the islands of Java and Borneo, from Oceanea to Socotra, India has propagated her beliefs, her genius, her tales and her civilization. She has left indestructible imprints on one-fourth of the human race in the course of a long succession of centuries. She has a right to claim in universal history the rank that ignorance has refused her for a long time, and to hold her place amongst the great nations, summarising and symbolising the spirit of humanity."

It was in the fitness of things that Calcutta took advantage of the presence of the encyclopædic Indologist to invite him to preside at the second session of the Indian Oriental Conference. His presidential address, though short, is characteristic of the scholar and savant. He could pass from the sight of Dhanushkodi to the Ramayana of Valmiki, to a Chinese and Tibetian version of one episode of it and could point out what an advantage for the proper understanding of texts a comparative study of these would be. No wonder that he could brush aside much that is external and accidental, and get to the true inwardness of things as the following view of Indian history of his gives us clearly to understand. "The multiplicity of the manifestations of the Indian genius as well as their fundamental unity gives India the right to figure on the first rank in the history of civilised nations. Her civilisation, spontaneous and original, unrolls itself in a continuous time across at least thirty centuries, without interruption, without deviation. Ceaslessly in contact with foreign elements which threatened to strangle her, she persevered victoriously in absorbing them, assimilating them and enriching herself with them. Thus she has seen the Greeks, the Scythians, the Afghans, the Mongols to pass before her eyes in succession and is regarding with indifference the Englishmen—confident to pursue under the accidence of the surface the normal course of her high destiny." His is a synthetic mind and takes hold of essentials to the neglect of the accidents. This is the result of persistent work and sustained effort to get at the root of things.

This feature is quite characteristic of the simple but typical scholar. He wrote his first paper on the Brihatkatha thirty-seven years since, and that mind remains open to receive new information. He asked me in Calcutta whether I knew of a man who wrote a short note in the *J. R. A. S.* about twenty years ago on a Tamil version of the Brihatkatha—referring to one of my own papers. I said I was the man. He adjured me, with all the fervour of youthful enthusiasm, not to relax in my effort to get to the original of the Brikaikatha, and wound up with the exclamation "If I could only see the original before I die!" There is the scholar whose own enthusiasm infects, and it is nothing more than due to him that his students exhibit almost an instinctive veneration for him such as I have witnessed in the course of the few days' stay at the Oriental Conference in Calcutta.

First Edition, 1,500 Copies, April 1922.
G. A Natesan & Co, Madras.